The
Custom-House of Desire

THE CUSTOM-HOUSE OF DESIRE

A Half-Century of Surrealist Stories

Translated with an Introduction

by

J. H. MATTHEWS

UNIVERSITY OF CALIFORNIA PRESS

BERKELEY   LOS ANGELES   LONDON

University of California Press
Berkeley and Los Angeles, California
University of California Press, Ltd.
London, England

Library of Congress Catalog Card Number: 74-16712

Copyright © 1975 by The Regents of the University of California

Printed in the United States of America

Designed by Ashton Geoffrey

2 3 4 5 6 7 8 9

The translations are for
E. Millicent Pool
Department of French
University College of Swansea
1926-1955

Contents

Acknowledgments

For stories that appear here for the first time, I am indebted to Jean-Louis Bédouin, Marianne van Hirtum, and Jacques Lacomblez. Vincent Bounoure kindly supplied two samples of parallel stories. For permission to translate material to which they reserve copyright, I am grateful to Leonora Carrington, Alain Joubert, Alain Jouffroy, Joyce Mansour, Marcel Mariën (for two of his own stories and one by Paul Nougé), Jean Markale, José Pierre, André Pieyre de Mandiargues, and Georges Sebbag. Special thanks are due Mlle Andrée Limbour. Mme F. van der Brecken-Demoustier granted permission and gave valuable assistance with respect to the work of her father, Fernand Dumont. Robert Lebel graciously checked my translation of his *L'Inventeur du temps gratuit*, while Joyce Mansour made striking improvements in versions of two of her stories. Illustrative material was made available through the generosity of Marianne van Hirtum, Jacques Lacomblez, and Joyce Mansour, who all provided drawings executed especially for this volume. Manina has been so good as to authorize reproduction of the drawings that illustrate Alain Jouffroy's *Double Envol*.

Acknowledgment is made to the following publishers for permission to translate the copyrighted material indicated:

André De Rache, éditeur, for Camille Goeman's *Les Débuts d'un voyage* (in *Œuvre 1922-1957*); Librairie Ernest Flammarion for Gisèle Prassinos' *Journoir, L'Arbre aux trois branches, Le Feu maniaque,* and *Le Gros Chèque* (in *Les Mots endormis*); Éditions Gallimard for Jean Ferry's *La Grève des boueurs, Le Tigre mondain,* and *Kafka ou "la sociéte secrète"* (in *Le Mécanicien et autres contes*), and for Georges Limbour's *Le Cheval de Venise* (in *L'Illustre Cheval blanc*); René Julliard, éditeur, for Fernando Arrabal's *La Pierre de la folie*; Éric Losfeld, éditeur, for Benjamin Péret's *Une Vie pleine d'intérêt, Un Plaisir bien passager,* and *Le Dégel* (in *Le Gigot, sa vie et son œuvre*); Mercure de France for Georges Hénein's *Notes sur un pays inutile* and *Histoire vague* (in *Le Seuil interdit*); Les Éditions de Minuit for Georges Hénein's *Le Guetteur* (in *Un Temps de petite fille*); Librairie Plon for Gisèle Prassinos' *La Robe de laine* (in *Le Cavalier*); Éditions du Soleil noir for Robert Lebel's *L'Inventeur du temps gratuit* (in *La Double Vue*); Jean Schuster, rédacteur en chef, *Le Surréalisme même,* for Leopoldo Chariarse's *Les Mélanges inadmissibles.*

Introduction

In the town of Aurillac, in the Massif Central of France, rises a statue to Gerbert (938-1003), who from 995 was Pope Sylvester II. The Michelin Guide does not record its presence, let alone recommend this monument to tourists' attention, yet scarcely seems open to criticism for ignoring it. His hand raised in benediction, the pope appears to have inspired the sculptor to no more than listless effort. In spite of this, in 1949 I found my students at the Lycée Émile Duclaux eager to take me to see Gerbert, by way of a side street that passed to the right of the statue. Knowing exactly where to do so, they stopped without warning, inviting me to admire the pontiff. From where I now stood, it appeared that he had been somewhat negligent when dressing to pose for posterity; unless, that is, I was being treated to the rare spectacle of papal exhibitionism.

Of course, the distinguishing feature of Pope Sylvester's statue is not unique, as those who have seen the memorial to Washington in El Paraiso can testify. It seems worthy of mention here because that monument and others like it have a few things to teach us about surrealism. The most revealing approach to reality, for instance, may not always be a frontal approach. We may have to come at it from a particular angle, and possibly with a special viewpoint, in order to discover aspects of the real that remain concealed from those content with the banal face of the familiar. Then we are likely to find that something which, in surrealism, becomes visible to all who are willing to look may well stand in defiance not only of common sense and even decency but also of that which serves as a basis for our estimate of what is decent and commonsensical. We find ourselves confronted with ingrained prejudices in favor of those things we believe can be and must be, as well as our prejudices against those we assume cannot be and therefore, we tend to suppose, are not.

The manner in which the unexpected, the unlikely, the improbable, the impossible are brought to our notice (what, one wonders, were the feelings of the first person who, without knowingly seeking to do so, found himself looking at the statue of Gerbert from an angle causing him to see the thumb on the Pope's left hand as that which it was not, could not be, and nevertheless certainly had become?) is symptomatic of a principle dear to the surrealist's heart, according to which chance helps bring about the precipitation of something surrealists call the marvelous, which we may define, provisionally anyway, as an enriched perception of reality.

A sense of provocation—to which we are introduced when surrealists set aside all reservations born of conventional morality, inherited or inculcated respect, good taste, and so on—to highlight the subversive pleasure of scandal is finally worthy of notice. Without acknowledging its appeal, we can progress but a short distance toward appreciation of surrealist writing.

The analogy I have drawn is intended to do no more than communicate, to those who have not experienced it already, something of the *atmosphere* of surrealism in which the texts assembled here take their place. Aware of its imperfections, I am especially sensitive to a major weakness. My analogy tends to impose limitations both upon the appeal exercised by surrealism for those who practice it and upon the effect produced by surrealism in those responsive to it. Above all, it may leave some readers with the erroneous impression that surrealism invariably tackles reality from the same angle, as though staking its claim to attention upon revelations of one kind only, that this approach apparently seems likely to provide.

A nodding acquaintance with surrealism, as the general public has heard it described, could well suggest that there is nothing at all wrong with this impression. In fact, it appears to find authority in the *Manifesto of Surrealism* published in Paris by André Breton in October of 1924. Was not Breton recommending a uniform approach, when he defined surrealism as "pure psychic automatism by which we propose to express either verbally, or through writing, or in any other manner, the true functioning of thought. The dictation of thought, in the absence of all control exercised by reason, outside all aesthetic or moral preoccupations"?[1] Nothing in the history of surrealist activity over a span of some fifty years indicates, however, that Breton intended—or, within the surrealist movement, was thought to have intended—to reduce the practice of surrealism for all time to the application of the automatist principle, thus limiting the use of language to the unfettered flow of words, released from the restraints imposed by reason for the control of rational discourse.

This is not to say that automatic writing cannot make an important contribution within the narrative framework. Automatic texts take their rightful place in the present collection. And they cover a significantly broad time span, from the earliest narrative presented, Benjamin Péret's *A Life Full of Interest* (1922), right up to examples of "parallel stories," written fully half a century later. All the same, it takes no more than a glance through this book to make clear to anyone believing that surrealism can be reduced to a recipe, or ought to be limited in this way, that he is mistaken. Such a narrow interpretation of the scope of the surrealist venture and of the freedom it grants the individual writer is incompatible with the practice of surrealism. The first step toward appreciation and enjoyment of surrealism, in its influence on storytelling as much as upon other modes of verbal communication, is recognition of the fact that there is a place in surrealist writing for fully structured tales like

---

1. André Breton, *Manifeste du surréalisme* suivi de *Poisson soluble* [1924] in his *Manifestes du surréalisme* (Jean-Jacques Pauvert, n.d. [1962]), p. 40.

Henceforth quotations will be identified in the text by parenthetical page reference only. Full reference to primary and secondary sources—magazines, catalogs, and books, in the edition consulted—is given below, under the rubric "Works Cited." Unless otherwise indicated, the place of publication is Paris.

André Pieyre de Mandiargues's *The Pommeraye Arcade* no less
than for products of the automatic method. And between the
poles marked here by the work of Péret and of Pieyre de
Mandiargues, surrealism has no difficulty accommodating
narrative forms of refreshing variety.

It looks as if a pendulum swing has taken us from one
extreme to the other, so that we must be prepared for anything,
when leafing through a collection of surrealist texts. But then we
should be left with as distorted an idea of surrealism as would
be gained if we assumed uniformity of technique among all its
writers. The wisest path is to begin by accepting that there can
be no exclusive prescribed recipe or pattern for the surrealist use
of language, and by accepting also that, to appreciate what
motivates a surrealist, we must begin by acknowledging his
indifference to the classifications of literary genres.

We face here an aspect of surrealism which, possibly, has
caused more confusion than any other. Because in their creative
texts surrealists use words, just like writers with purely literary
aspirations, it seems natural to suppose that surrealists share
these aspirations and that, therefore, their work is subject to the
evaluative assessment that is taken to be the prerogative of
critics. But if the product of surrealism's use of language may be
treated indeed as literature, this does not alter the fact that
literary criteria and preoccupations are at very best of no more
than secondary concern to the surrealist writer.

In one sense, then, surrealists may seem open to accusations of self-indulgence, when they decline to submit their
writing to judgment by literary standards. In fact, at first sight
we feel inclined to treat these accusations as well founded and
fully justified. Like the hero of Georges Limbour's story *The Horse
of Venice*, the surrealist "is never lost, for the path he follows is
always toward what he does not know." It would be foolish,
however, to think of a surrealist creative artist as destined for
inevitable success, in whatever his chosen medium. And so we
may best arrive at some intimation of the range of surrealism's
profoundly optimistic ambitions by conceiving of the surrealist
as in pursuit of something that lies just over the horizon of the
visible, the habitual, the predictable, at a point forever receding
before him as he moves forward. Other writers might describe
their own ambitions in the same way, of course. Hence the dis-

tinguishing feature of surrealist effort lies in the orientation it gives the pursuit of the ineffable. Far from inculcating facility, surrealism places a heavy burden on the writer. This is why authors such as Georges Hénein, Alain Jouffroy, Jacques Lacomblez, Jean Markale, and Georges Sebbag are particularly noteworthy in the context of the surrealist short story. Their experiments with narrative form record attempts to reach out to embrace the elusive and so, to a greater or lesser extent, celebrate the tantalizing inadequacies of language.

Often the surrealist narrator stations himself on the periphery of the comprehensible and takes us to the confines of the improbable, or even beyond. His distaste for the habitual and the banal spurs him on toward exploration of the impossible. Meanwhile, in everything surrealists write, diversity of form and substance is assured by contempt, as old as surrealism itself, for literature as an activity authorizing the exercise of acquired skills—by contempt for the agreed basis for the viability of literary genres. Indeed, so opposed are surrealists to the idea of genres that speaking of the surrealist short story means beginning with a compromise that places the unwary in a trap likely to close at any moment.

The line of demarcation may well be faint, and may even seem arbitrary, between some of the texts selected for inclusion here (those by Bédouin and Lacomblez come to mind first), and texts that by conventional literary criteria would be termed more readily poems in prose. Readers of these short stories must be prepared to discover that a surrealist writer frequently allows his grip to slacken upon the very elements the public generally associates with the short story form. Occasionally, anyway, it may seem to the author—so far, that is, as he is inclined to articulate his motives—that what matters in his work stands in inverse proportion to narrative unity. In consequence, it sometimes happens that, far from bowing to the conventions of a genre, the surrealist writer consents to give no more than a slight nod. We should not be surprised, by the way, if that nod is less a token of appreciation or respect than of irony.

We cannot understand why this is so until we take up the central question with which surrealism's rejection of literature faces us. If surrealists assert their independence of literary ambition, what then are the aims they elect to pursue through their writings? Whatever the answer, it must give a sense of purpose to the surrealist use of words, while yet permitting individual writers a degree of freedom that, among other things, dispenses with the need for respecting literary genres. At the same time, it must point to a definite orientation in surrealist exploration through language, conducted toward ends that surrealist aspirations invest with importance.

Surrealists answer our question by drawing a distinction between literature and poetry. Whereas literature is considered within surrealism to be a pointless exercise, having no better than aesthetic pretensions, poetry is regarded as the only valid justification for taking up pen or brush.

Someone hearing for the first time the word *poetry* used in its surrealist sense may well conclude that either the answer surrealists propose is anticlimactic or that, willfully practicing obscurantism, defenders of the surrealist ideal are merely playing with words. One has only to listen to a surrealist speak of poetry to realize that neither conclusion fits the situation.

As an example, let us take Alain Jouffroy paying tribute to André Breton in an article that appeared in 1967, the year after Breton's death. Talking of the moment when, at the age of eighteen, he first met the author of the surrealist manifestos, Jouffroy commented: "Until that moment, as with most adolescents, poetry stood in my mind for an antiworld: In it I mentally organized the conquest of the impossible. I couldn't imagine that it might manifest itself *really* in the very thread of my daily life, in the places where I ate, slept, felt bored. . . . Poetry stopped being an 'absence,' an 'evasion,' since the most immediate reality became one with it, for me."[2] In other words, as contact with Breton helped Jouffroy understand the word, poetry is not a branch of literature, not the use of verse in preference to prose. It is not a substitute for living, but a perspective upon reality.

"We know now that poetry must lead somewhere." When Breton, as a young man in his twenties, proudly made this claim in *Les Pas perdus* of 1924, he was not paying homage to an established literary mode. He was not even concerned with redefin-

---

2. Alain Jouffroy, "La Fin des alternances," *La Nouvelle Revue Française* (April 1, 1967), p. 639.

ing poetry as content rather than form. His intention was to make clear that content was possessed of value, for him, only to the extent that it promised to lead somewhere. In surrealism the principle to which Breton referred, when opening up discussion of painting in his *Le Surréalisme et la peinture* (1928), is no less applicable to poetic expression through other media: "And so it is impossible for me to consider a picture other than as a window for which my first concern is knowing what *it looks out upon* . . ." (p. 2). The central preoccupation in surrealist endeavor is this. The painter or writer is intent upon providing his audience with a window. Its shape and its conformity to specifications generally considered appropriate to well-proportioned windows are of no consequence to him. What counts is that his window should be so placed as to look out upon something to which surrealist ideals lend importance. Attention must go, therefore, not to the form but to the revelations that form helps make possible. Hence we can best expand our understanding of poetry in surrealism by asking what is visible through the surrealist window. And this calls for examining what surrealists mean when they refer to the marvelous—the "heart and nervous system of all poetry," to quote Péret.

The marvelous, asserts another surrealist, Pierre Mabille, in a book titled simply *Le Merveilleux*, "expresses the need to go beyond imposed limits, imposed by our structure, the need to attain greater beauty, greater power, greater pleasure, to endure longer" (p. 68). Needs of this kind have to be weighed, if we aim at full realization of the significance attaching to the surrealists' iconoclastic attitude before accepted standards in all forms of artistic expression. Thus the antiaesthetic stance adopted by the surrealist writer is comprehensible only when we recognize that his "need to attain greater beauty" must lead him away from traditional aesthetic paths he feels no inclination to tread.

Certainly, we are wasting our time, so long as we entertain the false notion that surrealists attempt nothing more than revitalization of aesthetics by the device of inversion. They have too many pressing concerns to indulge in juggling aesthetic theories. They reject all aesthetic preoccupations because they believe these stand between a writer and perception of a world Mabille has described in *Le Merveilleux*: "A world that some call reality but which is only incessant discovery; a mystery reborn

indefinitely, that imagination, armed with calculation and precision instruments, shows us differently from the way our senses
perceived it on first contact, a universe about which it is possible
to wonder whether it is not altogether other than we conceive it
habitually" (p. 17). Imagination is promoted over observation,
for the surrealist's world can be reached only through our
powers of conception and projection, and not through submissiveness to habit and routine. This is why we hear Fernand
Dumont declare, in *The Influence of the Sun*, that "official recognition of the marvelous would give the signal for the final
collapse of all values currently prevailing."

In a very important way, surrealism is initiative. Like the
story by Camille Goemans, it aims to offer us at least *The Begin-
nings of a Journey*, by granting imagination an essential role in
revealing the marvelous.

According to the first surrealist manifesto, only imagination
can give us an account of "what *can be*" (p. 17). And so, officially
launching the surrealist movement, Breton affirmed his unre-
served confidence in imagination, declaring his belief that it
would never lead him astray. So far as imagination fascinates all
surrealists, it does so by leading directly to the marvelous,
playing an important part in arresting the "cancer of the mind"
which the *Second Manifesto of Surrealism*, written in 1929, tells us
lies in thinking that certain things "are," while others, which
could very well be, "are not" (p. 221). Hence the conclusion
advanced in Breton's *L'Amour fou* (*Mad Love* [1937]): the greatest
weakness in contemporary thought resides in "the extravagant
overestimation of the known compared with what remains to be
known" (p. 61). Hence too the analogy drawn in the second
manifesto between the aims of alchemy and those of surrealism:
"the Philosopher's Stone is nothing other than that which was
to permit man's imagination to take striking revenge upon all
things" (p. 207). Everything, Breton stated in a 1935 essay on the
political position of art today, *"depends on the liberty with which
this imagination succeeds in putting itself on stage and in putting only
itself on stage."*[3]

Commenting on poetry in the course of an interview

---

3. André Breton, "Position politique de l'art d'aujourd'hui," in his *Manifestes
du surréalisme*, p. 258.

published in the magazine *La Tour de feu,* André Breton asserted in December 1959: "Its greatest privilege is to extend its empire well beyond the boundaries marked by human reason." This then is the close link surrealist thought establishes between imagination and the marvelous: the latter, Breton assures us when prefacing the short stories of Jean Ferry, "is kept from communicating with everyday life only by a sluice gate, the state of which, we must in fact note, is more and more precarious." It is imagination, surrealists believe, that will finally bring that sluice gate tumbling down. As they view the situation, imagination is a persistently potent force, ever working against reason. As such, it is called upon to play a capital role in the surrealist poetic program. "Abandonment pure and simple to *the marvelous,*" remarked Breton in the ninth number of the magazine *Minotaure,* "is the only source of eternal communication between men."

The material gathered in the present collection illustrates how these. theoretical principles influence narrative form and structure. They take us a step farther too, by helping to show what Breton meant when, citing Sigmund Freud in his second manifesto of surrealism, he talked of compensating for the inadequacies of so-called true existence and of realizing our desires (p. 192).

Breton spoke in the name of all surrealists, when confessing in *Les Pas perdus* that he had no other challenge in the world to offer than "*desire*" (p. 8). If it is really vital, he was to argue in *Les Vases communicants* (*The Communicating Vessels* [1932]), desire "denies itself nothing" (pp. 148-149). Seen from the perspective imposed by this insistence upon desire, imagination is an expression of the surrealist's profound need to communicate his desires. Imagination erects a bridge to connect desire with the marvelous, doing so in a way that treats desire in a distinctive manner. This is why we hear Breton confide in *Nadja* (1928): "I have always to an incredible degree wished to meet at night, in a wood, a beautiful nude woman, or rather, such a wish having no meaning, once expressed, I regret to an incredible degree not having met her" (p. 46).

The value of Breton's statement is that it makes very clear that one cannot afford to be impatient when looking for a definition of desire in surrealism. In fact, of the three terms to which surrealist theory now has introduced us—the marvelous, imagination, and desire—it is the last that needs to be handled with the most caution, because this is the one that, on the surface, seems easiest to grasp. For Breton and those who share his conception of poetry, expressing a wish means confining desire to the foreseeable. And this entails restricting one's expectations within less than acceptable boundaries. In the circumstances, a clear definition of desire, in the context of surrealism, would be inconsistent with all that surrealism stands for. Desire must always command the surrealist's attention in its virtual state, while it has no need to define itself through acknowledgment of any limitations.

So far as the reader is concerned, to enter the world revealed by surrealist writing, he must be willing to present himself at the "custom-house of desire" of which Lacomblez speaks. Only if he is not weighed down with rationalist and aesthetic baggage can he expect whatever he brings with him to be passed without delay and duty free. Not until the frontier is behind him will he be able to appreciate why Péret wrote in his *Anthologie des Mythes, légendes et contes populaires d'Amérique* (1960) that "the practice of poetry is conceivable collectively only in a world liberated from all oppression, where poetic thought will have become once again as natural to man as seeing and sleeping" (p. 28).

Underlying the surrealist use of language, the theoretical ideas summarized above offer three focal points of attention. As it governs surrealist practice in storytelling, surrealist theory helps place the work of authors represented here in the only perspective they consider appropriate to enjoyment and evaluation of the written text. To be sure, the principles defended in surrealism still seem lacking in precision. This is because their practical application needs to be examined, before they can take on fuller definition. Hence, as my introductory notes indicate, attention must go to the nature and scope of the contribution made by each of these authors to the pursuit of aims originating in surrealist ambition. An explanation is in order, therefore, regarding the range of material brought together in this volume.

All the texts assembled here appeared originally in French. They were not written, however, by French and Belgian authors exclusively. Included are a few stories by writers of other national origin—Egyptian, English, Greek, Peruvian, and Spanish—whose medium for storytelling happens to be the French language. Texts by Fernando Arrabal, Leonora Carrington, Leopoldo Chariarse, Georges Hénein, Joyce Mansour, and Gisèle Prassinos will serve, I hope, to correct the impression which otherwise might be communicated: that surrealism is the province of the French and Belgians. It is true that all the writers mentioned made contact with surrealism while living in France. All the same, their presence here should encourage readers to broaden as well as deepen their exploration of the surrealist story: to take into account, for instance, the work of Michael Bullock in England, Alberto Savinio in Italy, Artur Manuel Cruzeiro-Seixas in Portugal, and Rikki in the United States.

Examples offered in this collection as an introduction to the surrealist short narrative are taken from a period beginning in 1922, two years before the *Manifeste du surréalisme* codified surrealist principles, and continuing to 1973, four years after the dissolution of unified surrealist group activity in France. Only complete texts have been selected, at the expense of extracts from longer works—one thinks of the famous *Les Champs magnétiques* (1919) by Breton and Philippe Soupault, or Breton's *Poisson soluble* (1924), or René Crevel's *Babylone* (1927), or Robert Desnos' *La Liberté ou l'amour!*, published in the same year. In consequence, some of the best-known names in the surrealist movement have had to be excluded. Similarly, dream transcriptions have been denied space, with the result that other names, like Éluard's, do not figure in this book. Copyright difficulties, unfortunately, have ruled out the possibility of granting attention to Louis Aragon, Jean Arp, and Antonin Artaud.

Surrealism as practiced by writers who enlisted in the movement during the twenties is represented by the work of five authors. Two are from France: Limbour and Péret; three come from Belgium: Goemans, Lecomte, and Nougé. Also represented by five names is the generation of the thirties: Leonora Carrington from England, Dumont and Mariën from Belgium, the Egyptian Georges Hénein, and Gisèle Prassinos, born in Turkey of Greek parentage. To the forties belong the French authors Bédouin, Jouffroy, and Pieyre de Mandiargues.

The Peruvian Chariarse's association with the surrealists occurred during the fifties, as did that of the Frenchmen Ferry and Lebel, and the Belgian Lacomblez. The fifties also saw a Spaniard, Fernando Arrabal, recruited to the surrealist ranks, as well as Marianne van Hirtum from Belgium and Joyce Mansour from Egypt via England. French recruits from the same period are Micheline and Vincent Bounoure, Joubert, Markale, and Pierre. Renaud and Sebbag entered the movement during the sixties.

No effort has been made to submit texts by all these writers to arbitrary limits designed to give one decade precedence over another in a whole half-century of surrealist endeavor. In fact, someone approaching this selection with statistical preoccupations must necessarily find it providing totally unreliable bases for deductions regarding productivity in surrealism, the appeal of the short story form at any one time, and so on. In some instances, we know when a text was written. In others, we know only when it appeared in print. Where both dates are accessible, it is clear that, now and again, a story may be assigned to one decade or another, according to one's preference for either the date of composition or the date of publication.

There is reason to be cautious, therefore, about concluding, for example, from the high percentage of texts appearing for the first time during the sixties, that this perhaps was the decade during which surrealists felt a special interest in the short narrative. One cannot make such an assumption, though, without weighing evidence of the following kind. In France, the two magazines *La Brèche: action surréaliste* and *L'Archibras* came to provide an outlet almost continuously through the sixties for material, some of which, at all events, may well have been denied a public during the fifties, when only *Le Surréalisme, même* (Autumn 1956-Spring 1959) could accommodate writing of the kind with which we are concerned. We may anticipate that the volume of comparable material coming out during the seventies will be a doubtful indicator of the degree of activity on the part of surrealist writers in France, and possibly in other countries as well. It is noteworthy anyway that the four texts by which surrealism in the seventies is represented in the present collection appear here for the first time. Launched in November

1970, the *Bulletin de liaison surréaliste* is of too limited scope, apparently, to find space for extensive texts.

A strictly chronological arrangement of the material gathered here would be speculative and, as such, open to question. And since surrealism in the short story had not been subject to any noteworthy evolution, chronological order has but questionable advantages, offset certainly by the disadvantages of having two or more tales by the same author separated because they belong to different periods of his life. Hence an alternative arrangement has been adopted, the one that seems the simplest, the most practical, and at the same time the least confining for general readers.

With no specialist knowledge of surrealism, the general public has its own reasons for turning to these stories, and its expectations cannot be assumed to reflect uniformity. I hope therefore that an alphabetical arrangement will be interpreted, as it is meant to be, as an invitation, extended to anyone so inclined, to browse, to begin where a title or an author's name attracts his attention, conscience-free to abandon a text for another initially more appealing or perhaps, on first contact anyway, easier to follow and enjoy.

For the benefit of those who may find in this book their first opportunity to make contact with surrealism, an approach might be suggested that possibly could facilitate their introduction to surrealist writing. They might begin, for instance, with one of the following: Leonora Carrington, Chariarse, Dumont, Ferry, Marianne van Hirtum, or Pierre. All the texts drawn from the work of these authors can be said to afford some immediate satisfaction, although their most subtle and most lasting contribution to surrealism is not in every case just as immediately discernible. Then, having sampled these, readers could move on to Arrabal, Goemans, Hénein, Joubert, Lebel, Lecomte, Joyce Mansour, Mariën, Péret, Pieyre de Mandiargues, and Gisèle Prassinos. These are writers whose stories contribute to the development of our appreciation of the range of surrealism's influence upon the short story. They leave us better prepared to understand what role has been played in giving voice to surrealist aspirations by the remaining authors, whose intent is not perceived so readily: Bédouin, Jouffroy, Lacomblez, Limbour, Markale, Nougé, and Sebbag.

If such an approach is useful, one may ask, then why was it not permitted to dictate the order in which these writers are presented for examination? There are two reasons for this. First, each reader brings to the experience of surrealism predispositions in favor of and confidence in some aspects of the world about him, as well as prejudices against others. It is one thing to make broad tentative suggestions for the guidance of those who may welcome these. It is quite a different matter to impose these suggestions upon people who do not need guidance or have their reasons—whether or not these be articulated—for resisting them. This is especially true when the effect of proposing such a framework—one that, in the event, necessarily reflects *my* reactions to the world and to surrealism's way of dealing with it—is restrictive in another sense also. Second, whether he knows something about surrealism or not, the reader must be left free, if he chooses, to come to the tales assembled for his enjoyment in a manner consistent with his curiosity, with the demands he makes upon surrealism no less than with his capacity to respond to it. He may wish to take up the thread of surrealism in such a manner as to be able to follow it thematically. Hence, the most serviceable arrangement, for his purposes, is not one such as is sketched above. Instead, he will be looking for guidelines of quite a different sort.

Let us suppose him interested, to begin with, in examining how surrealists turn humor to account. He will need to read Chariarse's *Unacceptable Mixture*, at least one of the stories by Mariën (*The Children's Marquis de Sade*), two by Ferry (*The Garbage Men's Strike* and *Kafka or "The Secret Society"*), a few texts by Arrabal, and everything offered below from the writings of Leonora Carrington, Marianne van Hirtum, Joyce Mansour, Péret, and Pierre. He will then have discovered that surrealist humor is never simply whimsical. In one way or another, it stimulates alarm in any mind entirely content with the rationalist status quo. It defies social, ethical, and moral codes—and does so, sometimes, even more aggressively than can be estimated from the examples presented here. If, alternatively, the reader is attracted to the theme of terror as it serves to bring the marvelous to light in surrealist writing, then he will turn to Arrabal and to Joyce Mansour, will give Ferry's *The Fashionable Tiger* special attention, and will take care not to pass over Pieyre de Mandiargues or Gisèle Prassinos. He will come back yet again to Joyce Mansour, should his intention be to observe what role eroticism plays in surrealism. And, naturally, he will have to proceed to an exploration of the erotic universe of Joubert, of Jouffroy, of Markale, of Pieyre de Mandiargues, and of Gisèle Prassinos. Supposing his next concern is to gain a better understanding of the surrealist marvelous. He now must concentrate on Dumont, Goemans, Hénein, Lecomte, Limbour, and Péret, while not forgetting all that he discovered when pursuing the themes of humor, terror, and the erotic. Thus he faces a complex but highly rewarding task. Even if content to ignore the fascinating question of surrealism's demands upon language and narrative form—as these find an echo in the work of Bédouin, Hénein, Jouffroy, Lacomblez, Markale, and Sebbag, as well as in surrealist "parallel stories"—he will find out that thematic study is merely the first step in the direction of appreciation of the richness of the surrealist short story.

FERNANDO ARRABAL

1932—

Two writers whose work has had an impact on twentieth-century western theater found sympathy and support among surrealists in France sooner than they won general approval. One is Eugène Ionesco. The other, born in Melilla, Spanish Morocco, is Fernando Arrabal, who settled in Paris in the mid-fifties. While Ionesco's plays were soon to draw criticism from within the surrealist movement, Arrabal passed through a stage of active participation in surrealism and has done nothing to make himself the target for attacks of a similar nature.

Arrabal's *La Pierre de la folie* (*The Folly Stone* [1963]), from which all the texts below are taken, belongs to his period of direct involvement in surrealism. The first four extracts were published originally in the third issue of the magazine *La Brèche: action surréaliste* in September 1962. The remainder were reproduced in Jean-Louis Bédouin's anthology *La Poésie surréaliste*. Since in surrealist circles distinctions on the basis of literary genres and classifications are considered artificial, as a surrealist Bédouin felt no obligation to exclude from his selection certain parts of *La Pierre de la folie*, which he saw as its author's "means of awakening from the nightmare haunting him" (p. 45).

In a book, *The Theatre of the Absurd*, where Arrabal himself feels discussion of his plays has no place, Martin Esslin unenthusiastically describes him as viewing the world with "childlike eyes" (p. 219). Whatever the disadvantage seen by the historian of the absurd in Arrabal's way of looking at things, no reservations need be expressed by surrealists, who follow André Breton in regarding childhood as an enviable state. More important to note, however, is that Arrabal's outlook scarcely offers the adult the prospect of nostalgic escapism. On the contrary, reading *La Pierre de la folie* one is particularly aware of a mood of anxiety, having as one of its recurrent expressions the sensation of being watched, or at least the fear of being observed, in an activity usually of a sexual nature. Anticipation of blame generates feelings of guilt, no doubt. Yet these feelings do not merely conjure up dread. They increase the narrator's desire for the forbidden, so sharpening his responsiveness, not blunting it.

Everywhere in *La Pierre de la folie* we face evidence of a sensitivity that remains indifferent to the distinction, drawn by reasonable caution, between the self-indulgent benefits of folly and the dangers of madness. Indeed, Arrabal leaves us wondering whether we are not entitled to question Michelet's belief that "l'illuminisme de la folie lucide" is the prerogative of women. The values that society treats as generally operative in the commonsense world of everyday existence lose their stability here, rocked to their foundation by Arrabal's humor, which must be disconcerting to everyone unacquainted with the surrealists' affection for a form of humor that Breton's *Anthologie de l'Humour noir* defined as "a process permitting us to set aside what is painful in reality" (p. 360). Specifically, surrealists favor the humor illustrated in Breton's anthology, where *black humor* is shown to be "par excellence the mortal enemy of sentimentality" as well as of "a certain short-term fancy" (pp. 21-22).

Clearly, Arrabal is not interested in short-term fancy. To the degree that his *La Pierre de la folie* is marked by black humor, it shares with the work of the Marquis de Sade a characteristic emphasized in the *Anthologie de l'Humour noir*: it becomes "ground that lends itself to a mutation of life" (p. 64). Mutant forms, both animal and natural, are not merely fanciful adornments, then. They bear witness to the resistance offered the

reality principle by another, in which we recognize the pleasure
principle of which Freud spoke.[1]

---

1. The exhibition of surrealism held in Brno, Prague, and Bratislava in 1968 was
offered under the title *Princip Slasti* (*The Pleasure Principle*), "in explicit homage to
Freud," as Vincent Bounoure stressed in the catalog. "This show," explained
Claude Courtot, "is but a window open onto the jungle of your desires. Break all
the compasses and throw yourselves out of the window!"

FERNANDO ARRABAL

The Folly Stone

The curé came to see my mother and told her I was a fool.

Then my mother bound me to my chair. The curé made a hole in the back of my neck with a lancet and extracted from me the folly stone.

Then they carried me, tied hand and foot, as far as the ship of fools.

*

Behind there is a nun and a big frying pan on the fire. I think she is making an omelette, for I see near her two gigantic eggs. I approach, she is looking at me intently and I glimpse beneath her habit two frog's thighs instead of legs.

In the frying pan there is a man who has an air of indifference. From time to time he puts a foot out—maybe he's hot—but the nun stops him. Now the man doesn't move any more and a sort of bouillon that smells of consommé covers him completely. The soup is getting very thick, I can't see him any more.

The nun tells me to come into a corner. I go with her. She begins to speak to me and to say dirty things to me. To understand her better, I come close to her. I feel her caressing my sex

organ but I don't dare protest. Someone is laughing behind us. I
look at the nun's hands and discover two frog's legs.

I am naked. I'm afraid I will be seen in this state. She tells
me to get into the big frying pan so that no one will take me by
surprise. I get in. The bouillon becomes more and more burning
hot: I try to put a foot out of the frying pan but the nun stops
me. Suddenly the consommé covers me completely and I feel
the heat increasing incessantly.

Now I'm burning.

*

The naked little girl on horseback told me to go to the square.

I went. I saw the people playing with spheres that they
would throw and catch again thanks to a strong elastic. When I
crossed the square they all stopped playing and pointed a finger
at me, laughing. Then I began to run and they threw some
spheres at me which rolled on the ground near me without
hitting me: These spheres were made of iron.

I plunged blindly into the first street I came to. I realized,
afterward, that I'd chosen a dead end. I returned in the direction
of the square.

A horse came charging after me; I hid behind a tree with
several trunks, to escape from it. The horse threw itself on me
but remained a prisoner of the tree, the branches of which
closed about it. I was raising my eyes and I saw the naked little
girl.

I tried to free the horse; it bit my hand, tearing off part of
my wrist. It whinnied and seemed to laugh. The people began
to throw iron spheres at me and the naked little girl on the horse
was hiding her face so as not to show she was shaking with
laughter.

*

"My child, my child."

At last she lit the tiny lamp and I was able to see her body
but not her face, lost in the darkness.

I said to her, "Mamma."

She asked me to take her in my arms. I took her in my arms
and felt her nails sink into my shoulders: soon the blood
spurted, wet.

She said to me, "My child, my child, kiss me."

I came close and kissed her and I felt her teeth sink into my neck and the blood flowing.

Then I realized she was wearing, hanging from her belt, a little cage with a sparrow inside. He was injured but he was singing: his blood was my blood.

*

She gave me a bouquet of flowers, put a red vest on me and made me climb on her shoulders. She was saying: "As he is a dwarf he has a terrible inferiority complex" and the people were laughing.

She was walking very fast and I held tightly to her forehead so as not to fall. Around us there were many children and it made no difference that I had climbed up her, I hardly reached the level of their knees.

When I felt tired she gave me a cup to drink, full of a red liquid that had the taste of Coca-Cola. As soon as I'd finished she began to run again. And the people were laughing, you'd have thought they were cackling. She asked them not to laugh any more because I was very sensitive. And the people roared with laughter.

She was running faster and faster and I could see her uncovered breasts and her blouse that was flying in the wind. The people were laughing louder than ever.

Finally she put me down on the ground and disappeared. A group of enormous red hens came up to me, cackling. I was no bigger than the beaks that were approaching to peck at me.

*

Sometimes my right hand detaches itself from my arm at the level of my wrist and joins my left hand. I hold it tight, to prevent it from falling, for I could lose it. I have to keep watch on it constantly so as to avoid, in some absentminded moment when the time comes to replace it, putting it on backward, with the palm facing outward.

*

I placed the compass point on her belly and I traced several concentric circles that ran some through her knees and some through her navel or again over her heart.

So as not to forget her face, I imagined it full of numbers.

Then it began to rain, and she got onto a horse, standing, naked.

I was holding the reins. Fish fell from the sky and they were passing, laughing, between her legs.

*

A man dressed as a bishop, a whip in his hand, told me to go into the church. It seemed to me the porch was formed by the two thighs of a kneeling giantess.

In a corner, in front of me, danced a woman, completely hidden by veils, so that I could only guess at her shape. I wanted to look for the altar but I was watching the woman dance. She came up to me and asked me to touch her breasts; I was afraid someone would catch us but I obeyed. Then she removed one of her veils and under my hand, in place of the breast, I felt the head of a newborn baby. The head was laughing. I withdrew my hand and the baby fell to the ground. He began to cry, but when I bent down to pick him up, he had disappeared.

Then the woman took me in her arms. I was afraid of being seen. I tried to break loose, but without success. As I struggled, I tore off one of her veils, and I saw that her arms were big leafless branches, and her face seemed to me very pale and all wrinkled. She laughed, showing a toothless mouth.

I heard the child's voice shouting, "It's him." I turned around and caught sight of his head on the hand of the man dressed as a bishop, who was looking at me intently. I wanted to run away, but the woman's branches imprisoned me like pincers.

*

I hit the old man's head with an ax and she emerged from the hole, naked. She came toward me and I handed her a toad which she suckled.

The old man closed his split skull with the help of his hands. Then flames began to shoot from his feet. She came forward and swallowed up the fire.

She and I both went into a house, but we soon perceived it was a big transparent egg. We embraced, and, when I wanted to step away from her, I felt we formed one body with two heads.

The old man blew on the egg which flew away, carrying us both off.

*

We were both in a movie theater. Instead of watching the film, I was watching *her*. I touched her curls and smoothed her eyelashes. Then I kissed her knees and put on her stomach a paper bird I'd made out of the tickets.

She was watching the film and laughing. Then I fondled her bosom and each time I pressed one of her breasts a blue fish came out of it.

*

Gentlemen:

With reference to your 8763 BM/PR of November 27, ult. Kindly excuse my delay, but violent pains in the back of the neck are causing me a lot of suffering at the moment, and leave me prostrate for days at a time.

Indeed I did hang two big violet drapes over the front of my house. Please believe me when I assure you they are absolutely necessary to give me peace. I recently received certain visits likely to disturb my serenity, and I find myself obliged to avail myself of a method for discouraging these. You will readily understand that I cannot stand guard night and day on my balcony. As for the different signs on the wall, they were put there for the same purpose, as was the notice: "Keep away from me, vermin."

The solution you suggest (placing those drapes and the signs in the entrance hall of my apartment) can be of no assistance to me. The visitors always come in through the window (often passing through the wall), and everything leads me to believe they come to me flying through the air.

Reassure my fellow citizens, then, and tell them they must not see anything that can offend them in my modest means of protection.

I thank you for your kind attention to my most intimate problems and remain, Gentlemen, respectfully.

JEAN-LOUIS BÉDOUIN

1929—

As used by certain surrealists, language may fulfill either of two complementary purposes. Whether the written text is anticipatory (projecting experience foreseen yet unprecendented), or whether it is recapitulative (serving to record something that has occurred; in diurnal activity or nocturnal dream, or in reverie, it makes no difference), language stands in the same relationship to the material that occasions its use. When the text is cast in the form of a narrative, narration seeks to embrace something language is but imperfectly adapted to transmitting. In these circumstances, it is in the nature of narrative to fall short of its aim. Yet its inadequacy serves as a tribute to the event in focus, all the more significant for being incapable of encompassing that event fully. Thus in surrealist stories like Jean-Louis Bédouin's *Plume pour les paradisiers,* reproduced below, the event lying at the core of the narrative is protected, as it were, by an aura that language is unable to penetrate and must be content to delimit in a somewhat clumsy fashion.

Far from feeling despair at the ineffectuality of language when it comes to dealing with subject matter so elusive as to mock his effort at communication, a surrealist like Bédouin finds in the challenge of a patently unequal struggle the necessary stimulus for narrative endeavor and its true significance. Language, he recognizes, cannot exhaust his subject. In fact, his best effort with words is required merely to situate that subject, to signpost the route—unfrequented by rational minds—by which one may hope to approach it. Hence the parallel to be noted between *Plume pour les paradisiers* and the poem *Vigilance* in André Breton's *Le Revolver à cheveux blancs* (*The Whitehaired Revolver* [1932]) is a significant one. Like Breton's text, although more explicitly, Bédouin's culminates in the optimistic image of the clew that guides us through the labyrinth.

If any one sentence from Breton's *Manifeste du surréalisme* seems to lend itself particularly well to characterizing Bédouin's efforts as a surrealist writer, it is surely the following: "Words and images offer themselves as springboards to the mind of the listener" (p. 51). This dictum has found many an echo within the surrealist group, since surrealists have been consistently as much concerned with the effect of words upon those who hear them as with the value of spoken words for those uttering them. One surrealist of Bédouin's generation, Vincent Bounoure, stressed this preoccupation in a manner that exemplifies surrealist thought on this matter, when he dedicated a copy of his poems *Envers l'Ombre* (*Toward the Shadow*, [1965]) with this assertion: "It is not the wind, it is the ear that brings the Aeolian harp to life." And no one has commented more forcefully on the surrealist position than Paul Éluard when he wrote in his *Donner à voir* (1939): "Poems always have big white margins, big margins of silence, in which ardent memory is consumed to create anew a delirium with no past. Their principal quality is not to evoke, but to inspire" (p. 74).

The drama played out in *Plume pour les paradisiers* lies in the struggle between conception and projection, on the one hand, and expression, on the other. One's impression is that the most important things Bédouin has to say are to be sought in the big white margins that frame his text without confining it. It is worth noticing, in this connection, that a volume of verse he published in 1967 bears the title *Libre Espace* (*Free Space*). Here the title poem begins, incidentally, with the declaration that all we need to "proceed further" is "a spoken word," "the right word."

One does not ask a writer as self-effacing before his work as Bédouin for comments of a theoretical nature. All the same, some indication is available to us regarding the values underlying *Plume pour les paradisiers*. We find it provided discreetly in the following paragraph from Bédouin's preface to the volume on Victor Segalen (1963) in Pierre Seghers' "Poètes d'Aujourd'hui" series: "At a time when the language of man resembles more and more a form of sad esperanto, with the syntax derived solely from the laws of immediate necessity, it is good to recall with Segalen that true communication, fruitful exchanges, a profound understanding of Nature and of living beings are directly a function of the differences and distances existing between things in the intelligible, tangible universe, of the faculty granted us to perceive and experience them. For it is these differences and distances that lay the foundation for the innumerable forms of *relationships,* and make possible, for that very reason, the life of the spirit. Just as it is the white and the empty space between words that permit the written sentence to become organized and to take on meaning, so too silence lays the foundation for the word and the distance between two realities provokes the flash of lightning of the poetic image.[1] Distance then proves to be the essential condition of all proximity. The unknown, the condition of all desire to know, and disparity, that even of all pairing" (pp. 14-15).

Jean-Louis Bédouin, born in Neuilly-sur-Seine, France, made André Breton's acquaintance and began participating in surrealist activities at the end of 1947. Written on January 12, 1965, *Plume pour les paradisiers* appears here for the first time.

---

1. Bédouin's indebtedness to Breton is clearly visible in this sentence. Cf. the *Manifeste du surréalisme* of 1924: "It is from the somewhat fortuitous bringing together of the two terms that a particular light has sprung, *the light of the image,* to which we are infinitely sensitive. The value of the image depends on the beauty of the spark obtained; it is, consequently, a function of the difference of potential between the two conductors" (p. 52).

JEAN-LOUIS BÉDOUIN

A Feather for
Birds of Paradise

These portals—or are they, rather, great transparent slabs, split by fire as one thumbs through the pages of a book, to make the idea of depth emerge at last; these portals which, seen close up, are made of antennas, and closer still from brass wire, braced by diagonal or triangular spokes, crossing their X accentuated by Spanish fly, lead directly, without fear of losing their way in the cloister where green lizards couple, to the heart of the vision. Of reality. Whether they appear to delimit it, whether in fact they frame it, they nevertheless open upon the unknown, which is in the center. They make much more air circulate and carry more cries than they enclose of mute space, jealous of its privileges. This is why, no doubt, they incite one as nothing else does to clear the handrail of the support, paper, cloth, sky, or mine-head, so as, with one leap, to jump to the other side, and, in the time it takes to establish that appearances have remained on this side, to find oneself once again in the haunted house, the famous dwelling with no façade, whose every window faces toward the inside.

One had indeed hesitated a little. Because it is not certain that there is no peril—but of what nature? Ask the drop imprisoned within a piece of crystal—in venturing into that gallery which opens so logically onto the surface but goes on well

beyond the limit where one penetrates daylight, with its intersections and its nooks, its clear angles and its bottlenecks, where
horizontal bars and rails shine, inexplicable. These make you
think of the well-oiled machinery of a theater, with the illusory
scenery of a trap. Could one just foil the snare, which everything leads one to believe has been set? One does not yet know
anything definite, before the leap, about the silence that cries
out, about the music that casts a spell. But one already suspects
they are necessary, indispensable aids to expectation and relaxa-
tion, the trigger, or the flash of lightning, taking to the point of
paroxysm the long agony of desire and the crazy pleasure of
being the equal of death, even if it should be at the price of
murdering a simulacrum, body or dummy.

To bring yourself to do it, or plunge into it, you have to
divest yourself of that envelope of shadow which marks for
itself the position of a living person on the sand, under the
lowering sky; you have to change your form, after the image of
someone who has no reflection, or image, in a spurt of pure fire,
of naked fire, forever fed by the splintering, a thousand times
repeated, of a bone on the skull of the void. Then, but only then,
the surface can light up with stars, and from between the wire
portals, as from between the young girl's legs, the black blood of
sleeping woods can extravasate. Then, but only then, where the
sources of our hearts dilated, it is possible to discover the high
stele of schist, bearer of inscriptions about which it would be
pointless to argue over whether they are immemorial traces or
attempts at new kinds of inscriptions, when the desert itself, the
beginning and probable end of this earth, is an incense-boat full
of black pollen, that slowly covers the eyes, the hands, and
chokes the pipes of the song. So that, by dint of searching for
myself here, I am brought back again to my point of departure,
which is a crypt; a crypt paneled with silky fascines, black as the
black hair of the Queen of Ethiopia; a crypt suddenly walled up.

The knot of silence at your collar; the cavern's paw on your
shoulder; the evening wind in your pocket: here you are. The
idol, but it is a stake, a stake of plain, unvarnished, knotty
wood, that supports the valleys, the nacelle of the hills, above
the abyss where poisons grow. Suppose it looks behind you, do
not turn around; suppose it stares behind you at the spectacle,
or the drama, unfolding there also, do not turn around. You and

it are between two mirrors, and one is starred with the red of your blood, and the other reflects back the dance of the night on the tower steps.

A night left swinging, a night suspended. A voice is reciting that we must go up the steps and down them, that we must climb the steps of our own lives and know how to follow back down its course. I listen to this voice, but my heart is a crypt completely full of the flight of a bird from that night, on the bosom of which the white faces of the two sparrow-owls are beginning to shine, the winged wheels of the tip-cart of light that the invisible has cast. My heart rises, as the voice speaks, but the head, my head with eyes turned within, plunges interminably into the depths of a sea saturated with salt, a very weighty sea, unexplored, where the explosions of the reefs turn in slow motion. And it is there that the silent shooting breaks out in bursts, that the fire-damp of dawn deflagrates, at the rising of a star unknown, unhoped for, against the high background. A ballet of trajectories, a dance of tracer bullets, bearing spiculae! All the arrows fired together from the same bow, and all the glances from the same eye! Enough to make them go pale, up there, the sun and its daughters, the queens and their sovereign! Meanwhile, the portals, faithful to the horizon, continue to hold up with nothing at all, with a thread like a cat's moustache, the thickness of the mental night, the tons of sidereal coal dust, and the sex organs seeking one another desperately around the Pleiades, with the gestures of somnambulists or marine animals. While during the most muted part of the nocturne everything that traces, slips by, breaks through, and spreads out converges toward the ideal vanishing point, in the direction of which the wings of the great sphinx, which is crucified on the display counter, are arranged, antennae open like a compass or like a woman, toward the sun of the depths.

All this, which has no need of cries, of movement of the air or shifts in perspective, to come into being, all this which is less produced than revealed, as from a negative, by some molecular operation, being but the effect of an extension taken well beyond ordinary limits. As if there were a sudden, ineluctable mutation, and as if night itself, for so long in labor, had slipped its moorings, had tied up of its own accord, the better to make fast to its sail the string of worlds, rockets of stars, and silex noiselessly split, and as if it had undertaken, so as to link more closely that which day separates, to wreathe the nerves, little by little.

But the testing stone exfoliates with each heartbeat, inviting us to close our eyes, to open them, to close them again, faster, always faster, until between night and day, the bed and roof of the vein in the mine through which we merely pass, that which lives in the medulla adapts itself to the unique note by which is announced the appearance of the great figures wearing tiaras, whose masks burn black through the pyramidal canopy of their chests. Around them . . . But around them there is nothing, nothing in any case of what I thought I could see; nothing, save that stridency, of such rare quality; nothing unless it be they themselves and the spreading waves, a direct emanation of those beings made of nets and lakes, isothermic curves and isobars, in whom are incarnate the powers of anxiety and the vertigo that takes hold of the mind when it sees itself on the edge of the world.

And this is why those figures seem motionless; this is why they seem mute, as if all they needed were, at long intervals, a few great, simple, suspended gestures, a few gestures that nothing completes, that nothing would be able to carry through. A few great mute events, incomplete, uncompletable, are all that is needed for the drama being played out there; between the two birds of paradise, between love and love, between the swift passage of time and the vertical spurt of space—the labyrinth of darting flame, the translucent enigma that hides the spectator from himself, that hides from me myself this face I scrutinize in vain, through the visor of a helm or a mask.

However, I am beginning to glimpse, in the dark night's eye, the flower of a fire that is throwing out sparks, that is dotting the curve of suffering with brightness; bonds are breaking that still hold me back, that will not hold me back any longer from going toward the woman sketching, against the high, grey excavations, in a style sharper than a glance, the arch of her body, thrown back on the river of time.

While neuropteran Eros murmurs.

And while the light, still, comes from the bottom, as from a conflagration beneath the earth's crust, as from a sun bricked up in the foundation of the tomb or the temple. And it is now, only now, that I fully hear the order, for here reigns a law, all the more imperious for not being written down: I must go still farther toward the inside, pass the herse hanging from the portals, the rain of meteors that defends the watchmen lying in wait, the great solitary figures about whom it is not known what they are contemplating, in the past or the future; what they are expecting or what they dread, the Totem that stands in the fine frosted mirror, or the great female come from another world, with innumerable pairs of feet, wings missing, and that heads straight for the star, from the concave surfaces of the oval sky.

Alone, doubled up like the black stone, the sturdy being with bilocular anther head, with all its taut energy keeps the Sorceress at a distance. Behind him the rooms line up to infinity, fish held by the gills on a spit. They send back to one another the image of the absence that is in them, and selects and inhabits them in turn, and that, desperately, calls for and provokes some presence, the arrival of which, still distant, is announced by a slight crackling. For an instant, the perfect equilibrium of this system of crystals, the redoubtable harmony of this ballistic construction seems on the point of breaking down. When the colossal shadow of the appointed time brushes against the water's gong, the tension becomes almost unbearable. It increases even more, it increases still, while the desecrator, with the same suspended gesture of the other ghosts, reaches out his arm and raises the final veil.

Does the end of this endless race, rushing headlong, come now? Or is the enigma, a boomerang, going to turn me back on myself, shattering the frost-riven light, closing off forever the way out of the labyrinth? Nothing stirs, though, even in the very heart of the unfathomable; nothing stirs. The stars, invisible because they are innumerable, have scarcely blinked, and the magnetic specter has scarcely quivered for a lightning moment.

Secret, although more exposed than ever, the great hieratic figures, woven from waves and cries, continue their interminable vigil. Around them the air becomes the bearer of murmurs and whisperings. I hear advice being given to close my eyes the better to see, to create total darkness so as to see clearly.

And now sleeping, or dead, the woman in whom all sap is gathered and all flight glorified, lies bowed at the foot of space.

But it is still she, the same and only one, who straightens up at the same moment, her nudity scumbled with muffled light, and, making sport of herself as she dances, advances on the screen in the background.

Between the one and the other, the impossible embrace, the abyss of what can always take place, the irruption of phantoms and of every conjuration. Between the one and the other, the archway of a body thrown across chaos; the archway of a body to be loved. But between the one and the other—and the one is perhaps life, and the other the dream of that same life—no choice is possible. Everything, between them, occurs by echo, by reflection, by harmonics. And the one is not different from the other, which, rising in one spurt toward the tympanum of the sky, suddenly enlightens me and shows me the way and opens the river to me.

A little later finally, at the time when the wind of dawn has its sharpest edge, and later still, when broad daylight is at its most empty, it will be necessary to pick up once more the thread that goes from yesterday to the present moment, the thread I know so little how to dance on, that extends from my life to my life, from my heart to my words. At least I shall not have lost the key to the labyrinth; and without opening my eyes I shall be able to follow the woman whose silhouette marks forever, for me, the ford to the heart of the world, signals and stamps the opening through which I am permitted to pass, freed, liberated, lightened of the formidable burden of time, at last reconciled with colossal shadows and ambiguous totems.

Even if she dissolves at last into pure transparency, her gesture trembles still and the torch of her youth continues to burn, susceptible to cold and proud, in the narrow opening of the camera obscura where is to be found the only light that will never be extinguished.

LEONORA CARRINGTON

1917—

Author of two plays, *The Flannel Night-Shirt* and *Penelope*, as well as of an account of her experiences during a period when she was pronounced incurably insane,[1] Leonora Carrington entered the surrealist movement in 1937. An artist whose painting recurrently evokes magic encounters, she brings to the practice of storytelling a sense of occasion that endows her tales with quite a special atmosphere. Her stories are not characterized by a mood of wonder or excitement. Rather, these celebrations of the marvelous are marked by a singular matter-of-factness; as they are, also, by an element so mysterious to the French that, in defeat, they refer to it helplessly as *l'humour anglais*.

The feeling communicated in the stories Ms. Carrington tells owes much to her distinctive point of view. This is not at all the viewpoint of militant feminism. It is, however, so character-

---

1. Published in English translation in the American surrealist magazine *VVV*, no. 4 (1944) as *Down Below*, this text appeared in Paris as *En Bas* (1945) under the imprint Éditions Fontaine, in the "L'Age d'Or" collection. The English version reappeared in 1972 as no. 5 in the "Surrealist Research and Development Monograph Series," published by *Radical America* under the direction of the Surrealist Group in Chicago. The crisis poignantly recorded in *Down Below* was precipitated by events surrounding Leonora Carrington's separation from Max Ernst, interned as a German citizen by French authorities upon the outbreak of the 1939 war.

istically that of a woman as to make Leonora Carrington's tales
noteworthy examples of how narrative may be approached and
handled under surrealist influence. In the most positive, creative, and revealing sense, her imagination is feminine. It
enriches her stories with numerous details that contribute to
undermining the barrier separating normality from the universe
where her characters are in their natural element.

At the same time, the appeal of her early tales—especially
those collected under the title *La Dame ovale* (*The Oval Lady*
[1939]), from which come both *La Débutante* and *L'Amoureux*—
results in part from the fact that when Ms. Carrington wrote in
French, during the late thirties, she still had not given up thinking in English. These texts are not difficult to put back into her
mother tongue, of course. Yet it is important for full appreciation of her writing to realize that, in English, they lose some of
the flavor they have in French. Reading them in the original,
one has the impression that they have been pieced together,
with little regard for tense sequence, from colloquialisms and
clichés, interspersed with linguistic oddities that betray translit-
eration. So, if Leonora Carrington's aspirations were merely
literary, the results she has obtained would appear less than
satisfactory. But, in the context of surrealism, her stories gain,
not lose, from the method by which they have been quite literally put together, in a way that makes the collages by Max Ernst
seem especially appropriate illustrative material in *La Dame
ovale*.

It is not just a matter of style, as, for example, Joseph
Conrad's English owes something to his prior knowledge of
French. On the contrary, what counts in Ms. Carrington's case
is a twofold effect. First, the availability of familiar hackneyed
turns of phrase, which leads her to advance her narrative most
readily by means of dialogue, has evidently played a role in
shaping her tale somewhat. The things her characters say and
do, even the situations in which they find themselves—all this is
influenced to some degree, if not exactly dictated, by the limitations imposed on her stories by her incomplete acquaintance
with the French language. Obviously, this is the very opposite
of automatic writing. Nevertheless, the necessary practice of a
technique that channels imaginative activity under the more or
less confining influence of preoccupations of a predominantly

linguistic order serves, in an important way, to help liberate Leonora Carrington from concerns of a rational nature and to foster reliance upon chance in the development of narrative sequence. Second, the conditions under which these stories come into being impress upon them a tone of simplicity, of naïveté, even, that—in the total absence of signs of surprise on the narrator's part—goes a long way toward authenticating the marvelous, as Ms. Carrington affords us glimpses of its operation.

"The task of the right eye," Leonora Carrington tells us, "is to peer into the telescope, while the left eye peers into the microscope."[2]

---

2. Quoted by André Breton in his *Anthologie de l'Humour noir*, where Leonora Carrington is represented by *La Débutante*.

LEONORA CARRINGTON

The Debutante

When I was a debutante I often used to go to the Zoological Gardens. I'd go there so often I knew the animals better than the young ladies of my own age. It was in fact to get away from people that I found myself every day at the Zoo. The animal I knew the best was a young hyena. She knew me, too; she was very intelligent; I taught her French and in return she taught me her language. We spent many a pleasant hour this way.

On the first day of May, my mother was arranging a ball in my honor; for nights on end I suffered; I've always hated balls, especially those given in *my* honor.

On the morning of the First of May 1934, very early, I paid the hyena a visit. "It's a damned nuisance," I told her, "I have to go to my ball this evening."

"You're lucky," she said, "I'd be glad to go. I don't know how to dance, but I know how to make conversation, anyway."

"There'll be lots of things to eat," I said. "I've seen trucks full of food coming up to the house."

"And you complain," replied the hyena, in disgust. "*I* eat once a day, and you should see the shit they give me!"

I had a daring idea, I almost laughed: "Why don't you go in my place?"

"We don't look enough alike, otherwise I'd go all right," said the hyena, a bit sad.

"Listen," said I, "under the evening lights it isn't too easy to see; if you're dressed up a bit, among the crowd they won't notice. Then again, we're about the same height. You are my only friend, I beg of you." She thought things over, I knew she wanted to accept.

"Consider it done," she said suddenly.

It was very early in the day, there were not many keepers about. Quickly I opened the cage and in a few moments we were in the street. I took a taxi, and at home everyone was in bed. In my room I took out the dress I was to wear that evening. It was a little long and the hyena had trouble walking on the high heels of my shoes. I found some gloves to disguise her hands, too hairy to resemble mine. When the sun reached my room she walked several times up and down, more or less upright. We were so busy that my mother, who was coming to say good morning to me, almost opened the door before the hyena had hidden under my bed. "There's a nasty smell in your room," said my mother, opening a window. "Before tonight you'll take a bath scented with my new salts."—"All right," I said. She didn't stay long. I think the smell was too strong for her.

"Don't be late for breakfast," said my mother, leaving my room.

The biggest problem was finding a disguise for her face. Hours and hours we tried; she turned down all my suggestions. At last she said: "I think I know a solution. Do you have a maid?"

"Yes," I said, perplexed.

"Well, there you are. You'll ring for the maid and when she comes we'll pounce on her and we'll tear her face off. I'll wear her face this evening in place of my own."

"That's not sensible," I said. "She'll probably be dead when she has no face left; someone will surely find the body and we'll go to prison."

"I'm hungry enough to eat her," replied the hyena.

"And what about the bones?"

"Them, too," she said. "Well, do you agree?"

"Only if you promise to kill her before tearing her face off; it'll hurt too much, otherwise."

"Right, it's all the same to me."

I was ringing for Mary the maid, somewhat nervous. I wouldn't have done so if I didn't hate balls so. When Mary came in I turned to the wall so as not to see. I admit it was over quick. A short cry and that was the end. While the hyena was eating, I looked out of the window. A few minutes later she said: "I can't eat any more; both of the feet are still left, but if you have a bag I'll eat them later in the day."

"You'll find in the closet a bag embroidered with the fleur de lys. Empty out the handkerchiefs in there and take that one." She was doing as I had told her. Then she said: "Turn around now and look how beautiful I am!"

In front of the mirror the hyena was admiring herself in Mary's face. She had eaten very carefully all around the face so that just what she needed was left. "Yes indeed, you've made a good job of it," I said. Toward evening, when the hyena was all dressed, she announced: "I feel in fine form. I've the impression I'll be a big success tonight."

When we had heard the music downstairs for some time, I said to her: "Go on, now, and remember not to stand next to my mother: she'd know it wasn't me, for sure. Apart from her, I know nobody. Good luck." I kissed her as she left but she did have a strong smell. Night had come. Tired out by the emotions of the day, I took a book and, near the open window, I gave myself over to rest. I remember I was reading *Gulliver's Travels* by Jonathan Swift. It was perhaps an hour after that the first sign of something untoward came. A bat entered by the window, uttering little cries. I'm terribly afraid of bats. I hid behind a chair, my teeth chattering. I was hardly on my knees when the sound of beating wings was drowned out by a loud noise at my door. My mother came in, pale with fury. "We had just sat down to eat," she said, "when that thing in your place gets up and cries,' I smell a bit strong, eh? Well *I* don't eat cake.' Then she tore off her face and ate it. With one big bound she disappeared through the window."

LEONORA CARRINGTON

A Man in Love

Passing through a narrow street in the evening, I swiped a melon. The fruiterer, who was hiding behind his fruit, caught me by the arm. "Miss," he said, "for forty years I've been waiting for such a chance. Forty years I've been hiding behind this pile of oranges in the hope someone will swipe one of my fruit. Here's why: I want to talk, I want to tell my story. If you don't listen, I'll turn you over to the police."

"I'm listening," said I.

He takes me by the arm and drags me into the depths of his shop between fruit and vegetables. We pass through a door at the back and arrive in a bedroom. There was a bed there that held a woman, motionless and probably dead. It seemed to me she'd been there a long time, for the bed was all covered in weeds. "I water her every day," said the fruiterer thoughtfully.

"For forty years I haven't been able to know if she was dead or not. She hasn't moved, or spoken, or eaten during that time; but, it's an odd thing, she stays warm. If you don't believe me, look." Thereupon he raises a corner of the blanket and I saw a lot of eggs and some new-born chicks. "You see, that's where my eggs are hatched (I sell fresh eggs too)."

We sat down, on each side of the bed and the fruiterer began to speak: "I love her so much; believe me. I've always loved her. She was so sweet. She had little nimble white feet. You'd like to see?"—"No," I said.

"Anyway," he continued with a deep sigh, "she was so beautiful. *I* had blond hair. *She* had fine black hair. (We both have white hair now.) Her father was an extraordinary man. He had a big house in the country. He was a collector of lamb chops. That's how we got to know each other. *I* have a little talent. It's this, I know how to dry meat with a glance. Mr. Pushfoot (that was his name) heard tell of me. He invited me to his home to dry his chops so that they wouldn't go off. Agnes was his daughter. We loved one another at once. We left together by way of the Seine in a boat. I was the one who rowed. Agnes spoke to me like this: 'I love you so much that you are my life.' And *I* said the same thing back to her. I believe it's my love that keeps her so warm now; she is dead, no doubt, but the warmth goes on.—Next year," he continued, with a faraway look in his eye, "I shall put some tomatoes in; I'd not be a bit surprised if they took well.—Night is falling, I didn't know where to spend our wedding night; Agnes had become so pale, so pale from fatigue. At last, when we had more or less left Paris behind, I saw a bistrot overlooking the river. I tie up the boat and we come to it by the dark sinister terrace. There were two wolves and a fox walking about around us, no one else.

*

"I knocked, I knocked on the door that held back a terrible silence: 'Agnes is tired, Agnes is very tired,' I cried as loud as I could. At last an old head hung out of the window and said: '*I* don't know anything. The fox is boss here. Let me sleep; you're bothering me.' Agnes began to weep. There was nothing else for it, I had to speak to the fox. 'Do you have any beds?' I asked several times; he answered not a word, he didn't know how to speak. And then the head once again, older than before, comes down gently from the window, attached to a string: 'Speak to the wolves; *I'm* not boss here. Let me sleep, please, Finally I understood that this head was out of its head and that there was no sense in going on. Agnes was still crying. I walked around the house several times and in the end I was able to open a window by which we got in. We found ourselves in a kitchen with a high ceiling and on a big oven reddened by fire were vegetables cooking all by themselves; they jumped by their own power into the boiling water; this game pleased them a lot. We ate well and afterwards we lay down on the floor. I held Agnes in my arms. We didn't sleep at all. That terrible kitchen contained all sorts of things. Rats in numbers had taken up position at the mouth of their holes and were singing in small, thin, disagreeable voices. There were foul odors that swelled and subsided one after the other and drafts—I think it was the drafts that finished my poor Agnes off. She never came to. Since that day, she speaks less and less." And the fruiterer was so blinded by his tears that I was able to make off with my melon.

LEONORA CARRINGTON

The Neutral Man

Although I have always promised myself I'd keep this episode a secret, I have written it down after all, inevitably. Anyway, the reputation of certain very famous foreigners being involved, I find myself obliged to use fictitious names, which disguises no one, for any reader familiar with the customs of the British in tropical countries will have no difficulty recognizing everybody.

I received an invitation, asking me to attend a masked ball. Caught unprepared, I buttered my face thickly with an electric-green phosphorescent pomade. On this base, I spread tiny imitation diamonds, so as to sprinkle myself with stars like a night sky, with no other pretensions.

Then, nervously, I slipped into a public transit vehicle that took me to the outskirts of the town, on General Epigastro Square. A splendid equestrian bust of the famous soldier dominated the square; the artist who succeeded in solving the strange problem posed by this monument resorted to a courageous archaic simplification, confining himself to making a marvelous portrait in the form of a bust of the horse belonging to the general. Generalissimo Don Epigastro remains engraved in the public's imagination.

Mr. MacFrolick's castle took up the whole of the west side of General Epigastro Square. An Indian servant showed me into a large reception room in baroque style. I found myself among about a hundred people. A fairly charged atmosphere at last told me I was the only person to have taken the invitation altogether seriously: I was the only one in fancy dress.

"No doubt," said the master of the house, Mr. MacFrolick, "you have had the artful intention of looking like a certain Princess of Tibet, mistress of a King dominated by the somber rituals of the Bön, fortunately lost in remotest antiquity? I would hesitate to relate in the presence of ladies the atrocious exploits of the Green Princess: suffice it to say she died in mysterious circumstances, around which different legends still circulate in the Far East. Some claim the body was carried off by bees that still preserve it in a transparent honey from flowers of Venus. Others say the painted coffin contained not the princess but the body of a crane with a woman's face; others again affirm that the princess returns in the form of a sow." Mr. MacFrolick suddenly stopped and, staring at me severely, "I'll say no more, Madam," he said, "for we are Catholics."

Confused, I gave up hope of an explanation and dropped my head: my feet were bathed in a rain of cold sweat that ran off my forehead. Mr. MacFrolick watched me with a lackluster eye. He had little bluish eyes, a big thick nose, turned up a little at the end. It was difficult not to notice that this very distinguished, devout man, of impeccable morality, was the human portrait of a big white porker. An enormous moustache hung from his chin, well supplied with flesh but receding a little. Yes, Mr. MacFrolick looked like a porker, but a handsome porker, a devout, distinguished porker. As these dangerous thoughts were slipping by behind my green face, a young man of Celtic appearance took me by the hand, saying: "Come, dear Madam, don't fret, there's no avoiding it, we all bear a resemblance to the animal kingdom; you are certainly conscious of your own horsy appearance, well—well, don't fret, everything is mixed up on our planet. Do you know Mr. D——?"

"No," I said, very confused, "I don't know him."

"D—— is here this evening," said the young man, "he is a Magus, and I am his apprentice. Look, there he is over there, sitting near a big blonde dressed in violet satin, do you see him?"

I saw a man of such neutral bearing that he hit you in the

eye as violently as a salmon with a Sphinx's head in a railway
station. The extraordinary neutrality of that personage gave
such a disagreeable impression that I tottered towards a chair.

"Do you want to make D——'s acquaintance?" asked the
young man. "He is a very remarkable man." I was going to
reply when a woman like a Sun King's shepherdess, with an
extremely hard glance, took me by the elbow and propelled me
right into the gaming room.

"We need a fourth for bridge," she said. "Of course, you
know how to play bridge?" I didn't know at all, but I kept quiet
out of panic. I'd have liked to leave, but I was too shy, and so I
explained I could play only with felt cards, because of an allergy
in the little finger of my left hand. Outside, the orchestra was
playing a waltz I detested so much I didn't have the strength to
say I was hungry. A high ecclesiastical dignitary seated to my
right pulled a pork chop from inside his rich purple haha.
"Look, my girl," he said to me, "Charity pours forth Mercy
equally upon cats, the poor, and women with green faces." The
chop, which had certainly spent a long time near the ecclesiastic's belly, didn't appeal to me at all, but I took it with the
intention of burying it in the garden. As I was taking the chop
outside, I found myself once again in the dark, faintly lit by the
planet Venus. I walked near a stagnant fountain full of bees that
had fainted, when I saw myself facing the magician, the neutral
man.

"Well then, taking a walk, are we?" he said in a very
contemptuous tone. "It's always the same thing in the homes of
expatriate Englishmen: everyone has a lousy time."

I admitted in shame that I too was English, and the neutral
man gave a little sarcastic laugh. "It's hardly your fault if you are
English," he said. "The congenital idiocy of the inhabitants of
the British Isles is woven so well into their blood that they
themselves are no longer conscious of it. The spiritual maladies
of the English have become flesh or rather pig's head cheese."
Vaguely irritated, I replied that it rained a lot in England, but
that that country had given birth to the best poets of our planet.
Then to change the conversation, "I've just made the acquaintance of one of your apprentices. He told me you are an adept of
magic."

"Indeed," said the neutral man, "I am a spiritual teacher,

an initiate if you will, but that poor boy will never amount to anything. You should know, poor thing, that the Esoteric Way is hard, sown with catastrophies. Many are called, but few are chosen. I advise you to confine yourself to charming feminine foolishness, and to forget everything that belongs to a higher order of things."

While the neutral man was speaking to me, I was trying to occult the pork chop that was dripping horrible spots of grease between my fingers. I managed to put it in my pocket. Relieved, I realized the man would never take me seriously if he knew I went walking about with pork chops on me. However, I dreaded the neutral man like the plague, while still wanting to make a good impression on him.

"I'd like to know something of your magic, to study under you perhaps. Up to now . . ." With a superb gesture he cut me off suddenly: "THERE IS NOTHING," he said to me, "Try to understand that, *there is nothing, absolutely nothing.*"

That was when I felt myself evaporated in an opaque mass, colorless, and with no way out. When I had my breath back, the neutral man had disappeared. I wanted to go home, but I was lost in that garden heavy with the scent of a certain shrub called here the Odor of Night. I wandered for a fairly long time through the paths until I arrived in front of a tower through the half-open door of which I perceived a spiral staircase. Someone was calling me from inside the tower, and I went up the stairs, thinking that all in all I didn't have much to lose. I was much too foolish, running away like the hare with triangular teeth. I thought bitterly: "At this moment I am poorer than a beggar, even though the bees have done everything to warn me. Now I've lost the honey for a whole year and Venus in the sky."

At the top of the stairs, I found myself again in Mr. Mac-Frolick's private sanctum. He received me in friendly fashion, and I couldn't explain this change of attitude. With a gesture stamped with old-world courtesy, Mr. MacFrolick offered me a plate of (quite delicate) china on which rested his own moustache. I hesitated to accept the moustache, thinking he wanted me perhaps to eat it. "He's an eccentric," I thought. Quickly I made an excuse. "I am deeply grateful to you, Sir, but I'm not hungry any more, after sampling the delicious pork chop the Bishop kindly gave me. . . ."

MacFrolick seemed slightly offended: "Madam," he said, "this moustache is not at all edible, it is a souvenir of this summer's evening, and I ventured to hope you would keep it perhaps in some chest appropriate to that use. I must add that this moustache has no magic power, but that its large bulk differentiates it from common objects." Realizing I'd made a faux pas, I took the moustache and put it carefully in my pocket, where it immediately stuck to the disgusting pork chop. Mac-Frolick then pushed me onto a divan and, weighing heavily on my stomach, said in a confidential tone, "Green Woman, you should know there are different sorts of magic: black magic, white magic, and the worst of all, grey magic. It is indispensable for you to know that among us this evening is a dangerous grey magician, one D——. This man, this vampire with velvety words, is responsible for the murder of numerous souls, human and otherwise. On several occasions D—— has slipped through the walls of this castle to steal our vital matter." I had trouble hiding a little smile, for I've been living for a long time with a vampire from Transylvania, and my mother-in-law, a wereshe-wolf, has taught me all the culinary secrets necessary for giving the most rapacious vampires a treat and for satisfying them.

MacFrolick weighed more heavily on me, hissing: "I absolutely must get rid of D——. Unfortunately, the church forbids private murder: I am therefore obliged to ask you to come to my assistance. You are Protestant, are you not?"

"Not at all," I replied. "I am not a Christian, Mr. Mac-Frolick. What is more, I've no wish to kill D——, even if I had the slightest chance of doing so before he pulverized me ten times."

MacFrolick's face became changeable with rage: "Well then, leave!" he yelled. "Unbelievers aren't welcome in my house. Leave, Madam!"

I left as quickly as the stairs permitted, while MacFrolick leaned out of his door insulting me in terminology very rich for such a devout man.

*

There's no definite ending to this story that I'm relating as a mere summer incident. There's no ending because the incident is authentic, because all the characters are still alive and each is following his destiny. All, except the ecclesiastic who drowned tragically in the pool of the castle: it's said he was enticed in by sirens disguised as choirboys.

Mr. MacFrolick has never invited me to the castle again, but I am assured he is in good health.

LEOPOLDO CHARIARSE

1928—

Leaving Chiclayo in northern Peru, where he was born, Leopoldo Chariarse first studied ethnology in his native country, then philology in Barcelona, then musicology in Paris. In the French capital, surrealists saluted in Chariarse the inventor of imaginary ethnology and a creator of myths. They published his story *Les Mélanges inadmissibles* in the third number of their magazine *Le Surréalisme, même* (Autumn 1957), illustrating it with photographs of Jivaro Indians, supplied by the Museum of Man, in Paris.

It seems especially fitting that *Les Mélanges inadmissibles* should be dedicated to Benjamin Péret who, during a fruitful period of residence in Latin America, demonstrated his sympathy for local customs and folklore.[1] And, in connection with Chariarse's story, it is appropriate to recall that, when asked to list his peculiarities for the *Nouveau Dictionnaire des contemporains*,

---

1. As well as his substantial *Anthologie des Mythes, légendes et contes populaires d'Amérique*, Péret published an article, "Du Fond de la forêt," on the game *berimbau* played among the poor of Bahia (see the second number of *Le Surréalisme, même* [Spring 1957], pp. 105-109) and another essay, "La Lumière ou la vie," illustrated by photographs of Camaiura and Caraje Indians (*Le Surréalisme, même*, no. 5 [Spring 1959], pp. 42-45).

Péret wrote "detests curés, cops, Stalinism, and tradespeople."[2] From *Les Mélanges inadmissibles* it is clear that, if asked to list his own peculiarities, Chariarse might well have mentioned the same ones as Péret. The text attacks religion as a force naturally allied with a certain form of imperialism, taking impetus from the profit motive. For good measure, it ridicules the military mind, for which Péret had nothing but contempt.[3]

Chariarse does not practice the distinctive combination of vulgarity and fancy with which Péret scoffs at institutions detestable to him. Rather, *Les Mélanges inadmissibles* is reminiscent of Jonathan Swift's famous *Modest Proposal*, which inevitably found its way into Breton's *Anthologie de l'Humour noir*. For Swift is the first author cited in Breton's anthology, where we read, "Everything designates him, in the matter of black humor, as the true initiator" (p. 25). Noting that someone once said of Swift that he "provokes laughter without sharing it," Breton commented in terms that permit us to measure Chariarse's achievement, as seen in surrealist perspective, "It is precisely at this cost that humor, in the sense in which we understand it, can externalize the sublime element that, according to Freud, is inherent in it and transcend the forms of the comic" (p. 26).

Through *Les Mélanges inadmissibles* Chariarse confirms that black humor takes on value by transcending the forms of the comic borrowed for surrealist purposes. He shows that a writer can be entertaining, while still criticizing, from the standpoint of surrealism, the customs and behavior that society condones. He helps us see humor as capable, in surrealism, of inviting profitable reflection, when it highlights social and ethical hypocrisy, infringing upon personal liberty. In so doing, Leopoldo Chariarse demonstrates that humor is a vital expression of the surrealists' sense of responsibility, manifesting itself even and perhaps especially when, by the norms of conduct set by

---

2. The eighth number of the first surrealist magazine, *La Révolution surréaliste* (December 1, 1926), reproduced a photograph showing "our associate Benjamin Péret insulting a priest." The photo reappears in the same issue of *Le Surréalisme, même* as *Les Mélanges inadmissibles*.

3. Péret's contempt is amply demonstrated in his explosive poetic collection *Je ne mange pas de ce pain-là* (*I'd Rather Starve* [1936]).

society, they appear to be acting irresponsibly. "The authentic art of today," Breton declared, "has joined forces with revolutionary social activity. It tends, like the latter, toward the confusion and destruction of capitalist society."

LEOPOLDO CHARIARSE

Unacceptable Mixture

During the summer of 1947, in one of the rare moments of lucidity permitted me by the routine of lowly bureaucratic employment, I decided to travel through the Amazon forests, to live in nature, among savages, to learn to handle the bow, to eat unknown animals, fruit of incredible shape, the larvae of insects and the roots of trees never seen.

After a brief stay in Yurimaguas where, despite the suffocating heat, I was able to sleep a little, I took my place in the cabin of the hydroplane that had brought me from Masisea and was to take me to my destination, when a traveler occupying the seat to my right—a bald man, with spectacles and something about him of the attorney or the ecclesiastic—asked me:

"Do you know how many planes have come down this year on our route?"

As I had no idea, I declared brutally:

"Ours will make it a half-dozen."

I told him not to worry, that it was a fair figure, in keeping with the air traffic in that part of the world—one to four per week according to the size of the airline and ours being one of the biggest had more accidents.

My reasoning seemed to offend him. He affirmed that he was not afraid, that he did not need to be calmed down with statistics (for I was explaining that according to the normal curve of accident distribution per unit of time, place, etc.) and that anyway, in spite of completely unfavorable probabilities, it was not death he feared, but desecration of his remains, that at the hands of the savages his flesh might be chopped, ground, salted, or submitted to other treatment incompatible with the dignity of his position.

"*I*, imagine, a representative of judiciary power, a man without vices, without debts!"

I had to assure him that cannibalism was dying out as evangelization made progress and that after all it was more useful to be eaten by other men than devoured by worms, ants, and piranha.

"Don't be too sure," he exclaimed. "You know very well that in this part of the forest, evangelization has made no progress since the Indians were obliged to work on plantations."

I confined myself to a nod, so as to be able to admire in peace the somber greenery of the forest standing out between the blue and grayish mist over the fiery line of the horizon.

I took a room at a little hotel near the river whose waters I could see from my window stretching away out of sight.

It was a quiet inn; scarcely any travelers were in the lounge and on the terrace, and I was already rejoicing at having come at such a favorable season when deafening cries, rising above the sound of the motor of a big bus, made me see my error.

They were getting out in herds, brandishing their movie and snapshot cameras, photographing in all directions, chewing gum, speaking English, noisily opening and closing doors.

They all asked for precise information on the Maracaburus, while the guide discussed the price of rooms with the proprietress.

I knew vaguely that the Indians of that tribe were the mortal enemies of the Carajones, from whom they had learned, however, the art of preparing a large number of magic philters and subtle varieties of curare. Every month, except during the rainy season, they would come down in their canoes, headed for the village markets along the river bank, to sell their well-known salted meats, their medicinal herbs, and also, though secretly, their poisons that earned them the respect of future inconsolable widows in the area.

While I was telling all this, one of the tourists came up and asked me if they sold shrunken heads here and how high the prices could run.

I was going to reply when the hotel owner, who spoke English too, intervened:

"Here, no. You'll find those in Lima, in stores selling antiques and native curios."

The moment I was preparing to contradict him—for a short distance away, according to what I had been told in Yurimaguas, there was an encampment of Jivaros who kept up a constant trade with the whites, to whom they sold shrunken heads, and with the other Indians from whom they obtained freshly severed ones—he took me by the arm and said to me in an undertone, in Spanish:

"Don't tell them anything. Don't you see that with their mania for carrying off heads they are setting off real massacres among the Indians? For fear of reprisals the latter don't dare refuse to sell any and, as they have none in stock, they are compelled to make them."

"Aren't they stimulated, rather, by profit? No merchant is obliged to meet demand completely," I observed.

"You don't know perhaps, but the Indians remember very well what atrocities were committed against them, when they didn't bring in the rate of rubber the English demanded of them. And now when a gang of Americans come insisting upon having the heads of whites, they fall into a panic and go looking for them where they can. They are dubbed savages for having decapitated a few monks and settlers. I don't wish to defend them, but if *my* head was cut off to be sold to tourists I'd know whose fault it was. The Maracaburus, for example, gentle and peaceable by nature, but tributaries of the Jivaros and obliged to supply them with heads, have become cannibals only so as not to let what remains of their prisoners go to waste.

At that moment a lady interrupted the hotel owner's speech to ask if, further into the interior, it would not be possible for her to obtain a pair of very little heads, children's heads for example, to hang in the rear of her car. White children, she was

saying, and French if any could be found. She adored little
French children ever since seeing and hearing the "little singers
of the wooden cross."

The hotel owner raised his eyes to heaven and left me alone
with her. She was a rather fat lady, still young and beautiful.
When she spoke there was such enthusiasm in her voice that the
sincerity of her love for children could not be doubted.

She told me she belonged to various philanthropic organi-
zations, societies for the protection of animals and waifs and
that, in her house in Miami, she had a large collection of tropical
fish.

I told her not to worry, that in Lima she would get all the
child heads she could wish for, at moderate prices and, who
knows, perhaps even French children's heads or Canadian ones
from one of the planes come down in the jungle.

I went out that very morning to walk along the river bank.
On the right, at the end of an embankment lined with trees,
there was a little square in the middle of which, towering above
the tops of the coconut palms, rose a sort of column slightly
curved. It was an immense cylinder of granite that gave the
disorienting feeling of an anachronism or of some monstrous
mixture.

Why, indeed, is that phallus—which would not have been
out of place in the ruins of Delphi or Mycenae—here, lost in this
Christian village on the banks of the Amazon? Was it not an
obscure mythological allusion linked with the Amazon seen by
Orellana?[4]

Stepping back a little to see from a better angle, I noted that
this gigantic member was without its testicles, something that
could easily be explained by the prudishness of the authorities.
Moreover the glans was missing also, or was hardly indicated
perhaps because of a praiseworthy effort at stylization by the
artist, tending to anticipate the zeal of an always vigilant
censorship.

An inscription similar to that which expresses the public's
gratitude to citizens who have fallen at the front only increased
my confusion.

---

4. The traveler who first discovered the Amazon and first followed it down-
stream.

It was a monument erected in homage to the martyrs sacrificed by the Maracaburus on the field of honor of Christian faith. There followed a long list of reverend fathers and monks of various orders and numerous military men comprising four lieutenants, fourteen noncommissioned officers, and innumerable soldiers and policemen.

While I was reading the columns set out in strict alphabetical order according to rank, there appeared, dressed all in black, a little old woman making her way sadly but with an indescribably graceful carriage. She approached the railing protecting the monument and dropped a few flowers near the plaque, into a sort of metal box put there for that purpose. Seeing her, I thought I could hear a military band in the distance and a feeling of great tenderness would have come over me if, raising my eyes to the sky, I had not seen that inexorable shape defying all pity.

A most passionate interest followed my initial curiosity upon seeing the old woman's hair combed in a manner that brought to mind irresistibly a Greek hairstyle.

I approached her—a bacchante or a weeping figure exiled at the foot of this last vestige of her divinity—and, to say something, asked her—this is explained by my complete confusion—what day it was and the name of that place.

"Martyrs' Square," she said smiling and she added, "Every time I come back here, it seems I am going mad. I couldn't tell you what day it is, Sir. Excuse me."

Back at the hotel I demanded that the proprietress tell me for what reason, in Martyrs' Square, a pagan sign commemorated the death of these holy men.

She explained that this monument did not represent a male member at all but a sausage.

Faced with my amazement, the good woman confirmed:

"It's because of the victims transformed into sausages by the Maracaburus.

"The best pork-butchers in the area," added the proprietress' husband who was reading a newspaper, his elbows on the counter.

"Did that event take place a long time ago?" I asked with a certain uneasiness, irritated by the hotel owner's remark.

"Exactly three years," he replied, giving up reading. "Since then the hamlet of Maracaburu, a couple of miles from here, is one of the most prosperous places of pilgrimage in the whole country. During the busy season, we don't have enough room to put up all the pilgrims."

"In spite of the new hotel that's been built," added the hotel owner's wife bitterly. "Just imagine, we have to put mats and hammocks out, even in the dining room!"

At lunch, I was introduced to Father Saravia. The hotel proprietor told him I had arrived from Lima and did not know the story of the miracle that the martyrs' remains had occasioned.

"Don Pedro Irribáuregui—a relative of mine—had just been appointed bishop of the region," said the father, "when he summoned me to come immediately so that he could ask me to inquire into an event of which the theological and practical implications presented the most unreal and grotesque appearance.

"It had been discovered that a group of Maracaburu Indians had cut up and mixed the flesh of numerous priests, soldiers, and policemen with that of pigs and dogs stolen from the farms in neighboring villages. I had to find out how it was possible to grant those remains Christian burial and, first of all, establish if such a thing had been possible."

A captain traveling in the direction of the frontier sat down at our table. Of indeterminate age, but fitting his uniform perfectly, he greeted us in friendly fashion, declared that his name was Mirasoles and that he was a member of a commission charged with determining where the frontier ran, through zones about which the treaties in force left some doubt. It was certainly not the least curious aspect of the question to see the two countries in dispute over regions inhabited by cannibal tribes, each claiming the land but affirming that the cannibals were natives of the neighboring country. This contradiction and others I could not grasp very well made the captain's work extremely tiring and complicated.

When the captain learned from the hotel owner's wife, who had come up to wait on us, that Father Saravia had begun to tell me a story, he asked to be excused for interrupting us and wanted to move to another table, but we invited him to stay, telling him there was nothing secret about this story and that he could, in fact, be useful to us in clarifying certain details.

He accepted gratefully and we prepared to listen to the rest of the tale.

"As I was saying," the priest went on, "the problem was agonizing. Could Christian burial be given remains in which it was impossible to distinguish the human from the animal, not to mention other ingredients it would be too painful to speak of."

"That's the easiest thing in the world," declared the soldier to whom every problem seemed simple. "All they had to do was determine the exact amount of each part of the mixture and divide each sausage accordingly, symbolically bringing together the parts corresponding to the clergy, the army, and the animal kingdom, and bury them separately, even though in reality the mixture was inextricable. It was all a matter of establishing the proportions exactly."

"You've said it: that was the whole problem. But the Maracaburus, jealous of their manufacturing secrets and fearing that other tribes might appropriate these and cut them out of the market, would rather let themselves be killed than reveal them."

"But how was it known that the Maracaburus' sausages were made of human flesh?"

"A few missionaries having disappeared, someone remembered that a comparable event had taken place about fifty years before, when the Dominicans found themselves obliged to change the route they used to take to reach their missions in Brazil. There resulted such a famine among the Indians, for whom they were the staple diet, that very few survived."

"I know," interjected the captain. "Driven by hunger, they crossed the frontier and began attacking villages and plantations. They'd have got as far as Iquitos if they'd not been stopped by the heroic resistance of our troops who, aided by the settlers, in the end exterminated them."

"To get back to my story, when the disappearances reached alarming proportions, the police scoured the whole region in question but with no other result than the disappearance of numerous policemen."

"That's when the army stepped in," exulted Mirasoles,

filling out his uniform once again so that it seemed to have more buttons than ever.

"The result was the disappearance of almost a whole regiment," the priest continued imperturbably.

I thought of that little old women's flowers and those four lieutenants, fourteen noncommissioned officers, and I don't know how many soldiers mentioned on the plaque that seemed to me terribly human, almost familiar.

But the captain replied:

"All the same, it was thanks to us that the Indians confessed to having killed the missionaries."

"Finally the dreadful version of the facts had to be admitted and some Indians confessed, spontaneously or out of fear of being interrogated, that they had taken part in the massacre."

"Immediate seizure of the meat brought in by the savages was then decreed," thundered Mirasoles again, taking the opportunity to explain his role in detail. "At that time I was just a lieutenant," he said modestly.

With dinner behind us, we went to sip coffee on the terrace. The man in spectacles, who knew Mirasoles and Saravia, came up to our table and joined in the conversation. We felt he was very agitated. He told us he had received several threatening letters over a case involving tradespeople, in which he was to act as mediator.

Father Saravia went on:

"As soon as confiscation had been completed in fairs and markets, interment of the remains was carried out, with no distinction, in a common grave, and the names of the victims were inscribed on a plaque. Mgr. Irribáuregui, who presided over the ceremony, pronounced a moving eulogy. He deplored the absence of the heads and regretted there was no hope of retrieving them, for the Jivaros were uncompromising and it would have been necessary to buy a large quantity from them to separate the heads of civilized people and identify them. This obviously called for special government funds and the cooperation of all the faithful in the province. He would take this matter up: he was counting on the understanding of the government and the generosity of all."

On the morning of the third day the grave was found to be open and there was complete consternation when it was known that the remains had disappeared. A mixture of terror and indignation ran through clergy and settlers. The military and the police were placed on alert. A curfew was imposed and several Indians shot down in the vicinity.

"The massacre threatened to imperil the whole district's economy if the native population, which does the heavy work and constitutes the main tourist attraction, was decimated," Mirasoles observed pertinently.

"Divine mercy," Saravia continued, "permitted a group of Indians to manage to get to the bishop and relate the event they had all witnessed. Returning to their huts, a little after midnight, they said, a blinding light took them by surprise and while the night was rent by lightning and trumpet music, they had seen the tomb open and the sausages rise up to heaven."

Mgr. Irribáuregui gave up his return flight to Iquitos that day, and, calling together clergy and people of standing, solemnly announced the miracle.

Great festivities were organized and, in everyone's joy, the Indians who were to be executed for having participated in the massacres and in salting the meat were allowed to escape. The erection of a monument was decided upon immediately and Mgr. Irribáuregui insisted upon its being given the shape of a sausage.

"Out of respect for his dignity as a prelate and his venerable age we accepted this idea that seemed to us absurd and terribly ridiculous. To our timid objections he replied that it would be a lesson in modesty to the flesh and an example of what man is capable of who has entered the bosom of Christianity."

Time has borne out what the bishop said, for the number of pilgrims has not stopped rising from year to year and there is already talk of building a basilica.

His story over, Father Saravia consulted his watch, declared he had to go to work, and left.

Scarcely had he gone when the man with spectacles turned to me and, with a sinister air, said:

"What the good priest doesn't know is that the next day, in all the markets and shops selling food, the famous sausages appeared once again. Housewives were buying them, we were eating them, and no one thought that those who claimed to have witnessed a miracle were the same ones who had sold them. Serious rivalry between tradespeople allowed me to learn the truth. In my capacity as magistrate I did all I could to conceal it, so as to avoid a scandal, but the explosion is inevitable."

FERNAND DUMONT

1906—1945

Born in Mons, Belgium, Fernand Demoustier wrote under the name of Dumont. In 1938 he cofounded with Achille Chavée a surrealist group in La Louvière called Rupture. After the dissolution of Rupture, in 1938 he created in his home town the Surrealist Group of Hainaut, which looked to surrealism in France far more than did the Brussels group.

Dumont's first publication, a volume of poems called *À Ciel ouvert* (*In the Open Air* [1937]) was followed by a collection of three stories, *La Région du coeur* (*The Region of the Heart* [1939]) and an essay, *Traité des fées* (*Treatise on Fairies* [1942]). He had just completed the manuscript of *La Dialectique du hasard au service du désir* (*The Dialectic of Chance in the Service of Desire*) when on April 15, 1942, he was arrested by the Gehein Feld Polizei. He passed through several prisons, where he wrote the poems entitled *La Liberté* and a narrative *L'Étoile du berger* (*The Shepherd's Star* [1955]), before his transfer to a succession of concentration camps. He is presumed to have died in Belsen in March 1945.

"After several years of trial and error," Dument wrote in his unpublished *La Dialectique du hasard*, "I finally discovered in 1932 that prose with poetic content, sustained by narrative plot, suited my temperament infinitely better than poems." In September 1933 he submitted a text to André Breton. In *La*

Dialectique du hasard he comments pertinently, "For the first time in ten years, I had discovered a way of expressing myself that belonged to me alone."

Elsewhere in *La Dialectique du hasard* Fernand Dumont remarks, "I have a real phobia of ugliness," confessing, "I attach to physical beauty the value of a moral sign." Thus, to him "the beauty of a face is in some way the reflection of the moral purity of the person in whom it is found." Or, as he puts it in one of his poems, "You came in / and all the light came in with you." This outlook clearly marked *L'Influence du soleil*, published in the magazine *Mauvais Temps* in October 1935.

La Dialectique du hasard advises us to see in Dumont's story "the image of absolute love practicing poetry, that is to say scandal." The socially disruptive role of love gives direction to this tale in which a variety of inexplicable phenomena bear witness to the intrusion of the marvelous in human affairs. Perhaps even more important to note is that *L'Influence du soleil* was written by a man who devoted himself to searching for the laws of the unconscious so as to prove, as he explains in *La Dialectique du hasard*, "that desire is never subordinated to chance, but that chance is always at the service of desire." *L'Influence du soleil* rests upon its author's belief that desire erects "a narrow footbridge" over "the comfortable precipice of positive realities." And no one has demonstrated better than Fernand Demoustier that creation of a footbridge of desire is the very opposite of evading one's responsibilities in the world of day-to-day reality.

FERNAND DUMONT

The Influence of the Sun

Recently the surprising story has been going around of a couple who decided to live without in the least taking into consideration what could be happening, thought, or said in the town where chance had brought them together despite most categorical opposition from their parents. They must have been, so people declare, in a best-of-three match with the sun, for it was impossible to meet them in any season without seeing on their faces, hands, and hair that special light generally there only on persons returning from vacation.

Certain individuals, who had had the extraordinary privilege of getting into their home on one pretext or another, affirmed that it was full of and even cluttered with shining objects of strange shape for which they had not been able to discover the use or necessity. Others claimed that certain rooms on the first floor (into which they had not had occasion to go, but had been able to steal a glance, on the sly, thanks to a door having been left accidentally half open) offered a spectacle such as you could not conceive, they were arranged in such a singular way, were decorated with such inexplicably phosphorescent wall paintings, and had such an unusual and novel appearance that, really, one had to give up trying to describe them.

These people were closely questioned all the same, but, as

was to be expected, their contradictory and confused explanations, far from allaying curiosity, aggravated it to the point
where soon, all over town, people no longer spoke of anything
else. Those who were most curious, the very ones who, for
personal reasons they could not admit to, had always defended
the principle of the inviolability of the home, went so far as to
advocate use of the worst pretexts, so as to be done with this
aggravating enigma.

It did no good.

The bogus beggars, the obsequious canvassers, the make-
believe bailiffs ran into the polite but categorical refusal of an
obstinately closed door. And so they had to bow to the facts,
whether they liked it or not, but with that unconfessed confidence they persist in placing in the outcome of events, with that
secret hope that in the end events one day will take a favorable
turn; but the days slipped by one after the other without
bringing the least response that that immense collective curiosity could feed on, and nothing, in truth, was more exasper-
ating than finding oneself everywhere in the presence of that
couple, telling oneself that all one had to do was question them
to get to the bottom of the matter, and doing no more than tell
oneself so and repeat it to oneself, for no one would have risked
doing this, since the couple seemed to have, in the highest
degree, that attitude made up of coldness, indifference, and
disdain which instantly discourages the most determined of
people.

Then people tried not to think about it any more, to tell
themselves they had been the sport of an illusion or victims of a
bad joke, that after all those two were like everybody else and
that one would have to be very credulous to lend an attentive
ear to such talk, but all that was to no avail, it was no use crying
"hoax," speaking of other matters, opening a newspaper or
going for a walk, people discovered with some amazement that
it was impossible not to think of it any more.

People were on the point of seizing control when, one day,
as if they had guessed it was important to strike an attitude, the
couple moved among the crowd letting something like a long
scarf float behind them, a wake in which all who passed could
not but think of the silence, scarcely interrupted by the distant

crowing of the first rooster, of an April dawn in an orchard full of dew.

The news spread like wildfire and gave rise, as you can imagine, to the most diversified comments. While some claimed it was a matter of the purely chemical production of a perfume with the distillation of which the shining objects glimpsed in the secret house must have something to do, others, on the basis of vague considerations of a psychic order, gave free rein to their confusional thought, deducing with a rough appearance of truth that everyone was facing a manifestation of an immaterial order that must be connected with the well-known phenomenon of thought transference, and most, with their customary pettiness, persisted in locating the importance of the whole question in the wretched point of knowing whether the phenomenon was material or not, in centering all their hopes on getting this trifling thing clear, incapable as they were of realizing for a single instant the overwhelming significance of this thing that had never come about before.

If it was quickly established through many witnesses that they were dealing with a phenomenon perceptible to everybody, no one proved capable of explaining its origin and nature. The depositions did not provide the conclusive element. Most of them betrayed almost total indigence so far as investigative means are concerned, but they made it possible nevertheless to establish that the phenomenon, fluid or perfume, acted in the same way upon everybody. No one spoke of dusk, or of a pine forest, of a farmyard, or of a September mist. The measure of agreement was surprising. It made no difference whether it was midwinter, whether one was in the midst of a crowd, in the hubbub of an intersection initialed by railroad switches, it made no difference whether one was taken up with the most absorbing preoccupations, with the most animated conversations, with the most secret women, all one needed was to pass through the couple's wake, as the earth passes through the cone of shadow during an eclipse, to find oneself in the presence of that reverie which encroaches like bindweed.

The authorities remained defenseless for, even showing that notorious bad faith they never fail to manifest toward anything that, in any way, can look like disturbing established order, it was still practically impossible for them to give the couple's movements the felonious interpretation that could have justified the inquisitorial measures impatiently demanded.

However, more scandalously beautiful than an indecent assault, more provocative than a shout of laughter in a lighted church, more indifferent than the path of a cyclone, the couple moved about the town letting that unforgettable atmosphere float behind them that corresponds exactly, I have said, to the silence (scarcely interrupted by the distant crowing of the first rooster) of the dawn of a very fine April day in an orchard full of dew. Then people decided to appeal to specialists and were astonished to find that not a single one existed in the whole world. Thanks to their insistence, a few mystified psychiatrists made it known that they would immediately hold an extraordinary convention in the town, with the purpose of examining the question, but the very morning of their arrival a thick fog suddenly came down over the town.

As it was the season for fogs, everyone thought this a mere coincidence, quite annoying no doubt, but a mere coincidence, yes, pure chance, in short . . .

The learned men landed in fog so dense that getting them without mishap to a downtown hotel gave all the trouble in the world. Local people of consequence apologized profusely and suggested that the obviously disappointed visitors devote the whole day to hearing the best witnesses, while they waited for more favorable conditions—which could not be long coming— for the experiments proper. So it was done, but the next day all the windows in town opened early in the morning upon an impenetrable screen of white mist. This was all the harder to understand because milkmen and market-gardeners from the surrounding countryside reported that, when they had set out, the sky had been splendidly starry. During the morning, the suburban motormen declared that the sun was shining brightly everywhere over the outskirts, and at noon a reading of the weather forecast, listened to in silence, gave rise to the conviction that it was not a mere coincidence.

People were beginning to live under the yellowish light of anguish.

They felt the urge to shout that it was not true, that the couple had nothing to do with that fog stretching before their exhausted eyes, that it was necessary at all cost for this not to be true. People felt the crazy urge to rip it apart, to destroy it, to tear it away, find anything at all to drive it off, invent a storm, telephone the sun. Only in their imagination could they be rid of it and find their town once again familiar, transparent, easy to live in. And yet, as happens when people find themselves facing a succession of unforeseen events in which they do not manage to make up their minds to admit the existence of a causal relationship that seems at the same time demonstrated by the facts and contradicted by their unusual character, people still hesitated to establish this feature, this slender causal thread between the couple and the fog, people still hesitated to erect that narrow footbridge over the comfortable precipice of positive realities, people still hesitated to register the short and terrifying conclusion, even with the most explicit reservations, people still hesitated, for it appeared only too clearly, all in all, that official recognition of the marvelous would give the signal for the final collapse of all values currently prevailing.

People still tried to be reasonable, to appeal to old good sense; old men would pretend to recall comparable situations and, in front of an open fire, shutters closed, under the lamplight, between two pipes of tobacco, people would once again find the little zone of bluish calm, as pleasant to the heart as an island to a shipwrecked man, but it was shrinking visibly and in the streets, if the fog had lifted, they would have been able to ascertain that the terror of living had inscribed its name everywhere on the walls.

At the end of the third day, the authorities held an emergency meeting and decided the only measure to take, to check this monstrous enterprise of demoralization, was to proceed to arrest the couple. Everything was prepared in secret, down to the smallest detail, and the most thorough precautions were taken to assure the success of this operation that was set for the following morning. And so, how stupefied they all were when they perceived in the early morning that the fog had dissipated completely. They had become so accustomed to it that they had difficulty believing their eyes, while the sun, still very low over the horizon, seemed to shine with singular brightness.

Already the authorities were beginning to ask themselves what on earth had managed to dictate those extreme measures that nothing, all of a sudden, seemed to justify any more, and they were beginning to hesitate, to tell themselves it was perhaps premature to act, that it would be wise to require additional information without which they ran the risk of leaving themselves open to derision from all sides. But the crowd was growing and its presence alone prescribed action, the long-repressed desire to violate an aggravating mystery and, above all, their preoccupation with not contradicting themselves in public, coupled with the petty vanity of playing an apparently courageous role, carried the day fairly easily.

They set off, then, with a little incoercible band of anguish around their hearts, and, when they were in sight of the couple's house, they saw it was already surrounded by a semicircle of interested spectators and heard at once that it was impossible to approach any closer, on account of the extraordinary heat given off by the house. This was all the more difficult to understand because no smoke, no flame, no sign at all permitted the eye to bow to the facts. The dwelling looked absolutely normal. However, the circle was widening more and more, pushed back by that invisible furnace and the light, the light that a while ago was already strangely bright, the light slowly became so dazzling, so terribly blinding that the street had to be evacuated and they had to shut themselves up hurriedly in the houses. From time to time, volunteers went out to reconnoiter, despite the entreaties of those around them, but not one returned.

Then no one ventured out any more and, after endless hours, night slowly came down on a deserted town.

Toward dawn windows were half-opened and, as nothing aroused suspicion, a few persons went down into the street and approached the house stealthily, hugging the walls.

The heat had abated and, as it was still very dark, they thought at first they were the sport of an hallucination, but a little later they realized this was not at all the case and then began to shout at the top of their voices for everyone to come, that there was not the slightest danger any more, that everyone absolutely must come to see this extraordinary thing.

The house was now nothing but an immense block of an incredibly transparent substance, softly luminous, something like crystal, but infinitely more pure than the one we know and, inside, beyond that admirable shell of which no breath could tarnish the brightness, the couple could be seen coming and going as in one of those dazzling dreams after which one retains, always, a painful hankering, they could be seen coming and going against a background of very old legend, much smaller than life size, splendid and shining as ever.

Soon the couple made their way slowly toward the mystery of a bluish forest and, at the very moment when they were about to be lost from sight, those who, to see better, had leaned against the shell fell crashing into a horrible piece of waste ground where, among the nettles and rubbish, an exceedingly rare rose was opening, for it was of the sadly prophetic color of the last dusk we shall be permitted to see before we depart this life.

JEAN FERRY

1906—

Among devotees of the enigmatic writings of Raymond Roussel, Jean Ferry, born in Paris, is best known for his painstaking elucidation of Roussel's work. His *Une Étude sur Raymond Roussel* appeared in 1953. Subsequently, he edited the special number of the Parisian magazine *Bizarre* devoted to Roussel in 1964. To other people, he is the writer of film scripts who worked with Clouzot on *Quai des Orfèvres* and the movie version, *Manon*, of Prévost's *Manon Lescaut*, but whose own surrealist scenario, *Fidélité*, published in 1953, has not been transposed to the screen. As a short-story teller, Ferry first reached only a very small audience indeed. His *Le Mécanicien et autres contes* came out originally in a limited edition of one hundred copies.[1] It was issued in more accessible form in 1953, accompanied by a long preface written by André Breton.

Breton's preface presents Jean Ferry as an artist "conscious of expressing a new dimension of the world." Identifying one of the sources of Ferry's humor in the fatigue affected by the narrator in tales like *La Grève des boueurs*, the one about certain unlikely events precipitated when garbage men go on strike,

---

1. Incorrectly dated 1947 in Breton's *Anthologie de l'Humour noir*, where Ferry is represented by *Le Tigre mondain*, the volume appeared in 1950.

Breton nevertheless recognizes that, however well it lends itself
to humorous treatment, fatigue is a tragic force in Ferry's world.
And indeed one notices that humor is not inconsistent with
Ferry's taste for situations deeply marked, as in *Le Tigre mondain*,
by panic. So we find Ferry naming his volume of stories after a
tale that refers insistently to the panic released when, inexplicably, an engineer drives his locomotive along without ever
stopping, while he ignores alarm signals from a few of the
passengers still optimistic enough to try, from time to time, to
bring the train to a halt.

When we hear Breton commend Ferry for his "faculty for
dreaming," ascribing to it Ferry's ability to identify with so
many dissimilar characters and to find his bearings in so many
places and under so many circumstances that he will never
know in his own life, there is no reason to think Breton is
confusing dream with evasion. Clearly, in Ferry's work an acute
awareness of existence, such as perhaps only feelings of panic
can generate, is by no means the fruit of an instinct for evasion.
What Breton means to do, therefore, is refer to dreaming as it is
always understood in surrealism, as a protest against the
confinement imposed by the rationalist spirit. In other words,
dreaming expresses in Ferry's stories a "taste for subversion"
that earns him Breton's praise.

In connection with the subversive inclination manifested by
Ferry, his story about Kafka calls for special mention. Breton
qualifies it as "the most unsettling" of all the tales assembled
under the title *Le Mécanicien*, one which, upon its first appearance, he himself did not hesitate to salute as a masterpiece.
According to Breton, *Kafka ou "la société secrète"* conveys a
conception of love that—with no pejorative intent, naturally—
he terms "sadistic." Recalling that we have Freud's word for it
that a sadistic disposition can engender virtues as well as vices,
Breton credits it with generating in Ferry's case a virtue particularly favored among surrealists: lyricism.

In his preface to *Le Mécanicien et autres contes* Breton does not
go on to define lyricism, no doubt because, in his view, the
lyrical quality of Jean Ferry's short stories is self-evident: Ferry
shows us that the marvelous is not apprehended best by those
in a state of passive submission, far less by those who remain
complacent about the inevitability of its manifestation. Ferry

treats sensitivity to the marvelous as the direct result of panic, in this anticipating Arrabal. And when he does so, he pays tribute to the marvelous as a supremely disturbing agent, of distinctly subversive nature.

JEAN FERRY

The Garbage Men's Strike

As people didn't know what to do with their trash, during the garbage men's strike, they burned it in the little central heating boiler. But ashes don't burn, and soon people didn't know where to put them. At that time I was very fatigued, even more fatigued than usual, and I couldn't summon up the energy to carry those accumulated ashes down to the heap in the square, where, not without pride, the concierges of the neighborhood watched over its growth. I poured the ashes between the boiler and the little recess and soon there were a lot of them because, to burn my garbage, I was burning up my supply of briquets. Now, because of some bad example, contagion, the fire going out one day, anyway, on our own little heap things were thrown in the end that weren't ashes and that it would have been better to burn. In a little apartment like ours, piling up trash this way was really unpleasant, all the more so because it began to run, to spread just about everywhere and we were sweeping up all the time, in the little room where the boiler is. Everything was put on that pile of ashes—oyster shells, banana peel, an empty tinned food can, scraps of cloth—in a word, a real garbage can run wild. But I was fatigued . . .

And, naturally, what had to happen did. One morning, in place of the pile, there was a poor old man, who looked at me

across the room reproachfully, because I didn't give him anything, no doubt. He had taken so much care to come into being
out of our garbage that, apart from him, everything was clean
and spotless, now, in the little room. Itemizing him in despair, I
could detect the ashes in the grime of his greyish complexion;
the banana peel he had made into livid fingers, deformed and
trembling, the white of the eggshells into that of his eyes, the
bits of rag into his tattered clothes. And he held out the tinned
food can, which seemed to him fine as a begging bowl. He filled
the little recess exactly, and I felt at once, with a heavy heart,
that there'd never be any way to get him out of there.

The following day, the strike was over, and the garbage
trucks ran joyously through all the streets. But my tramp's still
there. I don't know what to do. We have to pass all the time
through the little room that gives access to half of our apartment; anyway, the fire really had to be relit, and where he is he
can't be feeling cold. He never speaks, he scarcely moves, only,
every time we go through, he holds out the tin at the end of a
slightly trembling arm, and, in spite of everything I can think of
against charity, if I have no change on me, I go back into the
kitchen for some. No one, now, would dare pass by him
without giving him something. The concierge says to me, "Why
don't you bring him down with the rest of your garbage, once's
he's in the garbage can, people won't be able to tell the difference between him and everything else!" That's easy enough to
say. I don't have a shovel big enough, and he looks so comfortable, against the boiler. Maybe he'll go away when the fire's out.

The cats are very lucky. They can't see him, they don't
know he's there, and sleep in the same place he does.

As if we didn't have enough troubles already!

JEAN FERRY

The Fashionable Tiger

Of all the music hall acts stupidly dangerous to the public as well as to those putting them on, none fills me with more uncanny horror than that old turn called "the fashionable tiger." For those who have not seen it, since the new generation does not know what the great music halls were like after the 1914 war, I recall what that training consisted of. Something I could not explain, or try to communicate, is the state of panic terror and abject disgust into which this spectacle throws me, as into suspect and atrociously cold water. I ought not to go into theaters where this number figures on the program, more and more rarely, incidentally. That is easy enough to say. For reasons I have never been able to get clear, "the fashionable tiger" is never advertised, I do not expect it, or rather yes I do, a vague menace, barely given expression, weighs upon the pleasure I derive from the music hall. If a sigh of relief frees my heart after the last act on the program, I know only too well the fanfare and the ceremonial that herald this number—always performed, I repeat, as if given without notice. As soon as the orchestra tackles the brassy waltz that is so typical, I know what is going to happen, a crushing weight grips my chest, and I have the thread of fear between my teeth like a bitter current of low voltage. I ought to leave, but I no longer dare. Anyway, no one moves, no one shares my agony, and I know the beast is already on its way. It seems to me also that the arms of my seat protect me, oh, very slightly . . .

First, there is total darkness in the theater. Then a spotlight comes up on the proscenium and this ridiculous lighthouse beam sends light into an empty stagebox, most times very near where I am sitting. Very near. From there, the pencil of light seeks out at the far end of the lounge a door connecting with the wings, and while in the orchestra the horns dramatically tackle "Invitation to the Waltz," they enter.

The animal tamer is a very thrilling Russian woman, a little jaded. As her only weapon she carries a fan of black ostrich plumes, with which at first she conceals the lower part of her face; only her great big green eyes appear above the dark fringe of undulous waves. In a very low-cut dress, with bare arms which the light makes iridescent with a winter's twilight fog, the tamer wears tight-fitting clothing suitable for a Romantic soirée, a strange dress, gleaming dully, of the black color of very deep water. This dress is cut from fur of incredible pliancy and quality. Above everything, the cascading eruption of flaming hair, spangled with stars of gold. The whole effect is at once oppressive and a little comical. But who would think of laughing? The tamer, using her fan, and so uncovering pure lips with a set smile, advances, followed by the beam of light from the spot, toward the empty box, on the arm, if one may put it that way, of the tiger.

The tiger walks in a fairly human manner on its hind legs; it is dressed up as a dandy of refined elegance, and this costume is so perfectly cut that it is difficult to distinguish, under the gray pants with straps, the flowered vest, the blinding white jabot with irreproachable pleats, and the frock coat waisted by the hand of a master, the animal's body. But the head with the dreadful rictus is there, with the crazy eyes rolling in their red sockets, the furious bristling of the moustache, and the fangs that sometimes glint beneath lips curled back. The tiger moves forward, very stiff, holding in the crook of its left arm a light-gray hat. The tamer walks with well-poised gait and if there is sometimes a curve in the small of her back, if her bare arm tenses, showing under the light tawny velvet of the skin an unexpected muscle, this is because, with a violent effort, she has straightened up her escort who was about to tip forward.

Now they are at the door of the box, which the fashionable tiger pushes open with a claw, before standing back to let the lady through. And when she has gone to sit down and rest her elbow negligently on the faded plush, the tiger drops into a seat by her side. Here, usually, the audience bursts into blissful applause. And *I* watch the tiger, and should so much like to be somewhere else that I could weep. The tamer bows in a stately manner, with a movement of her curly fire. The tiger begins its work, handling the props laid out in the box for its use. It pretends to examine the public through opera glasses. It takes the cover off a box of candy and pretends to offer some to its companion. It takes out a fancy silk handkerchief, that it pretends to sniff; it pretends, to the great amusement of one and all, to consult the program. Then it pretends to become gallant; it leans toward the tamer and pretends to murmur some declaration in her ear. The tamer pretends to be offended and coquettishly places between the pale satin of her beautiful cheek and the animal's stinking snout, set with saber blades, the fragile screen of her feather fan. Thereupon the tiger pretends to fall into deep despair, and it wipes its eyes with the back of its furry paw. And throughout this dismal pantomime, my heart beats excruciatingly beneath my ribs, for only I can see, only I know that this whole tasteless show hangs together but by a miracle of will power, as they say, that we are all in a state of frightfully unstable equilibrium, which a mere nothing could destroy. What would happen if, in the box adjacent to the tiger's, that little man turned out like a lowly office worker, that little man with the livid complexion and tired eyes, were to stop willing for one moment? For *he* is the real tamer; the red-haired woman is just a super, everything depends on *him*. *He* is the one who makes the tiger a marionette, machinery more surely connected than by cables of steel.

But what if that little man all at once were to begin to think of something else? What if he died? No one suspects the danger that is possible each second. And I who know imagine, imagine, oh no, it's best not to imagine what the lady in fur would look like if . . . It's best to look at the end of the number which delights and always reassures the public. The tamer asks if someone in the audience will kindly entrust her with a child. Who would refuse anything at all to a person as pleasant as this? There is always someone unconscious of the nature of her own actions who holds out a delighted child toward the demoniac box. The tiger gently nurses him in the crook of its bent paw, turning toward the little piece of flesh the eyes of an alcoholic. In a great thunder of applause, the lights come up, the baby is returned to his legitimate owner, and the two partners bow, before withdrawing by the same route that brought them.

Once they have passed the door, and they never come back for a curtain call, the orchestra bursts out with its loudest fanfares. Shortly after, the little man wilts and mops his brow. And the orchestra plays louder and louder, to cover the roaring of the tiger, become itself once more, now that it has passed the bars of its cage. It howls like hell itself, rolls around tearing to shreds its fine clothes, that have to be replaced for each performance. Now come the outcries, the tragic curses from a rage driven to despair, furious, smashing leaps against the walls of the cage. On the other side of the bars, the bogus tamer is undressing in a great hurry, so as not to miss the last subway. The little man is waiting for her in the bistrot near the station, the one called 'Never, Never."

The storm of cries released by the tiger entangled in its shreds of material could make a disagreeable impression on the public, from however far away. This is why the orchestra plays the overture to "Fidelio" with all its strength, this is why the manager, in the wings, hurries the comical cyclists on stage.

I detest that fashionable tiger act and will never understand the pleasure the public derives from it.

JEAN FERRY

Kafka or
"The Secret Society"

Joseph K——, around his twentieth year, learned the existence
of a secret, very secret society. It truly resembles no other
association of this kind. It is very difficult for some people to
join. Many, who ardently desire to, never succeed. On the other
hand, others are in it without even knowing. One is, by the
way, never quite sure of belonging; there are many people who
think themselves member of this secret society, and who are not
at all. It makes no difference that they have been initiated; they
are members even less than many who do not even know of the
society's existence. Indeed, they have undergone the test of a
bogus initiation, intended to throw people off who are not
worthy to really be initiates. But to the most authentic members,
to those who have attained the highest grade in the hierarchy of
this society, even to those it is never revealed whether their
successive initiations are valid or not. It can even happen that a
member has attained some real status, in the normal way,
following authentic initiations, and that, afterward, without
having been warned, he is submitted to bogus initiations only.
The object of endless discussion among members is to find out if
it is better to be admitted to a low but authentic grade than to
occupy an exalted but illusory position. In any case, no one is
sure of the stability of his grade.

In fact the situation is even more complicated, because certain applicants are admitted to the highest grades without having undergone any test, others even without having been informed. And to tell the truth, there is not even any need to make application; there are people who have been given very advanced initiations who did not even know of the secret society's existence.

The powers of the higher members are limitless, and they carry within a powerful emanation from the secret society. Their mere presence suffices, for example, even if they do not show themselves, to transform a harmless gathering, like a concert, or an anniversary dinner, into a meeting of the secret society. These members are responsible for making, upon all sessions at which they have been present, secret reports that are examined closely by other members of the same rank: there is in this way a perpetual exchange of reports among the membership, permitting the highest authorities in the secret society to keep the situation well in hand.

However high, however far initiation goes, it never goes so far as to reveal to the initiate the aim pursued by the secret society. But there are always traitors, and for a long time it has been no mystery to anyone that this aim is to keep things secret.

Joseph K—— was very frightened to learn this secret society was so powerful, spreading so wide that he could perhaps, without knowing it, be shaking hands with the most powerful of its members. But unfortunately, one morning, emerging from a painful sleep, he lost his first-class ticket on the Métro. This bit of bad luck was the first link in a chain of jumbled contradictory circumstances that brought him into contact with the secret society. Later, so as to protect himself, he was obliged to take steps to be admitted to this formidable organization. That happened a long time ago, and it is not yet known where he stands in this endeavor.

CAMILLE GOEMANS

1900—1960

In 1925 Camille Goemans, born in Louvain, Belgium, settled for
a time in Paris, where he participated in meetings of the surrealist group, from which he broke away around 1930.

If Goemans is remembered in France, in connection with
the history of surrealism, it is no doubt as one of those who
contributed most to bringing surrealist painting to public attention. At one time he had Arp, Tanguy, and Magritte all under
contract. He introduced the work of Dalí to the French, and was
the first to show Ernst's *Histoire naturelle* in Belgium. In 1929 he
organized the first big exhibition of collages in Paris, giving
Louis Aragon the opportunity to write, in the form of an
extended catalog preface, a major text of surrealist theory with
respect to painting, *La Peinture au défi*. In Belgium, Goemans's
status is somewhat different. There he is most likely to be
known for his collaboration with Paul Nougé in launching *Correspondance*, a magazine in the form of a succession of tracts, from
which surrealist activity in Belgium derived its origins, and for
his involvement in the magazine *Distances* (1928), also with
Nougé. Neither in Belgium nor in France can Goemans be said
to be well known as a writer.

Goemans produced a lot, but published little, apparently
quite content to write for his private satisfaction. It is only since

his death in 1960 that the work of Goemans has become available, thanks primarily to Marcel Mariën, first under Mariën's imprint, Les Lévres Nues, and then in a substantial collection of texts, *Œuvre 1922-1957*.

Written in 1928, *Les Débuts d'un voyage* was serialized in *Distances* (Nos. 1, 2, and 3, February, March, and April 1928). In this story Camille Goemans brings meticulous care to evoking an experience set against an exotic background whose strangeness fosters a mood of anticipation of events to which the narrative is no more than a prelude. In structure and content, this tale is a faithful reflection of the author's idea of surrealism, as summarized in a lecture he delivered in La Louviére in January 1949: "surrealism is itself youth, in this sense that it takes revolutionary feeling at its moment of birth and from the first stage, the one where ridiculous, odious constraint, stupid social conventions, the tragic opposition of dream and reality awaken in the adolescent the first eddy of revolt that goes with his first fairly clear perception of injustice and of offensive inequalities."[1] It demonstrates his belief in surrealism "as a grasp on existence and as endowed with the most direct means of acting upon it" (p. 205). What is more, it expresses his conviction that "if surrealism is an action, . . . one must not, for all that, be able to take it for an amusement, without real consequence and without danger" (p. 207). But, most of all, it does all this with the characteristic discretion displayed in a reply Goemans once sent to a letter from André Breton: "My position is exactly this (and I am a bit vexed with you for asking me to give it this air of importance) that if it should happen to find definition, or if I were able to define it, I should have to abandon it at once." Caution recommends letting *Les Débuts d'un voyage* speak for itself.

---

1. "Expérience du surréalisme," a lecture delivered in La Louvière, January 29, 1949, on the occasion of a Pol Bury exhibition, reproduced in *Œuvre 1922-1957*, pp. 214-215.

CAMILLE GOEMANS

The Beginnings of a Journey

We are assured, before we leave, that the region through which we are going to pass is extremely dangerous on account of the natives, whose mood is unstable. One cannot say whether they are, really, warlike or in fact peaceable. They are both, by sudden and unforeseeable changes. They do not seem to like strangers much, though they have given some a magnificent welcome and have sent them away laden with gifts, after conducting them back to the boundaries of their territory.

There could be nothing more attractive to us than this risk.

. . . .

Dawn was slow coming and the wind made a great noise stirring the forests that spread before us. A vague apprehension weighed on our shoulders, and our eyes, wherever they turned, could discover nothing but a darkness most favorable to surprise and ambush.

. . . .

With daylight, forms took on definite shape. The blue color, the one we had become acquainted with already, on our previous journey, and of which one sees in these parts only light or dark shades (this submits us every time to the operation of giving back to reality that which, at first, appears only a delusion), was the cause once again of incredible mistakes that made us stumble very often, or fall into some quagmire before we had recovered from our surprise.

. . . .

He used the leisure time left us by our preparations to tell me of his first adventures and of how he lacked experience then.

Besides a magnificent double-barreled rifle, of the best English manufacture, for each, they had brought in their baggage a few heavy caliber Brownings and enormous hunting knives. The ammunition alone filled one very heavy packing case.

When the moment came, they assembled for a last confabulation. It had to do with leaving where it was all the equipment which, because of its weight (for they had at their disposal only a very limited number of bearers) was likely to be cumbersome and, in consequence, to slow them down.

Neither he nor his companions had any taste for hunting and had never done any. There was no fear of running out of provisions in a country where edible plants and fruit grew within reach. Was there any need to encumber themselves with accessories so heavy and, when you thought about it, of so little use as rifles, pistols, knives?

The unlikelihood of having to use them, complete inexperience in handling these things (something which, if doing so proved necessary, would have deprived them of an advantage that can be expected only of skill, leaving them to rely on chance), everything inclined them to leave these behind.

What use is there for a hunting knife and its heavy leather sheath, where a pocket knife will suffice? What false security is in a rifle that may not fire or may misfire, in a Browning likely to jam.

Very unlikely, a meeting with prowlers in an area where nature is at her most generous. A few wild animals, at the very most, but hardly dangerous, all in all, if not attacked, and against which, anyway, in unpracticed hands no firearm gives any guarantee.

It was best to rely only on themselves, upon prudence, upon

a few movements, very simply and unforeseen, that instinct holds in reserve for difficult circumstances.

They were deciding to leave their weapons behind when they pictured a starving leopard before which they were going to find themselves defenseless.

. . . .

If I judge it necessary to report what follows, this is because it seems to me that this brief episode in our journey exercised a decisive influence upon succeeding events. When later we had occasion to speak of it, we never did so willingly. Some emotion gripped our throats so tightly as to make it painful to bring our voices out, a sudden alteration came over our faces. Perhaps, too, we attributed to one another a certain responsibility in this matter. But such is the fissure by which was revealed to us the existence of another world, an unknown world.

Light penetrated the forest only subdued by foliage without any chinks through which the sky might be visible. We walked along a corridor effected by the regular spacing of the trees, beneath a sort of dais for which the framework was made of delicate leaf nervure. The branches were not so high that one would be unable, with a jump, to catch hold of one of them and to hang from it. They could be seen, at moments, gliding one across another, and sometimes relaxing, but no bird had taken flight at this, for nothing, not a cry, not a free movement, revealed the existence of birds.

The temperature, despite the fairly deep shade, was perfectly mild and we were preparing to take advantage of this favorable circumstance to lengthen our day's march and to cover, at an even pace, more ground than we had done so far. After the plain, exposed in all directions to the sun, and bare, we had dreaded meeting that stubby inextricable vegetation of which explorers speak, humidity, or a more stifling heat. But all our apprehensions were quickly dissipated. Level terrain and that atmosphere favorable to deployment and the exercise of physical strength allowed us to believe no obstacle would stand in the way of the execution of our plans. An optimism we had hardly had occasion to experience, up to then, made us as usual put complete faith in advances of this kind on nature's part. She owed it to herself to undeceive us in the end.

We had been marching but an hour or two under the
forest's covering when an immense fatigue overwhelmed us.
We could not imagine its cause, but the air seemed to take on
unaccustomed consistency before us and offered us progressive
resistance. We had the feeling of being bathed in oil. The
movement of our hands and arms—which we thrust ahead of us
only to draw them back behind us, in turn, as swimmers
do—helped us only slightly. It became more and more painful to
move.

Thanks to a phenomenon about which we could not have
said whether it was or not a consequence of the other, our eyes,
although they tolerated being kept open, were detaching themselves from the spectacle around us. Little by little, they were
losing the power to discern objects very well, and almost their
taste for looking and seeing. We experienced the horrible sensation that they were going to die in our living bodies. That they
should in this way evade their natural duty, the feeling that an
irremediable night was approaching, soon brought our disappointment to its highest pitch.

We began to feel strangely lacking in energy and our
thoughts ceased to be lucid, even though, at different times, we
resorted to alcohol in the hope that it would manage to dissipate
our dangerous torpor.

If, in the beginning, we were tempted to believe we were
succumbing to the treacherous emanations that induce fever
and which, in certain parts of the Tropics, grip you before you
are able in any way to take precautions against them, our experience of bouts of this kind had quickly taught us we were mistaken. And that discovery had only increased our discomfort
and given it a character upon which were shattered all the illusions we had still contrived to retain about its origins in nature.

We could not have put up with a position as demoralizing
as ours was in those moments. We had been tested enough by
loneliness and it had already happened before that one or other
of us, after a long day spent in silence, by some fortunately still
harmless eccentricity would betray the serious disorders loneliness encourages and fosters. Our new situation could well make
us fear the worst. By common consent, we stopped. Apart from
violent solutions, we could no longer imagine any other
resource than lying down and closing our eyes. No action, not

even the most ordinary one, suggested itself to us, any more, with that appearance which renders it, in other circumstances, valid or necessary, and we were without the strength to accomplish the smallest action. We let ourselves drop, here and there, to the ground, convinced, it must be added, that sleep itself would bring us no lasting relief.

*

If we had been able to doubt the evidence of our watches, we should not have been able to believe it was night, so imperceptible was the change. Little by little, however, our senses became more acute, we perceived, as happens when a whole orchestra settles on a half-tone higher or lower without the harmony seeming at first different, a few slight and later surprising modifications of the former ordering of things. It was not the darkness, nor even anything that was evocative of it. If an opinion has to be expressed, it was rather a matter of some sort of concentration, or again of things coming into focus. The sky remained invisible.

We had started off again, quite listlessly, then with real eagerness. Shapes appeared to us to have an outline unsuspected in daylight, the slightest rise in the ground, a branch, a fallen leaf took on an aspect such that we felt them capable of holding our attention a long time. We had the impression one has when looking through the wrong end of opera glasses, the reduced size of objects and the limitation of the field of vision confer upon them an appearance at once firm and immaterial. But without effort we could see clearly into the whole expanse of the countryside, while with the same look, from the foot of a tree to the point where the foliage intercepted our glance, it was possible to embrace the irregular small cracks on its trunk, as if these were ornamentation, a little more complicated but quite visible, in a general effect.

The ground was covered in a light springy moss over which we were advancing so rapidly it seemed to be carrying us. We made more progress than we could realize. Some had struck up conversations, pleasant, sometimes harsh. These would start from nothing. Recollection of that day had suddenly faded away.

But also this was no longer the possibly exhausted nature

upon which, earlier, our energy had collapsed. Plants we had
not noticed until then emerged from the soil, under our feet,
and admirable flowers, just like eyes shaded by long lashes,
mouths revealing the flash of shining teeth, white hands,
weighed down with rings, opened slowly as we approached.
Some breath of wind, from one knew not where, caressed us as
we passed. A whole multitude of birds, singing and uttering
cries, came down from branch to branch and flew around us.
Animals passed between the trees, escorting us in silence. They
were of the size, more or less, and had the facial features of our
domestic cats, but nothing could compare with their majesty,
the softness of their long hair and their tawny gold color.

Our strange powers of perception seemed to increase from
moment to moment. Sounds, shapes, voices harmonized so
perfectly that this could have been surprising. Whatever unique
revelations we controlled, whatever mysteries, whatever secret,
to us mattered only their power, which we felt strongly.

This is how we were brought to the edge of an immense
clearing, and it was only from that moment that we became
conscious of the night's reality.

*

The sky now to be seen was of that dark blue assumed by
certain glances from an attentive woman. It was studded with
big stars whose stillness and symmetrical arrangement
impressed us. Their brightness lessened the heaviness of the
sky and touched its uniform color with a golden shimmer.
Halting at the edge of the forest and still protected by the
luminous shadow of the most advanced line of trees, we looked
at a house outlined against the far side of the clearing, apparently spacious, architecturally very simple, with only one story.
Its skillfully calculated proportions, its general appearance were
not like those which, in cities, give off that unbearable melancholy and inescapably prompt us to flight. It seemed unoccu-
pied, even though through all its wide-open windows we could
see it brilliantly lit from within. Upstairs, and at the far end of a
room that appeared to us immense, a 'cello was resting, with its
bow, against a chair, brass instruments gleamed in corners.
Other windows revealed empty white rooms. Downstairs, a

table, with scintillating crystal glasses, seemed to await guests. We did not doubt that we were those guests.

We stayed there, though, without impatience, as if to soak up the spectacle, tarrying over the contemplation of all its details. My companions were becoming visibly transfigured. There was no longer any doubt in my mind that I had not known them up until then, and I have never been so sure that their feelings corresponded to mine. We had never felt in one another, I think, anything but a moderate interest, confined to the necessities of a life that, if we had taken the trouble to think about it, would have inspired us to nothing but disgust. The lack of curiosity to which action gives such poor pretexts had cut us off more surely from the existence we were beginning to treat with suspicion than a great infirmity would have done, or death. Perhaps a ridiculous modesty, but not—fortunately— incredulity, had held us back from believing in the reality of other exchanges than those of a knife, a watch, or a cigarette lighter. And it is true that our tanned faces, our highwayman appearance, and our awkwardness could have dissuaded any- one, and us too, from thinking us capable of reaching more complex feelings and grander designs. All we men who treated one another like children a bit stronger than other children, better cut out for self-defense, found ourselves again, beneath the tan, the ragged beards, the free and easy ways of the encampment and the march. It could not have been chance alone that had brought us together in that place, from the four corners of the globe, at that precise moment. What was best in us, no doubt, some profound instinct, some madness, had prompted us to trade our relative peace for definite risks and dangers.

"My child, my sister, think how sweet it is."[2] Who among us—the one you would least expect, for sure—was bringing up that forgotten poem with magic promise. In any other circum- stance we would not have tolerated hearing it recited. But nothing was out of key here, neither the voice nor the place. "There everything is just order and beauty, luxury, calm and

---

2. The first two lines of Charles Baudelaire's poem "L'Invitation au voyage," originally published in *La Revue des Deux Mondes* on June 1, 1855. Reprinted in his *Les Fleurs du Mal*.

delight to the senses." The song came to an end on a serious note which, with a long soft vibration, seemed to bring to life the 'cello and the brass instruments in the abandoned house. Neither did the cries of the birds that had bewitched us a while back disturb the silence any more, nor did any living form break the line of stillness when a nude woman, in cycling socks, came down the flight of steps to meet us.

GEORGES HÉNEIN

1914—1973

Born in Cairo, Georges Hénein discovered surrealism while a
student in Paris, joining the movement in 1934 at the age of
twenty. Promoter of surrealist activities in Egypt, he was
co-founder there, in 1947, of the surrealist magazine *La Part du
sable*.

Like others before him, Hénein shows himself in his
writings to have felt the impulse to create a world that, departing from the norms of familiar reality, is animated and sustained
by imagination. This is the world on which he reports in his
Notes sur un pays inconnu. Hénein displays greater originality,
however, when undertaking to explore the borderland between
everyday reality and another reality, capable upon occasion of
casting its shadow upon the world in which we live. It does not
matter to him that, in the process of exploration, he must find
himself relating incidents less than clearly defined, as in *Histoire
vague*, originally published in the fourth issue of *VVV* in
February 1944. Of necessity, he finds his attention drawn to the
periphery of habitual experience. Inevitably, he walks the outer
perimeter of reality. Here everything is almost quite common-
place. And yet Georges Hénein makes us feel the tug of the
improbable, experienced as the promise of desire fulfilled.
Illumination seems to come most often from the magic proxim-

ity of woman in whom, faithful to one of the dominant myths of surrealism, Hénein sees the mediatrix between man and the surreal. Thus *Histoire vague* bears comparison with the surrealist poems of Paul Éluard and with André Breton's *Nadja* and *Arcane 17*, which all testify to the sense of wonder liberated in the surrealist when he is privileged to be touched by the presence of woman.

Histoire vague takes its rightful place in a volume called *Le Seuil interdit* (*The Forbidden Threshold* [1956]) that owes its title to a story in which we read, "On the prohibited side of the threshold, we live the dreamy life of pariahs." In the tales collected in *Le Seuil interdit* Hénein reveals his preference for marginal figures whose preoccupations and aspirations set them apart from society. The same is true of *Le Guetteur* (*The Watchman*), from *Un Temps de petite fille* (*Little Girl Weather* [1947]). What impresses in every case is that awareness of the existence of a forbidden threshold inculcates restlessness, not inertia. Although banal reality is insistently and even intrusively present we encounter also an impulse to look, at least, across the threshold that current living conditions seem to make it impossible for us to pass. Everything communicates Georges Hénein's sensitivity to the existence of things that cannot be grasped firmly *from this side.*

Hénein's use of language, then, expresses faith in the ability of words to lend themselves to something that, revealing his early training to have been in medicine, Breton called "the auscultation of the imaginary." This means that Georges Hénein probes the equivocal, not so much with the hope of deducing precise meanings as in order to measure the equivocal's fascinating ambiguity. For him, a sense of existence remains incomplete, and therefore devoid of interest, if one's attention is not directed to the extreme limit of the tangible, with the purpose of penetrating as far as possible, through language, into the intangible that lies beyond. "Henceforth," he once wrote, "we must no longer play with the words that fall from the void of the mouth and construct on ground impatient to germinate worlds impatient to die."[1] This affirmation of confi-

---

1. "A Contre-Cloison," published in the English surrealist magazine *London Bulletin*, no. 17 (June 15, 1939), p. 21.

dence in the austere instrument of language goes with another, formulated on the same occasion: "Now the precise hour is striking when chance closes the parenthesis it opened for us . . . when all we can do is choose between the tools of despair and the vile balm of consolation." Hénein's use of words as a less-than-adequate tool may give a hint of despair. All the same, he finds in the promise extended by language something preferable to the "vile balm of consolation" with which so many of us are content.

GEORGES HÉNEIN

Notes on a Useless Country

How could I have known that these people blinked their eyes when dreaming?

And yet, when that was explained to me, I understood why, waking up, they appeared so scatterbrained and without a comprehensive view of things. They are dreaming, I am assured, of "real countries" where men they do not know vegetate. They never speak of the matter among themselves, but in the end you can guess it from the way they excuse themselves all the time for not amounting to a "real country."

"We are an accident," they say in a tone they try to render detached. "You mustn't be angry with us. Do you cavil about an atoll rising the height of a tooth above the line of the horizon?"

A country with gestures that fade quickly. Everything, about us, that is undertaken anew remains methodically unfinished. It is not unusual, in the morning, opening a newspaper, to discover that the editorial comes to a halt in the middle of a sentence, on the threshold perhaps of an idea, for no other valid reason than the extreme fatigue of the editor . . .

On the screen, it is much better. The main outline of a story is presented in successive flashes. In the orb of each face—like a hat veil of words—are laid out the themes, storms, the fever of which it would have to give an account, if the moving pictures had the right to live out their lives.

One day, I experienced a shock from which it was quite a time before I recovered. Around the bend in a street of severe countenance, I came upon a shop window where in Gothic script the following promise was traced: EVERYTHING FOR LOVE. Thanks to these words the locality was as though suffused with mystery. I went in, full of illogical plans, but the devil of a silence extended all around me, slipped handcuffs on me, enlaced me in the manner of those protoplasms that take the form of foreign bodies and close about them forever. Just about all I could see was, arranged in a semicircle around a nun with features ravaged by leprosy, a family of alembics in which the bitterness of time dripped away.

Close to the frontier, the ground loses its consistency. There banks of quicksand absorb, with greedy lips, dozens of desperate people every day. These quicksands are a sort of official institution; to forbid or modify their use would seem sacrilege.

They are edged with well-beaten paths where, a contemplative look on their faces, tourists take up position, equipped with folding chairs and supplies of food. From time to time, these spectators make comments in a low voice, respectfully, on the exceptionally pathetic physiognomy of a suicide.

Charitable souls have managed to install, in these disquieting regions, nightingales whose melodious song soothes the last moments of those being sucked down. These birds live in a world apart. They live between the imaginary landscapes that cover the walls of their cages. They hover indolently above the drama and everyone is envious of their state.

A useless, useless country, this, where the women are too fragile to be loved from up close.

GEORGES HÉNEIN

Vague Story

There are some things that can happen only in the rain. Or at the very least with the quiet complicity of rain . . . For example, feeling light, light to the point of disputing the regulation that the elements believe they have the right sometimes to exercise over the to-and-fro movement of people's hearts. A downfall during a rainstorm means a date missed—a date that will not necessarily be reborn from its own ashes, everything needing to be begun all over from the first kiss, other occasions to implant it upon other lips—a hat veil which, for want of being raised in time, will crystallize into permanent latticework over the incomplete face of anticipation. A beautiful face to which rain gives the illusion of weeping, to which tears recall inexplicable infractions of certain orders to be cold on the platform of departing railroad stations . . .

It rains and the large sentimental posters, where two people from the movies embrace in vain, softly become unstuck from wall to wall. Subject to no attraction in particular, a woman advances through the heavy beating rain, a woman in no hurry at all and whose gentleness, all at once, walks ahead of her and spreads its contagion right and left in the way illuminati distribute their tracts every time the question of changing the world comes up. No one could say exactly if she is beautiful but everyone has seen her beautify the places through which she passes, everyone has seen her capture distressed outlying districts of the town with the mother-of-pearl lasso of her breath. Do not ask her the color of her eyes. She will lift her head to the sky, brush the clouds with an absent-minded eyelid and reply, if she really wants to reply to you, that all she knows of her eyes is that "during rainy weather, they are striped on the inside."

Keep her company before she fades away like a rapid image on a temporary window pane, before she breaks like the thread of a dream picked up again a moment ago and for a moment only. Take her hand so that people will move out of your path and stop exposing, in the name of the seriousness of their own attitude, all that is absurd in yours. Take her hand and let each of her fingers have its story, have its ring of thrills to be lost in the labyrinth of silent shared secrets. You have perhaps only an hour left to share, the time it takes the rain to tire and the first lightening of the sky, perfecting it again, to separate inconsiderately this couple brought together by inclement weather!

Whatever you do, do not try to entice her into one of those cafés where people speak of business, idleness, and women in the same pallid tone, their cigarettes dangling, their thoughts on other matters. When it is raining in the street, the café owner cranks up his phonograph and voyages aboard the "Comparsita," a captain at the same time attentive and woolgathering, with a word for no man, with not a glance for the sea. Something's got into him again, the waiters say. Something—the accordion with clenched teeth, the chorus that lays bare the bellies of women, the struggle with life or uncovering the right side of the theatrical set, the real names of hated things— . . . stop the music, you're wanted on the phone, Sir! As if he still had the courage of his voice. . . .

No, cafés like that are not for her. No "Comparsita" with hanging dagger. No captain whose glance is stabbed in advance. All those destinies traced with a drawing-pen, the lucidity of the condemned man, the poet's rapture, the picnic on the grass, those she freezes with one gesture; with the mechanical gesture of falling rain. She will never claim, as do so many laughable individuals, she will never claim that she "has been through worse than that." Her strength comes probably from the fact that she has not been and will never be through worse.

With her striped eyes she tirelessly combs the world like hair, understanding which matters little. And her heart beats too lightly to be interested in events of passion on which the infinite resources of human violence are so readily expended.

If you wish to speak to her, if you believe in the taming influence of the spoken word, she will let you set up your stall, lay out your lace, spread out your frivolities, hold out even the symbolic fears of your childhood, after which all she will need is one incisive little question, one very little question, to raze to the ground the delicate structure of your lies. What is, this is all she will ask you, what is your relationship with bad weather . . .?

If it were only a matter of breaking her silence, a giant step would have been made already. But it is a matter of much more than that, it is a matter of what this woman has in mind and of what obstinacy and adventurousness the rain adds to a forehead decidedly that of a child. Others before you, worn out by solitude, have tried to make of her at least a wife, at least a frequenter of their dreams, this woman one is sure to find everywhere that her image is necessary, this woman who in destroyed towns dresses in broken stained glass windows. It is a waste of time, time that will always be wasted, each new shower of rain, so far as each new supplicant is concerned. In truth, nothing could divert her from her hermetic, insulated, insoluble path. The more she advances, the more her feet stir up eddies in bloom, the petals of a bouquet which, for you, can signify only her farewell. Your childhood memories sleep at the bottom of puddles already deep. The café owner's phonograph is going rusty with incoherent words. Try out on it your projects meant for reciting, while it is still going.

*

The rain has just stopped, for no reason. Around you, things seem to have remained just as they were. However, now an agitation that is not natural to you takes possession of you. You search anxiously for the woman who moved like a ship at your side. She exists no more and soon you will doubt she ever existed. Nothing in the street, nothing in the sky . . . What are you complaining about? You are taking your first steps in love at first sight; she is taking hers in disappearing. You are quits. No indeed, you have not quite given up. A last shred of hope sends you toward that big dark dwelling where the main entrance seems to have admitted something extraordinarily slender and stealthy. The concierge blocks your path at once. You describe your companion, your vision. And without even letting you finish, the concierge replies, gazing at you despondently, "Don't you see, poor man, it's over . . . In a moment the side-walks will be dry. The rain has done enough work for today. I advise you not to offend its rest . . ."

On the top floor, though, black drapes are being drawn behind a proud lone window.

GEORGES HÉNEIN

The Watchman

There are some women without contacts in towns too large for them.

One day, in the street an unknown man slaps them, out of hate for their unimportance, and their splendor is what responds to this outrage. Their splendor like the spark under the horse's shoe. Their splendor that people did not suspect the existence of and are not sure ever to recover from, being themselves so unprepared for so little affectation, and even more outweighed in the scales than is the prayer by the sin corresponding to it. People will persist though, do their best, throw the ashes of slander upon that splendor, the intractable ashes of families where something is still at stake.

This is when the questioning begins:

"You have no friends?"

"I have no friends."

"So-and-So though, you know all about his misconduct; how are we to know that he doesn't get prompting from you for his wrong doing?"

"We found ourselves sitting next to one another at school, he rested his head against my shoulder, for five minutes he slept . . . there's nothing more I can tell you; if the water in the ornamental lakes was less forgetful and the children less serious in their play, maybe they could be called to witness . . ."

"And what about the drunken Portugese of the other evening, you're not going to deny that you were pressing drinks on him . . ."

"I've little chance of convincing you we had nothing in common, our paths crossed, that was years ago, in the turnstile of a beerhouse, in Central Europe."

"Well, anyway, what are your responsibilities, what are your resources?"

"My responsibilities? I think you mean my weaknesses: not to spy on those I love . . ."

"You are simplifying, Mademoiselle."

This is the way people reproach certain persons with "simplifying" when they are in fact embroidering with no purpose in mind, when they are in fact embroidering out of a need to slip a thin down of illusion between themselves and the insensitive plate of society.

People would like to make them place their trust in some useful vulgarity, limit them to comprehensible behavior.

Oh, if only these persons were to lodge a complaint . . .

I knew a man who used to open doors, endlessly, tirelessly, because he was looking for someone.

Despite his evasive air, no one would have dreamed of accusing him of killing time. He was looking for someone, and that was an exclusive activity which put up with no joking.

The doors followed one upon the other without surrendering anything of the person he was following. He almost ended up going around them. He would tackle them with ridiculous precaution and each one in a peculiar fashion, in, one could say, a peculiar style. He would slip through askew, he would take up as little space as possible, sometimes he would wait until the door had been opened from the inside. He would pass, necessarily, again and again through the same places. His life resembled an obstinately circular route. Even chance repeated itself in all his life. All that continued to elude him was the treasure for which he begged with the humblest gestures. We had nicknamed him "the watchman." *He* too possessed that faculty for "simplification," use of which makes one so unsociable. We were sure a night would come when he would utter the old cry announcing the passing of the hours.

When fatigue came over him, he would grant himself a brief rest. He would take up a position between two river banks, at mid-bridge, as he used to say, and he would envelop the countryside in the tissue paper of a chilly glance. Seeing him refresh himself this way, as others slash their veins or allow themselves to be stood against a wall, folks would arrive in droves. They insisted on having confirmed before their eyes the quite artificial alliance of despair and newspaper headlines.

It was at mid-bridge, during breaks in his pensive siesta, that it was easiest to start a discussion with the watchman and to strike up a rather shaky conversation with him, the reflection of a conversation in the sensitive hearing of the water flowing by.

He readily employed antiphrasis and one had to restore their true intention to most of the terms he used. When he ran aground, touching bottom, and the mud came up to his lips, he would take pleasure in recommendations of which the most frequent was: LIFE MUST BE EDULCORATED. And each person was free to think that this was a dying man's prescription.

And at the end of an afternoon when I had piously escorted him throughout one of his methodical sterile rounds, I made bold to ask him where he stood in his search and what its purpose was.

"Oh," he replied, as if there were no choice in the matter, "one of those women with diamonds suppressed, perpetually at the bedside of a choice they don't make—forever nurses to the imposture of the passions:—one of those women about whom you say that they have contacts and whose loneliness, I am ascertaining, comes most often from the clumsiness of our desire.

"I shall take care not to forget her little engrossing face, her little unmarked blotting paper of a face. It was on a café terrace. She was sitting, quite a way from me, preoccupied with a contumacious pencil in which the lead kept breaking. This little game had already been going on for some time and there was no reason why it should not continue, except that, a customer having left his table, a quick move on my part allowed me to get close to this individual. I saw then she was weeping. She remained like this for a moment—on a gentle slope—maybe not even possessed by her tears, then she raised her head and looked me up and down across some waste ground or other, the way you gaze at rusted scrap iron in the courtyard on the outskirts of town. Finally she threw down her pencil and slipped away. In the crushing fog that hit me and it took me hours to cut through, hers were footsteps it didn't seem to me one could follow in.

"How long can it be since then? I've no idea any more. Such apparitions have no date. But, now as yesterday, I persist in the belief that things are going to work out—I believe she will be returned to me, that for the good order of the world my individual on a gentle slope will be returned to me, with all her reasons for crying, and others too that she doesn't suspect . . ."

He consulted his watch, took me by the arm and suggested we push on to another establishment we rarely visited on the Rue du Liseron.

He took advantage of the trip to explain to me, in great detail, several of his edulcorative projects. The principle was the same in every instance. They were all based on great severity toward the ways of man.

The lights were coming on, one after the other. There was beyond a doubt nothing in sight. And I thought, I know not why, of those railroad employees who, when night has come, wave lanterns among the jumble of tracks. No one takes the trouble to thank them. They no doubt are part of the rite.

MARIANNE VAN HIRTUM

1935—

Born in Bricniot, near Namur, Belgium, Marianne van Hirtum met André Breton in 1959. That was the year the surrealists dedicated to Eros an international exhibition held in Paris, while Breton announced in the newspaper *Arts* (No. 754, December 23-29), "L'Érotisme est le seul art à la mesure de l'homme" ("Eroticism is the only art that measures up to man"). Shortly afterward, the surrealist Robert Benayoun, editor of an *Anthologie du Nonsense* (1959) and, later, of an *Érotique du surréalisme* (1965), was to point out, during a BBC Third Programme discussion "In Defence of Surrealism" (broadcast on February 9, 1960): "We have always depended on chance, which is the great regulator of nature, and we accept with joy all the hazards of coincidence, the accidents of thought and language. At the same time, we consider humor as a very potent weapon against society, against restraining forces of society. We use the cruel, the direct impact of black humor, 'humour noir' as Breton called it, but we also use nonsense, the far-fetched detours of disappointment of the critical mind."

Surely, one of the characteristic features of nonsense is the gravity with which the improbable and the impossible are presented as though they were faithful reflections of everyday experience. An unpublished story by Marianne van Hirtum,

Euthanésie (1972) displays this feature, turning it to account in an attack upon accepted social and moral values. In *Euthanésie* the narrative tone is beguilingly unsophisticated and matter-of-fact, as the storyteller draws upon numerous details that are immediately recognizable as true-to-life. However, we can accept her opening statement (that what she has to tell is really very simple) only on condition we allow the real to be compromised to the point where confidence is weakened in that aspect of reality to which habit and education have accustomed us.

L'Histoire drôle de la semaine des trente-cinq jeudis (1973), also unpublished, is noticeably different, in one important respect at least. It challenges common sense from the outset, imperturbably advancing in defiance of so much that seems to lend permanence to the familiar façade of the real. Introduced when the narrator is listing witnesses to the fact that—the most conclusive evidence to the contrary makes no difference—Madame Louismille's marriage has not been consummated, an enumeration that defies translation[1] offers a helpful clue to those wondering how *L'Histoire drôle* came to be written. Open to assistance by chance, when assembling words Marianne van Hirtum willingly lets the progress of her story be influenced by verbal associations beyond the control of rational sequence.

Following a surrealist like Marianne van Hirtum into the "far-fetched detours of nonsense" may give some readers the annoying feeling they have been tricked into losing their bearings in the byways of frivolity. This is because they do not appreciate that, as Marko Ristic has shown, to the surrealist humor is "the disinterested and direct expression of the unconscious."[2] As such, it is "in its essence an intuitive and implicit criticism of the conventional mental mechanism" having as its effect removal of facts from their so-called normal context "to

---

1. "La courte-pointe, la courte-vue, le court-bouillon, le temps qui court."
2. Marko Ristic, a response, under the title "Humor in 1932," to a survey opened in the first number of *Nadrealizam danas i ovde* (*Surrealism Here and Now* [June 1931]) on the theme: "Is Humor a Moral Attitude?" Ristic's response appeared in the second number of the same Yugoslav surrealist magazine (January 1932). Under the title "L'Humour, attitude morale?" and over the signature "Marco Rististch," it was reproduced in French translation in the sixth number of the Parisian magazine *Le Surréalisme au service de la Révolution* (May 1933), pp. 36-39, and not, as reported by Yves Duplessis (*Le Surréalisme* [Presses Universitaires de France, 1950], p. 21), in *La Révolution surréaliste*.

precipitate them into a vertiginous play of unexpected surreal relationships." The stories of Marianne van Hirtum illustrate the principle laid down by Ristic: "In contact with poetry, humor is the extreme expression of a convulsive irreconciliation, of a revolt to which restraint and repression only give more strength."

MARIANNE VAN HIRTUM

Euthanasia — A Cat Kidnapped — Thirty Francs — The Veterinarian

This was very simple, really. At noon, the Lady from the fourth floor, meeting the little young woman from the sixth in the hallway, asked her to be kind enough to come up with her, for she had a favor to ask. "It's this way," she said, "It's very simple. I'd like you to agree to take my cat to be put to sleep. That poor animal is suffering. She's seventy-two years old now. I don't have the strength to take her down there." Little Emie agreed at once, because of her usual willingness to help. The appointment was set for two the following afternoon. "There's five francs in it for you," added the Lady with a gracious smile.

At two o'clock, then, the next day, Emie rang the bell on the fourth floor. The other side of the door there was a commotion, then a fairly long silence reigned. "Well," Emie said to herself, "they're in no hurry." At last the door opened and the Lady exclaimed with a bewitching smile, "Oh! Poor little Emie, you've chosen a very bad moment: it had completely slipped my mind that we were baptising our little boy today, could you come back tomorrow at five o'clock?" Emie acquiesced—what else could she do?—and went away. Back in her own room, she took off her pretty red hat and her gloves, and, rather listlessly, went back to work.

The following morning, returning from an errand in town,

HiRTUM 73

Emie met the Lady from the fourth floor in the hallway. "Oh my dear girl," said the Lady, "would you be so sweet as to kindly do me a big favor. It's this way: our dog isn't at all well. He's over a hundred fifty years old, would you be so very good as to take him down there for me, to have him put to sleep: we don't have the heart for the job, ourselves." Emie, who was kind, said yes. The appointment was set for the following day at three o'clock. When, the following day at three, Emie rang the bell on the fourth floor, the Lady joyfully opened the door and at once cried, "Oh you poor child! You've come at such a bad time! I'd quite forgotten we were celebrating today our hundredth wedding anniversary, my husband and I. Would you be so kind, please, as to come back tomorrow evening at six o'clock?" Emie answered that she would be there. The door closed quietly. Emie had to go out that day: so she did not take off her pretty red hat.

When she came back from town, at the front door of her house she met the Lady from the fourth floor who tugged sweetly at her sleeve, saying, "My little child, I find it hard to ask you to do me a very big favor. This is what it's all about: our horse Robert is sick. He's just over three hundred thirty-two years old. Would it please you, to spare us that hateful trip, to take him tomorrow down there where they put animals to sleep? Let me add—without wanting to hurt your feelings—that there's five francs waiting for you, Emie." Emie, kindhearted as always, replied that such a favor did not bother her. As early as five o'clock in the morning she put on her pretty red hat. Then, as she still had a little time left, according to her alarm clock, she prepared herself tea with milk and drank it very thoughtfully. Then she shut her door and went down to the fourth floor. She waited a while after ringing the bell. The Lady cautiously opened the door a crack. "Oh!" she said, upon seeing little Emie, "my dear child, what a bad time you've chosen. Just imagine, today—my Goodness! I'd completely forgotten, scatterbrain that I am—we have to celebrate our last little boy's solemn communion. Couldn't you come back tonight at ten o'clock?" Emie, with her customary graciousness, replied that, indeed, there was no problem, she herself had so much to do that morning, anyway, and went off, her pretty red hat a little askew.

At ten that evening, Emie courteously rang the bell on the fourth floor. The door remained closed, but the Lady's voice reached her, muffled, from behind the door: "Do please excuse me, gracious child, we're celebrating such a great event, you understand: tonight's the marriage of our grownup daughter to her best friend from school, I can't allow myself . . .": the rest was so unintelligible that little Emie went off on tiptoe.

A few weeks went by. Emie was ill in the meantime. She went to the best specialists for treatment. When she was better, on sick leave, one fine morning she was very happy to go to the milliner's to treat herself to a new little hat, which she chose in red, this time. Just for a change, she said to herself, filled with joy. Returning from that happy errand, she ran right into the Lady from the fourth floor.

The Lady had put on a considerable amount of weight, so Emie did not recognize her right off. When she had got over her surprise and greeted the Lady in a friendly fashion, the Lady took her hand and asked her in a low voice if she would consent to come up with her to her apartment for a few moments, since she had a little favor to ask. She added in Emie's ear that if three francs would be welcome . . . Very happy with her pretty red hat, Emie accepted at once and went up behind the Lady. The latter, because of her new corporeal opulence, walked more slowly, so the climb was long and difficult. Emie was dreaming of meeting a mirror in which she could admire herself at her leisure.

When they had reached the fourth floor the Lady collapsed in a chair. Feeling tired, Emie did the same. A moment went by, each getting her wind back.

Then the Lady spoke to Emie in a low voice. "It's nothing," she said, "Nothing, or nothing much, anyway. My poor husband has just had his five hundredth birthday. He's at the end of his tether. Between you and me, whatever you do, don't repeat this to anyone: he smells these days. Would you have the civility, Mademoiselle, to take him, with the usual precautions, to those people to have him put to sleep? That would save us all sorts of worries . . ." "When?" asked Emie. "Well, right away, if you like. I'll go into the toilet, for the sight of all that business would be too painful for me, you understand. My husband is hidden in the kitchen closet. His basket is on the chair, all you

have to do is get him into it: that won't take but a moment.—
Oh, please don't forget to wash out his dish as you go
through.—Thank you."

Emie carefully closed the front door and went off toward
the kitchen, while the Lady took care to shut herself in the toilet.
The whole business took a little more time, though, than it takes
to put an old man of five hundred in a basket.

Nevertheless, the following morning, Emie, wild with joy,
was able to buy a new little hat, in red this time. When she went
home, joyfully, she had a shock, seeing a great crowd standing
in front of her house. The firemen were there in full uniform,
nothing was missing. Emie went up and questioned the neighbors. "Oh my poor girl," was the response, "a very painful
thing has happened.

"There's been a huge leak on the third floor. A real flood,
you know. It didn't do any good to ring the doorbell on the
fourth floor, no one answered. Then the Concierge had the marvelous idea of calling in the firemen; they broke the door down:
oh! what a smell! Just imagine, there wasn't anyone there. But
the Fire Chief had the wonderful idea of forcing the toilet door
that seemed to be jammed from the inside.—You know . . .
they found Madame so swollen and dead in there that the
doorway had to be widened to be able to pull her out, and while
the firemen were dragging her over the rug in the entrance hall,
her stomach burst under too much pressure and you know out
of it came . . . a little dog, a very big cat, a tiny horse . . . oh,
Mademoiselle! Is her husband going to be flabbergasted when
he gets home from work! . . . Madame loved him so . . . he
loved Madame so. Times are bad, Mademoiselle!"

The next week, Emie decided that red hats did not suit her
any more so well as before. With the three francs from the Lady
on the fourth floor, she bought herself a pretty black hat.

MARIANNE VAN HIRTUM

The Funny Story
of the Week with
Thirty-Five Thursdays

Madame Louismille adored her son, Louiscent. The poor little
boy deserved it with all his heart. He was a precocious child.
Even before he was born he had given dazzling proof of this.
Two weeks from his conception, as his mother felt strange
ocular disturbances, the consulting physicians diagnosed in the
fetus third-stage schizophrenia. The birth took place at two
months. At once the little boy was enrolled in the psychiatry
section of the École du Louvre, where his great-uncle was a pro-
fessor emeritus. Louiscent's father would have preferred a
career in firearms, seeing that he himself belonged to the
managerial staff school for retired wild boars, of which he was
bursar-gendarme. But Madame Louismille had other ambitions
for her son. She had by the way never been able to love her
faithful courteous husband who barely touched her once a
Sunday. She asked for a divorce, which was granted in no time
at all, in view of the nonconsummation of the marriage, recognized by various witnesses to the fact: the counterpane, short-
sightedness, fish served in wine sauce, things as they are these
days. It was plain to see that Madame Louismille preferred her
son to her husband, she swore to make her son her lover. At
that very moment, Louiscent was studying Oedipus, in the
company of the Volga boatmen, hurriedly summoned.

It was wintertime: the Seine was rising with a menacing air and haste was necessary. In the morning, the little boy would put on his boots and breathe the air with great strides as he went to work. In the square courtyard of the Louvre those two or three hundred hysterical women would wait for him with unconcealed impatience, all come from the suburbs, for this disease is getting to be rare in the capital. Louiscent made the acquaintance of all those nurses registered by the Turkish state. They marched past, each morning, in serried ranks, holding tightly under their thin arms the annals of contemporary psychiatry, which contains, everyone knows, as many folios as the future will and testament of Jesus Christ, late King of Prussia. Louiscent did not pay them any attention. On the other hand, his heart at once fell in love with the kitchen maid. A young trainee nurse secretly suckling a cat plastered from head to tail, that mewed in French. Louiscent would have gladly given the girl a present, as a declaration of love. She was quite blonde and so delightful to see. But he used to hand over all his pay to his mother, Madame Louismille, who, on the other hand, fed him like a little pigeon. She would make him, every morning, adorable slices of bread and jelly so that he could eat his lunch thinking about her.

But Louiscent thought only about Louisette, the young trainee nurse so full of beauty, with whom he was hopelessly smitten. Then he resolved to devote himself to some great action to win her heart. He stole his mother's blue necklace to present to her, on the second of the year one thousand. Louisette immediately put the necklace around her neck and presented Louiscent, who was filled with wonder, with the most burning love kiss there could be on earth. It was a kiss composed of an amethyst surrounded by big real pearls, which was worth, at the lowest estimate, at least all the riches of the potentially over-developed countries.

Faced with so much acknowledged love, Louiscent lost his balance and had to have it restored by being put on the winner in the third, something that at once brought the pink back to his cheeks.

Now they were friends, Louiscent promised Louisette he would take her Sundays to the Camargue country. But that was not an easy thing to do, given the close supervision maintained by Madame Louismille over the free time of her son, that son whom she wanted to keep in her arms and get into her lonely woman's bed. She had a padlock made by her protégés at the Court of Miracles. This padlock kept the door of Louiscent's bedroom closed tight, so that the poor young man had to make do with spending his Sundays at home and had to give up his short-lived amours. His mother, who was a stout woman, did her best to make detention bearable for him. She called in General Motors' Mechanic,[3] Pieds Nikelés, the Ego, the Here, the There, Robin Hood, and the Marquis of the Marquesas, who all performed an aubade for Louiscent, under his window, every Sunday between three and six in the afternoon. After which, Madame Louismille would open the door and release her beloved who, exhausted by so much sacred music, would end the day falling asleep on his tender mother's knees, shared incidentally by the faithful Lazarus, a dog swathed in bandages, like a Minion from the time of the Edwards. Then Madame Louismille would daintily carry her love into her lonely woman's bed and relieve herself, shedding all the tears on earth.

However, Louiscent prospered, increasing in size and weight. He carried *his* right in front and had a hard-on like a fine Arabian horse. So as to reward him, his mother decided, therefore, to take him on a vacation in the kingdom of Latin Arabia, where there is so much to see. They left hand-in-hand.

The heat was so great, though, that Louiscent very quickly lost his appetite. Urgently called in, a magician made it clear he had an acute neurosis, the effect of prolonged parental insolvency, and said it would appear to be time to have Louiscent psychoanalyzed, if, that is, he would consent to this.

But Louiscent vigorously refused to let himself be psychoanalyzed. And so the Institute of Psychoanalysis, of such celebrated renown, lost the most famous of its potential adepts, badly in need of love.

"Jesus Christ will not forgive me for this," thought Madame Louismille, who was as religious as all the monuments in Paris and she ordered Louiscent a priest's cassock, so as to make atonement before the divine Pro-Evidence. But the divine Pro-Evidence refused the sacrifice. There was a totalitarian and

---

3. I.e., Charlie Chaplin, in *Modern Times*.

vestiary storm and the cassock was burned alive before the assembly of their Majesties of Europe. Madame Louismille was beginning to despair of winning her son's love. Then, in secret, she decided on the worst thing she could have done. She cut off her dear son's allowance, put him on Madeira sauce only, something that is very bad for reincarnated uncles, and had his three uncles come from America. In their company, she went on a cruise to the Super Westward Islands, on the ship *The Monthly Rose*.

She was very angry to find no mail from her son at general delivery anywhere she went with the rapid stride of a hungry wild beast. The voyage was a fiasco and they returned home three weeks late.

Alas, it was to find Louiscent in an ominous condition. He was dying of hunger, frightfully thin; ashamed of his own appearance, he had taken cover under the bed, where his mother had to capture him with a flower-prod.

It was time to move the poor young man to hospital. There, things did not take long. Louiscent was laid out on a dissecting table, trepanation was rapidly carried out. The Sylvius bridge was shaky, the Rolando fissures had been carried away by the flood of poisoned humors that flowed down from the cerebellum. It was decided that they would proceed to ablate the whole head.

Madame Louismille sobbed in the corridors of the hospital. The hours went by slowly, anguish was at its most acute. It was then that an intern dressed in scarlet came to lay on the knees of the lady, still in tears, a box puffed out with rose petals, containing her beloved son's penis, all that was left of that great love, too great and too passionate, alas, to find fulfillment on this earth.

Madame Louismille was awarded the Martyr's Palm, on the final ballot. A bubble, emerging from the mouth of our very honored Holy Father, made her blessed forever.[4]

That is what you call a well-recompensed effort.

---

4. *Bulle*, the word for "bubble" is also, in French, a papal bull.

ALAIN JOUBERT

1936—

In the course of the broadcast discussion "In Defence of Surrealism" (February 9, 1960), the moderator, Jacques Brunius, invited the participants, Robert Benayoun, Joyce Mansour, Nora Mitrani, and Octavio Paz, to comment on the significance of eroticism in surrealism. Nora Mitrani stressed the taste for scandal, commenting: "I think that scandal is very important for surrealism. For us surrealists, scandal is a provocation, a challenge. It consists in tearing the mask off what society and conventional morality only tolerates when it is camouflaged." In corroboration, Octavio Paz added, "We can say that both poetry and eroticism are means to destroy the maze of mirrors that is the so-called moral life of modern man," explaining, "Well, surrealism tries to regain for eroticism and for all the activities of man the mystery—or perhaps mystery, that's not the right word—the marvelous part of man, and that is always private, secret."

All three texts by which Alain Joubert is represented here show him to be in agreement with these views: *Le Sens de la fête* (*The Meaning of the Treat*), taken from *La Brèche: action surréaliste* (No. 8, November 1965); *Le Naufrageur des sens* (*Wrecker of the Senses*) from the first number of the Brazilian magazine *A Phala*, which served as the catalog of the thirteenth International Surrealist Exhibition (São Paulo, August 1967); *Moiteur des plages qu'épointe le baba* (*The Moisture of the Beaches Blunted by the Baba*) which appeared in the surrealist magazine *L'Archibras* (No. 6, December 1968).

Born in Paris, Joubert first made contact with surrealism in 1952, when he was no more than sixteen. Three years later he met Breton and began participating in surrealist activities. By 1959 he was declaring, "I have the good fortune to possess a mind generally attentive to the daily expression of a certain form of imbecility; the one externalized through a perpetually defensive state, the supreme faculty available to the man who wishes to avoid at all cost contact with the marvelous."[1] Consistently opposed to imbecility of this kind, and sensitive to man's need to enjoy the benefits of the marvelous, he remarked, that spring, "I am not a mathematician of the unknown, at very most a dreamer."[2] This statement is a modest one that gives little intimation of the direction in which his dream takes him. It does not emphasize, for instance, that in Joubert's estimation dreaming, the contrary of escapism, relates to something he terms "ferment of the mind": "If the only weapon at our disposal is ferment of the mind, this is no less capable of provoking various forms of uneasiness, and, at the apogee of its curve, of *reviving the revolutionary concept by restoring its mythical strength and luster.*"[3] As Joubert goes on to explain, in order to free mankind, "we must already awaken in man, far from the sole ambition of a more satisfying *standard* of living, the need for a greater *sense* of living."

Alain Joubert's own contribution to the program outlined in his essays takes the form of a succession of short stories that give special prominence to gesture. Whether it be the gesture giving "The Meaning of the Treat," or the ritualized act executed with gravity in the course of a ceremonial, the significance attaching to gesture lies in its linkage of the erotic to the marvelous, in scandal.

Commenting on the graphic work of Robert Lagarde, Joubert once observed, "We too often miss noticing that each

---

1. ". . . Comme une rare fleur . . . ," *Bief: jonction surréaliste*, no. 13 (January 15, 1959), no pagination.
2. "Les Parfums Lourds," *Le Surréalisme, même*, no. 3 (Spring 1959), p. 56.
3. "Demandez le programme," *BIEF: jonction surréaliste*, no. 7 (June 1, 1959).

instant whose duration we make vibrate really exists only as a function of the gesture accompanying it."[4] And so—just like the men and women in *Le Naufrageur des sens*—"We must play with passion, while remaining ignorant even of the rules of the game." This is because, as Joubert pointed out on another occasion, "in the measure that a person's sovereign desire tends toward constant modification of the *ego* by a very extensive system of references to the outside world, the breaking point is situated on the level of gesture and its echo."[5] For this reason, Joubert sees the echo of our gestures as more important than gesture itself: "it speaks to our sensibility as clearly as pain or pleasure, it is the best *developer* for bringing out our physical reality, since upon it rests knowledge of our tangible *weight* on what surrounds us."

The world opened up to us in *The Meaning of the Treat* is evocative of that painted by Paul Delvaux, in which so many naked or half-clothed women appear, and, even more, of a painting, *Her geracht* (depicting a nude woman cycling through deserted streets), by the Dutch surrealist J. H. Moesmans.

---

4. Untitled text published in *Phases*, no. 7 (May 1961), p. 31.
5. "Le Geste a la parole," *La Brèche: action surréaliste,* no. 3 (September 1962), p. 25.

ALAIN JOUBERT

The Meaning of the Treat

It is summertime. Three o'clock in the morning. She is stretched out, nude, alone, on the unmade bed. The sheets have lost all their coolness and stick to her skin. Sleep has eluded her so far and she thinks it is now too late to drop off. Her body, which she can make out in the semidarkness of the room, is a source of discomfort to her: on her stomach, her arms tucked under the pillow; on her back, diagonally across the bed; sitting, her knees drawn up to her chin. There is nothing she can do, the heat is everywhere, *throbbing*. Since her body imposes its presence so much, she must take it into account. She rises, picks up a light-weight dressing gown, hesitates, throws it down. She feels the need to *go out*. She just has to go out, *as she is*.

Her hand on the door knob, her head framed in the doorway, stealing a glance through the shadows. Timidly, she creeps as far as the stairs. At this hour, she is in danger of meeting few people. She does not especially want to, anyway, she does not wish to *be seen*. The very opposite. What she wishes is this: to go on as long as possible through the streets round about, her body free of all hindrance. To feel the weight of the city, without nylon and silk armor. To run, her hair falling loose, beyond the limits of the crosswalks. To hide, when she catches sight of someone so as to take better advantage of *the treat* she is giving herself. She knows, of course, that behind the windows faces will appear sometimes. But she will not see them, and so will not have the feeling of being seen. *She will not see herself "seen."* This is what she is looking for. The nakedness of her body is a challenge to the city, at the same time as a tribute. Subjugated, concrete, steel, brick, stainless steel, ashlar will become her finery. In exchange, the firmness of her breasts, caressed by the warm July air, the tropical forest beginning on the border of her thighs, the hollow of the back and the hardness of the buttocks on a body rinsed clean will give the deserted city in return a dimension of which she often has a presentiment without ever really finding it.

She has just come down the four flights of stairs. At the bottom, the main entrance. She has taken care not to set off the night bell. The tiles of the entry offer a contrast with the rug on the stairs. She shivers. Pressing the button that controls the solid door, she knows she is going to carry through an essential operation, *for herself alone.*

It is still very dark. No one, at such an hour, is abroad in the neighborhood where she lives. There is in the immediate vicinity no tavern, no bar, no restaurant for people out at night and those who, for the most part, work early in the morning do not stay out late. Moreover, vacation time has already begun. She walks through the doorway, stands squarely, legs apart, in the middle of the sidewalk, hands on hips, and breathes in greedily. Her heartbeat, and this seems to her as it should be, quickens. She shakes her head, sending her black hair tumbling about her shoulders, looks at a scrap of starred sky between two apartment buildings and notices deep within herself a slight dizziness. The other side of the boulevard draws her. She crosses calmly, stops an instant in the middle of the roadway, detects no movement, continues walking. After crossing, she decides to go on as far as the first street to the left. In spurts, she starts to run very fast, taking pleasure in seeing her breasts bounce, in feeling the muscles of her thighs tighten in turn. She is going to round the corner. A glance. In the distance, the noise of a motorized cycle. Here it comes now. She draws back, presses herself against the glass of a bakery, pointlessly holds her breath, *for the fun of it,* and waits. The cycle passes like a whirlwind, the man has seen nothing. This episode has suddenly increased her pleasure. The experiment is taking on its meaning, the *gain* is certain.

Once again, the corner of the street, which this time she follows around. She is happy to be disporting herself in this way, accessible but secret, without visible defense but not wishing for any inopportune meeting. She is taking the city's measure, and her body is the standard of a new system of feeling unknown to others.

On the left, a street comes up. She takes it. A little further, on the other side, a night watchman is checking the door of a Radio-Electrical Supplies store. He has his back to her. She is not worried because she will have passed level with him when he continues his rounds, in the other direction. She takes a chance and walks with short steps, without trying to hide. It is getting less dark and the dawn mists will not be long coming. The air is getting more chilly too. She must do something. She stops in front of a half-open door, gives it a push, sees that it leads to a courtyard, enters. Four trees in the yard. The low branches of one of them makes it possible to climb up; she does so. The bark scrapes the skin of her stomach, of her thighs. Nine feet up, she is watching the first-floor windows. Several are open, few of them show bedrooms. A disappointment. She can make out only one sleeper when she had hoped to see a crowd of them—or better still some insomniac a prey to his condition. Footsteps on the gravel of the courtyard. A man, head bent, is making for Staircase B, to the right of the tree where she is ensconced. He will not see her either. The situation is gaining still more intensity. She is happy, even happier, and feels her body blossoming.

Daylight is coming, it is time to go home. She jumps from the tree, runs as far as the street, rushes blithely into it without the slightest precaution, and comes face to face with a passerby. The man, about thirty, stands open-mouthed, his limbs slack. She looks at him, bursts out laughing, and goes on running in the direction of the road to the left which will bring her back opposite the apartment block where she lives. And so she *has been seen* after all. By chance, without trying to *show herself*.

She must go quickly now. The effort makes her tipsy. The man still has not moved, she discovers, turning around. He is watching that silhouette flying by him, *breathtakingly*. Perhaps he understands, too, the importance of this moment. Will the *operation* have produced two initiates? She asks herself the question as, breathless, she goes in through the doorway. She hopes so.

The staircase. Quick, the four flights. The half-open door through which she passes, closing it, against which she leans her back for a moment. Her breathing, calming down, becomes regular again and leaves a taste of sugar in her mouth. Her mucous membranes are burning. She stretches out on the cool sheet, too cool now, for morning has come, runs her hand over her brow, her cheeks, her neck, her breasts, her stomach, her sex, her thighs, all in one movement. She gives a long sigh, then falls asleep, at the same time excited and serene.

ALAIN JOUBERT

Wrecker of the Senses

The room is an oval one. The ends farthest from one another, thirty-nine feet apart; maximum width, twenty-five feet. The height is only just over seven feet. The floor, walls, and ceiling are entirely covered with aluminum (great sheets of metal riveted edge to edge). All the objects assembled in the room— three small low tables, about fifteen chairs, two semicircular benches—also. The only light comes from three oriental spot- lights set in the ceiling; forming a triangle. A frolic of frost. The light from the cold scraping the bone of reservations. Thirty- three persons are present in this supreme space. Sixteen white men, dressed the same in steel-blue suits; sixteen white women, each wearing a mesh garment ending at mid-thigh; one black man, naked to the waist, in spangled tights—as serious and tense as a dancer in a big spectacular shortly before the finale. He is the one who holds the threads of possible relationships between the thirty-two others, he alone knows what *must* happen, the crystal of desire, the treflé cross of the passions that vibrate beneath the skin. As though emanating from the metal walls, the stream from a spring—moving against the current— imperceptibly fills the air in suspense, where the bodies move about. Little groups of four or five have formed and are speaking in hushed tones, while the black man moves rapidly between them, on the tips of his bare toes, weaving an invisible net by the mere play of his perpetually evanescent gestures. A counter-fugue.

*

A little later, the black man picks up a little casket of varnished wood that stood out clearly on an aluminum table. At once all conversation ends. Spontaneously, as if secretly no one's attention has been on anything else, all eyes converge on the black man's hand which, meanwhile, is taking out of the casket only a pack of cards. Lips burn with silence. In response to a nod, the sixteen men and sixteen women present themselves, in turn, before the black man who makes each of them take a card, any card. This apparently meaningless ceremonial goes on for a moment, interminable in the minds of those who are submitting to it. Thirty-one times a white hand, with trembling fingers, will pick out from the rest a card that attracts it, the thirty-second having no other choice but to leave the black hand, which holds all power, as bare as thunder. The gibbet of waiting. A horde of fears breaking like waves, to the blood's rhythm. Gleaming indistinctly, the infinite number of eyes wound themselves on the metal's reflection. There is already no more time to regret *intoxication*.

*

Now the black man is asking a question. Will the one, man or woman, who holds the 7 of hearts kindly step forward? The sentence. A woman steps slowly out of the group, a torrefied smile on her porcelain lips. Two-thirds of the way down the room, on the axis of the oval, she comes to a halt. The black man trains one of the spotlights right on her eyes, then puts out the other two. He circles the woman several times. He takes up position behind her. He orders her to take off her mesh garment. He watches the coat of mail, unhooked along the left side, slip like a fish down over the woman's hips. He remains for a long time motionless, silent, observing a drop of sweat that runs from the hollow of the back toward the chasm of the buttocks. He gives another order: the woman is to turn around. He can now see her whole body on display: insolent breasts and pimento sex, stomach on the alert and extortionate thighs. Of her face he sees only the eyes, making holes in horsehair, as a piolet does in ice. Apostle. Confines. Kilogram. Success. Expedient, Deviation. Fascine. Navajo. Sodium. Springboard. Proximity. High relief.

*

From the casket of varnished wood the black man now takes two little bottles of ink—red and blue—a set of needles of various lengths, a little cotton, a stylet. He asks each person to reveal to him the wildest erotic desire he has ever imagined without being able to fulfill. He waits. A moment goes by, a cathode of promises. The current is established. A man comes forward and confides in a low voice what his senses crave. The black man takes a needle, uncorks the bottle of red ink, dips the needle and tattoos, below the woman's left breast, what deep down inside the one who has just spoken wished most of all. The woman scarcely quivers under the slight prick of the needle, but closes her eyes and clenches her fists. Several hours will be needed for the slow procession of bodies to distill, without holding back, the unctuous alcohol of unreason. Several hours during which the skin of the nude woman will be covered with signs—red and blue—charged with extreme excitemen and indescribable fear, pain, and joy. Several hours during which the needles will rapidly slip beneath the nude woman's skin their indelible ink, forming the chain of secret passions, tapping desire, ennobling the body with their points of steel. Several hours during which the nude woman will remain standing, legs apart—to permit access to the darkest parts of herself—without a cry, without impatience, with all the explosive serenity of someone who accepts others' desire as a priceless gift.

*

The ceremony is over. Only the face and the upper part of the neck have been spared. The body seems completely sheathed in a veil of lacework, giving its nakedness a yet keener edge. The black man helps the woman on with her coat of mail, then kisses her lips. Her clothing adjusted, she heads for the metal door that dominates the room and goes out, held in the beam of glances. She knows herself to be, for always, the repository of the mystery of man and woman, the habitation of their real strength, the *cathedral of flesh* where they will want to commune with their thoughts. *She exists.* There is nothing more to be said.

ALAIN JOUBERT

The Moisture of the Beaches Blunted by the Baba

. . . in a few days' time, she will receive a large envelope already waiting for her at her hotel desk. She will find in it the draft program for the July 10 soirée, an invitation, a car park ticket, and a letter of advice to candidates, in which she will read among other things: "If your name is announced at the close of the ceremony, concentrate at once upon trying to throw off as quickly as you can the lethargic ecstasy into which this news will have thrown you. Then gather all your strength to reach the rostrum, forcing your way through the crowd of people who will have decided at least thirty seconds earlier—and whatever their sex—to become your lovers." The tone of this advice is intended to reduce nervousness in candidates condemned to take part in a ceremony during which the women who triumph are often their closest rivals. But this warning does not hold much meaning for her: she has no taste for competition. Of the chosen she may be the one who gains most, she will certainly be, of the losers, the most active. The serenity of puddles. Methodically stepped across. She contemplates her own destiny as if someone else were involved. With interest, but without passion. With, also, inattentive amusement. First, she will go into the bathroom of the suite reserved for her. Bathing is part of the rite. She will add salts, oils, and bubbles. After a lengthy stay in the soapy water, she will use a white unctuous, light cream, the purpose of which is to restore the smoothness and the softness of the skin by use of the properties of the avocado. Very easy to spread on, this cream is not greasy. The odor, not a disagreeable one, is rather reminiscent of that given off by a shandygaff. She will notice, however, that the bottle, striped lime green and white, with a pretty gilt stopper, would be improved if it had little notches in it or a partially non-skid finish. In bathrooms, in fact, hands always wet become clumsy upon contact with a runny cream. Precisely these hands that will play such an important role as the ceremony proceeds. Wrist, palm, thumb, index, middle finger, little finger, ring finger. Warm hand. Hold out a hand. Raise a hand. Force someone's hand. Have a LUCKY touch.[6] Have one's hands tied. Be in good hands. Pass from HAND TO HAND. Cash book. Manumission, MORTMAIN. Later, she will wander about the apartment. Luxurious. Lots of marble, mahogany, ashlar, and used right. A transistor radio for a moment, as one lights a cigarette. ". . . After tilling the soil for man, for two thousand years, is the plow going to end up as a museum piece? The promising results obtained with a herbicide, Gramoxan or Paraquat, leads us to think so: it plays the same role and, sometimes, replaces the plow to advantage. Discovered in Great Britain . . . bilingual nursery schools have meaning only . . . men are now at the stage where the administration has not been afraid, a few months before the elections . . ." Parenthetical music. Serious reflections on her own conduct. He had taken liberties, a lot of liberties, and she had had to put him in his place. She was afraid he would not keep his promise. Preoccupied, she had gone to bed. She had taken the dagger in her sleep and left her compact in its place. The next day, she had found the dagger in the bottom of her suitcase and discovered she no longer had a compact. He was the only person who could save her, she thought. The whole story. He had laughed at her. He was going to telephone to put everything right. On one condition. She will give in, since it was the only thing to do. The dozen red roses will conceal the sidewalk opposite when she wants to check if

---

6. In translation, it is impossible to sustain this sequence of words and phrases centered on the word *main*, "hand."

the car is still there. Municipal butcher. Tomahawk toast. Arctic. Sand moleskin. Waiting. There will be a knock at the door. She will say come in, slipping her clenched fists into the pockets of her dressing-gown. A man will arrive, carrying a tray. He will have a white twill jacket a little too big for him (on the tray, a cold meal). She will think she recognizes in him a swarthy little man, dejected, with sad moist eyes, whom she had seen repainting a boat, when crossing the docks. She will be mistaken, of course. The ceremony. Standing in front of the flames, without really seeing them, she will wonder why the blonde had given her money, the brunette dug her nails into her shoulders, the redhead kissed her. But what is that? A woman is waking up and a long sentence is becoming alert in her, at the same time as she, and will be with her throughout the day, and will not stop growing, swelling, as the cell germines[7] until the conclusion. The avowed aim is emotion, feelings, prominent people. That they become fixed, immortal. Deep down, one wish: "Try at least to remember not why things happened that way, but how . . ." She will return after a long vacation spent noting a reply, knowing fear. "Yes, that's how it is, that's exactly how it is," she will catch herself saying when she comes out of THE BABA, brandishing her number seven like Flash Gordon his disintegrator gun. An uncomfortable homily, if ever there was one. To prove it, this Parisian woman, tanned by the Gstaad sun, who regularly confides in her masseur the disgust she feels for game. She will remain riveted to the spot, dazed, waiting for Number 7 to be called. The pool will send back her reflection. Even as far as her lips: prestige. When she arrives, in a few days' time, she will receive a large envelope that is already waiting for her at her hotel desk . . .

---

7. The author introduces a neologism, the verb *germiner*.

ALAIN JOUFFROY

1928—

1949   "As a desire for suicide, my poetry is the sublimation of a crime rendered (by my unused aggressive exigencies) infinitely renewable and perfectible. The suicide, a repressed criminal, makes of his own obsession an instrument for extrapolative exploration and, like the poet, the dawn of his antipode; tracks down the unthinkable, a marvel null and void to comprehension and limitlessly extensible."[1]

1959   "What, essentially, does this [surrealist] revolution consist in? What distinguishes it from so many forms of revolt, and from all the whims of sensibility, suddenly raised to the status of dogmas, is its *Copernican* character. . . . It is no longer human reason that is considered the spiritual centre of the universe, it is no longer human consciousness about which the world is organized into a measurable kingdom, it is the *unknown*. . . .

"Thus the artist, formerly a demiurge, has become an instrument. . . . he sees himself condemned to registering as faithfully as possible, like a seismograph or a tape-recorder, the tremors and sounds whose vibrations reach him *in this hole*. The

---

1. "Clé de contact," prefatory statement, dated 1949, in Alain Jouffroy, *Aube à l'antipode* (1966), p. 15.

unconscious, which has been reduced to slavery by man, has become his master, his black sun, his greatest source of renewal. The Copernican revolution, on the spiritual plane, is total."[2]
1963   "More than a school or a sect for initiates, surrealism was for me the fundamental structure of all that I undertook or wanted to undertake. But, within this structure, all the contradictions of my thought never ceased to take effect and manifest themselves."[3]
1966   "The rationalists and their criticism always presuppose the precedence of 'thought' over 'writing'; the one heading toward the other like a shipwrecked man toward the shore, to join the world of men once again, *to save himself.* But how could the poet not see that thought is contemporaneous with the act of writing, that it arises from the direction and trajectory of words, that it is the dictation of words in action?"[4]
1966   "Surrealism presents itself as a preface to future thought, as the threshold starting from which man is going to cease to be sequestered in defunct categories, in that iron-collar of culture that asphyxiates his mental life, his love life, his life on the practical plane, his political life."[5]
1967   "Since surrealism opened up before me like the widest objective road to liberation, I mean since my adolescence, the aim I have set myself has never ceased to be exploding the individuality itself, opening up to every chance, *taking a leap.*"[6]

*

All these statements were made by a man born in Paris, who, joining surrealism in 1946, was excluded from the Paris group just two years later, when he was still only twenty. While finding group activity irksome and unorthodoxy better suited to

2. "Le Rayon invisible du surréalisme," in Alain Jouffroy, *Une Révolution du regard* (1963), pp. 29-30.

3. Statement supplied by Alain Jouffroy on May 24, 1963 for J. H. Matthews, ed., *An Anthology of French Surrealist Poetry*.

4. "Saint-Pol-Roux, premier poète baroque," preface to Alain Jouffroy, ed., *Saint-Pol-Roux: les plus belles pages* (1966), p. xiv.

5. Alain Jouffroy, "Introduction au génie d'André Breton," in André Breton, *Clair de terre* (1966), p. 14.

6. Alain Jouffroy, "La Fin des alternances," *La Nouvelle Revue Française* (April 1, 1967), p. 637.

his temperament, Jouffroy has never betrayed the spirit of surrealism, either in his poems, in his art criticism, or in his novels.

Alain Jouffroy's brief narrative *Double Envol* was published
in *Le Surréalisme, même*'s fifth number, in the spring of 1959,
illustrated by his wife, Manina, who had had an experience upon

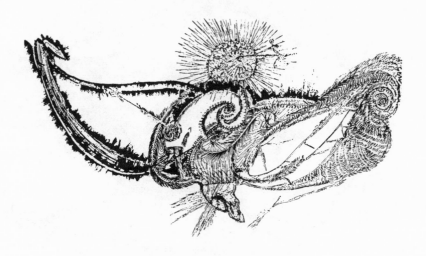

which the text is based. In a "Letter to Manina," prefacing *Les
Quatre Saisons d'une âme* (*The Four Seasons of a Soul*), a volume of
his poems that reproduces Manina drawings by which they
were inspired, Jouffroy wrote in 1955, "In your eyes as in mine,
the destiny of every man remains in the darkness of what is not
said," adding, "Your drawings, which reveal the successive
states of mind through which you pass in your life, are veritable
interior mirrors, where each of us can interrogate the symbolic
images of his own destiny."

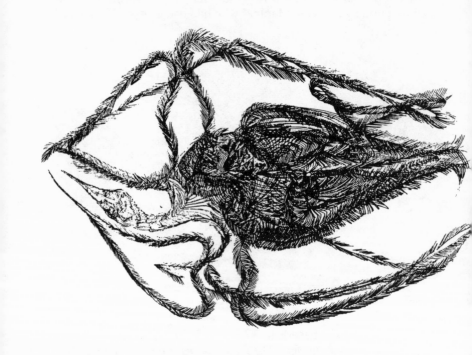

ALAIN JOUFFROY

Double Flight

And first I was crowned. The beds were unmade. All the windows, above the black trees, were swinging in the wind.

They dressed me in a long tunic of blood. I pronounced—very low—the words dictated by the Moment. And with my knee on the cushion of gold, I thought about the hand that had first slid under my dress.

And then—that Man's glance was my only weapon for the battle—I was ordained. Smiles came few and far between. My fingers were kissed. My eyelashes trembled.

There were suddenly several boats on the shore. Cries. I was pushed into a car and the chauffeur didn't turn around to me a single time. The road followed the lake in frightening hairpin bends.

I was free. I was a woman. I was thrown into a crater from which I shall never get out. I was thrashed, adored, insulted.

I was alive.

But the doors of the house in the city were quickly bolted. The servants surrounded me at the head of my bed as soon as the first light of day came.

A watch was kept on my hands. My feet were bathed in rose water. I was forcibly fed almond paste.

I thought things over. That went on for long months,

perhaps for several years. Regularly, every five or six weeks, a feast was held in my honor. The most surprising flowers abounded in my room. The Man with eyes of steel whispered, "You are our prisoner, don't forget. But do what you wish. Our love is merciless and unconditional." He'd come to see me, sometimes, at night, and I'd draw him into my dreams.

One day I discovered a door. It had been kept hidden from me. I'd been told, "It's nothing. It's a closet for the cook's linen." I looked feverishly for the key. And I opened the door. What I saw (this is the first time I "can" say it): the Man standing, a red-headed woman kneeling in front of him, giving him pleasure.

From that moment a sharp cold spread through the house. The garden made me shiver. Flowers of hoarfrost, cubes of ice—everywhere—and a white bitch, silent as the North Pole, took up a position by my side. I held it close, petrified.

This was a period of silence during which I drifted in slow motion along an endless iceberg.

I kept silent as long as I could. I'd go every afternoon into a waiting room in the annex, my hands crossed on my knees, waiting, waiting. I'd receive letters from distant friends; I found it hard to understand their tenderness, their allusions, their playfulness. Every day, the stairs to my room were becoming a little longer. I'd go up and down ceaselessly.

I'd forget the time. I'd forget my book (*Le Livre des Quatre Cercles*), I'd forget my gloves (even if I wasn't "going out," I often wore them, fearing the touch of a sticky object). I'd forget too my little silver toothbrush.

And, suddenly, the voices, in the next room, increased in volume. The Man slammed the door and I heard him weeping in the room upstairs, where he worked.

This weeping was recorded.

Something snapped inside me. I went out naked on the terrace, under the leaden sky, like a stone exposed to thunder on an evening road in Brittany. I looked at my mouth—and I thought of my closed "mystery."

In the distance, the dogs were mounting she-wolves. War was thundering near the port. Police roadblocks had been set up.

That was when I reached my decision. I went out and

walked by the long funeral line. The men watched me from behind the glass of their big black limousines. It was raining a little. I walked a long time, without becoming disturbed.

When I'd forgotten my name, my house, my birth, my childhood, my daily cares; when I'd forgotten the forbidden door, and the white bitch, I got at random into the first car stopped by the side of the road and embraced its driver violently. He looked at me as though he'd been waiting for me. He said, "It will rain comets tonight. Come watch with me."

He wasn't surprised at my being naked under my summer coat. He wasn't surprised at my submissiveness. When he at last reached the square, he asked me, "Right or left?" and calmly, without hesitation, I turned my head to the right, toward the sea, where the high tide had been calling us for such a long time.

I belonged to him. He looked at my hands and said, "Your eyes are mad. Your lips, your fingers too are mad. I love everything that is mad in you."

I felt myself "respected."

Raped, but giving my consent, and respected even in the moment of rape, I gave and surrendered myself to him without remorse, beneath the rain of comets. I worshipped him.

JACQUES LACOMBLEZ

1934—

Born in Ixelles, Belgium, Jacques Lacomblez first exhibited his painting in 1952 and brought out his first volume of poems, *L'Aquamanile du vent* (*The Ewer of the Wind*), at the end of 1961. Between 1956 and 1966 he participated in Movement Phases.[1] His magazine *EDDA* was the Belgian counterpart of Edouard Jaguer's Parisian magazine *Phases*, bearing the same subtitle: "Cahiers internationaux de documentation sur la poésie et l'art d'avant-garde." Beginning in 1959, a temporary alignment of the surrealist and Phases movements led, in Lacomblez's case, to a meeting with André Breton and participation in the 1960-61 International Surrealist Exhibition at the D'Arcy Galleries in New York City.

In 1963 disagreement over Pop Art resulted in the dissolution of the alliance between Phases and surrealism. Lacomblez's contribution to the quarrel took the form, notably, of an essay in the tenth number of *Phases*, worth mentioning because it makes clear an attitude toward external reality that helps situate the two texts by which its author is represented here.

---

1. The most complete information on Phases generally available is to be found in the catalog *Rétroviseur Phases*, relating to an exhibition that ran between September 8 and November 11, 1972. It covers catalogs, magazines, books, posters, and documents extending over the period from 1951.

Lacomblez, whose painting Robert Benayoun has described aptly as leading to "a sort of speleology of thought,"[2] violently attacked those who "consecrate a sordid *return to the object* and, with this, a particularly feeble submission by man to the very indications of his alienation."[3] Condemning in those artists a "frightful acceptance of the world as it is, of society as it is imposed upon us," he evidently interpreted their conduct as expressive of a "will to maintain established order" (p. 74). "In a world reduced more and more to nothing but definitions, to nothing but the discoveries made by mandarins in white coats, the poet's gesture (the hand holding a pen, the hand holding a brush, it matters little . . .) can no longer confine itself to exploration, but must culminate in the *invention* of a universe where the man of science can never find his five-legged calf or his giant frog again" (p. 77).

L'Orfèvre puni, dating from March 1967, has not been published before. As for the other text offered here, this appeared in the fifth number of *La Brèche: àction surréaliste* (October 1963) as "Un Cahier d'Eugénie." Revisions reported to the editor, André Breton, were not incorporated into that version. The definitive text was printed subsequently as *Fragments pour une vie d'Eugénie,* in the undated fourth issue of *EDDA.* In both versions the dedication is to Breton.

Comparison of the two printings brings to light a noteworthy fact. Apart from textual changes, the revised version departs from the first in being preceded by a quotation extracted from Breton's *Nadja,* referring to *Les Champs Magnétiques.* The latter, written in collaboration by Breton and Philippe Soupault as early as 1919, is regarded in surrealist circles as the first authentic surrealist text, and is the first extended piece of writing to result from the deliberate practice of verbal automatism. In part, then, Lacomblez surely wishes to draw attention to the special virtue of words, as he reminds us how one Sunday, as reported in *Nadja,* Breton found that shop signs, indicating where coal and wood might be purchased, gave him

---

2. Robert Benayoun, "Images pour le voyageur égaré" ("Pictures for the traveler who has lost his way"), preface to the catalog of an exhibition of paintings by Jacques Lacomblez at the Galerie Saint Laurent, 1962.

3. Jacques Lacomblez, "Le Donjon et la basse-fosse" ("The Castle Keep and the Dungeon"), *Phases,* no. 10 (September 1965), p. 73.

an opportunity to exercise "a bizarre talent for prospecting," thanks to which he discovered in himself the gift for predicting in which Paris streets, and where on those streets, coal merchants had their place of business. Moreover, as an indication of a rationally incomprehensible necessity making itself felt in human affairs, in *Eugénie* the word "coal," borrowed from Breton and Soupault, stands as an invitation to us to advance beyond "the first custom-house of our desire," after we have left the sinking ship of familiar reality.

JACQUES LACOMBLEZ

Fragments for a Life of Eugenia

> The words COAL & WOOD that
> are displayed on the last
> page of *The Magnetic Fields* . . .
>
> —André Breton, *Nadja*

Daughter of a methodical volcano, she recognized herself in that glass of water placed before her like a cry. Her wings spread there with secret precautions. Taking care of bubbles . . .

A certain snow began to spring from below.

Eugenia's footstep is still a little space.

*

The bottom of the sea has been cleared of birds, Eugenia goes walking in the mirror. She sees herself in it very far away, baring her breasts as the soldiers pass by. The city is burning and drying her mouth.

Tomorrow people will cut off her hair, her head under severed arms.

*

When Eugenia is asleep, her legs lay siege to a doorway of feathers. Bristling with very edible forests, a tractor often comes to fold the sheets with scrupulous precision.

Eugenia's friends think her a dreamer.

*

The woman, so beautiful in proportion to being unexpected, who, her eyes rubbed with young dawn, gets out of a
berlin strayed onto a race track, is she not the image of Eugenia
multiplied for her alone by the power to be of little account in
this century and the fringe also of that fog of whirling immobility one scarcely dares name love, for the somnolence of very
erectile volcanic ash? Living in this fog guarantees us such
complicity with Dreaming that indifference comes over us from
judging if the tiny bursts of pollen suspended in its peacock tail
are the verge of a woman offering herself or the first custom-
house of our desire. For it is a matter of *living in* that place,
intangible here, without resistance to astonishingly virginal
instigations, like the poet who had set up house on the casks of
the warehouse for Indigenous Sugar in the big city's foam and
who, taken off guard by one of Eugenia's strolls, was concealing
under his fresh-butter gloves the postcards from foreign parts,
like that adolescent too, night companion of women who died in
childhood, who used to live in fresh graves so as to offer some
warmth to their young cadavers and whom the family bedroom
could no longer contain in the embrace of the drapes.

Dwelling-places without walls above the breath of the sea,
dwelling-places vitrified by the willful damage of reason on the
slope of a head of hair or other broceliandes, desolate dwelling-
places where absence fastens its rapid icebergs as during those
imperious itineraries of atlases in which on colorless days
Eugenia would give herself fertile devastations, we recognize in
you the eternity of man.

When Eugenia was dismissed from her "position"—the
infinite tenderness she showed useless machines was to lead
her to that exclusion—she could not be satisfied with looking
again for work (it really was a question of *looking* where the veil
cannot part or half-open even around the curve of a street
through the sudden wedding of a frightened night peacock with
the eyes of a woman only too foreshadowed). Working, invoked
by some people for the renewal of life that plunges its barometer
deep into the stomach, appeared to her, now that she was
leaving behind the factory railing and a moment in her existence, as one of the most ominously justified of human
misapprehensions.

From clandestine visits to public gardens, those expedients

which alone until that day used to mime a life crossed out by the daily pruritus of social function, she no longer knew how to extract that crazy gem in which without the least curve of vacillation availability shines at every meeting. From that moment, the resolve easily was born in her to "leave the ship" in a wreck during which it was the rats, this time, that stayed on board.

And when she caught sight again of the Coal Shed, barded with shivering sheet metal, a long flow of alluvia took place within her; down to the deepest interstices of her body, she felt calm ocean flowers opening like hands. The word COAL, long drawn out, black and green, on the newly lime-washed wall caressed her eyelids with the plectrum of its rhythm. Eugenia described it as a fugue with a certainty that only her practice of not reading it any more could make possible. Each evening of her former status, she had stopped in front of this inscription, at that time abandoned and destined for obliteration, with the wish, that she knew to be absurd and puerile, for a dazzling reappearance of the indistinct word, a perspective all the more useless because the ramshackle shed was no doubt about to be put to another use.

And so on that day of opening up to the world, the term born of the most heartbreaking banality and renewed with no other motive, it seemed, than a precious negation of all necessity, imposed itself upon Eugenia like the sign of a mysterious intervention, resting, under the authority of confusion, upon the familiar countryside, with the luminous arrogance of liberty.

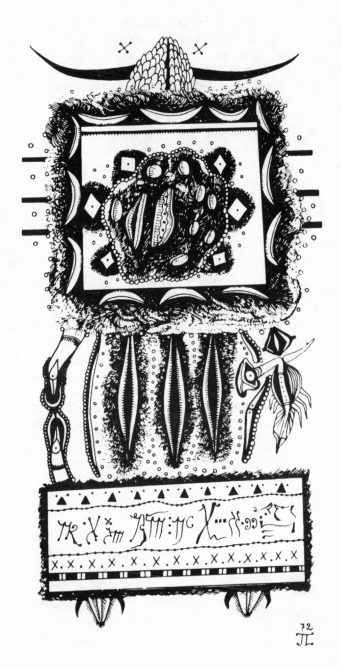

JACQUES LACOMBLEZ

The Punished Goldsmith

A window banged ceaselessly a few inches from my closed eyes. Now, the house was made of glass, the windows were ridiculous. It was precisely this dwelling's state of absolute transparency that obliged me to keep my eyes closed all day and in the least glimmer of nocturnal light, so that the predatory outside should not catch sight of me.

An odious transparency. That is true in both ways . . .

*

Reduced by prudence to blindness, I found it impossible to know if the banging of the window was indeed the procession of burned trees announced as early as dawn by the barely clothed rain. I placed a lot of hope in the great combustion that, the day before, had decimated all the forests with the precise savagery of a hummingbird. Disguised as a young female lace-maker, it had at first uncovered its breasts before the passing regal fern, then tearing up its skirts to screen several fox holes, it imitated the crackling of sulphur with the skill for which it is known.

Converted by the fatality of the conflagration, the forests took fire with one razor stroke.

*

According to my desire, the smoke held for an instant beneath the wings of partridges sitting on eggs was to trace, between earth and sky, new routes that would be useful to me for debauching stars of medium magnitude.

Fire, like despair, always retains an irretrievable flame for the unforeseen cloud. The latter, arriving early in the morning above the main entrance to the town, brought its threats into play, a vast range of violently colored muscles that covered its torso. A flame with the pallor of a dried-up river adopted the absentminded manner of a rope ladder and rose up to the cloud. A few moments later, there was nothing in the sky any more but an octopus of dead branches.

The forecast, at least, had remained favorable.

*

But now the sudden change of fortune and expectations seemed to me so distant—and memory itself so buried in ashes—that all that still matters to me is this window thumping like a useless heart. Calcinated forests never come up to the hope born in the black instant of the first flame. Indeed, they say in the valley that I practice the evil art of purposeless hopes, I shall never open my eyes from now on, even if it is naked night: I know the sun is an old jewel caught in ice.

ROBERT LEBEL

1904—

In 1953 Parisian-born Robert Lebel edited a volume of essays on contemporary art, a *Premier Bilan de l'art actuel*, introduced by a brief preface in which he wrote, "Is it not ludicrous to claim to have surveyed the real when ceaselessly perfected means of investigation reveal it to be, on the contrary, inexhaustible? Antinaturalism, if it comes from disgust for a 'déjà vu' identified with the sordid in daily life, only anticipates the eye's future conquests. It aspires only to be the realism of tomorrow" (p. 15). André Breton might well have been offering a summary of this statement, in surrealist perspective, when he spoke of surrealism as "what *will be.*" As for Lebel, discussing surrealism on the same occasion, he did not neglect to place emphasis upon its "disturbing role" (p. 95).

Lebel's story *L'Inventeur du temps gratuit* shows how closely he resembles in outlook the surrealist painter Toyen, as he describes her in *Premier Bilan*, "fascinated by a world where identity cards do not circulate" (p. 96). The meaning of his tale runs deeper than appears to those attentive above all to its veneer of geographical exoticism. It would seem that, when the story was originally published in the second number of *Le Surréalisme, même* (Spring 1957), ironic exploitation of its elementary appeal led to the choice of photographs of New York's Elevated as illustrative material. At all events, when reprinted, beside a longer text that lent its name to the volume *La Double Vue* (*Double Sight* [1964]), *L'Inventeur du temps gratuit* was illustrated, instead, by two photographs showing an object, "La Pendule de profil" ("The Clock in Profile"), designed for the occasion by Marcel Duchamp.

As a tribute to Duchamp, *L'Inventeur* had a special claim on space in a surrealist magazine. The character of its central figure owes a great deal to the example set by Marcel Duchamp, whose name, even before the appearance of the first surrealist manifesto, represented in Breton's view "a veritable oasis for those who are still *looking*."[1] In fact, those wishing to be fully responsive to the meaning attaching to the Inventor's conduct might well begin by examining Robert Lebel's book *Sur Marcel Duchamp* (*On Marcel Duchamp* [1959]), where we read, for instance, "Expurgated of all elements of exterior picturesqueness, his strangeness comes rather from his smiling but firm refusal to situate himself on the plane of immediate causality" (pp. 1-2).

Robert Lebel's purpose is not to provide a portrait from life but a transcription of aspects of Duchamp's work, and especially of his behavior, which made Duchamp an unfailing inspiration to surrealists.

The Inventor's readiness to use materials left in the warehouse he occupies by previous tenants presents an analogy with Duchamp's invention of the ready-made as a challenge to the idea of egocentric artistic creation.[2] Speaking of ready-mades in *Sur Marcel Duchamp*, Lebel remarks, "It is a matter of sacralization" (p. 35), and interprets Duchamp's motive as follows: "to depreciate the common and tacitly recognized notion of value, to glorify the strictly individual and *sovereign* choice that has to render an account to no one" (p. 36). Is it going too far to see in the Inventor's three clocks the equivalent, on the temporal plane, of the *Trois Stoppages-Étalon* (*Three Standard Stoppages* [1913-1914]) that correspond to the fundamental law of the "new physics," as conceived by Duchamp?—"a straight hori-

---

1. "Marcel Duchamp," in André Breton, *Les Pas perdus* (1924), p. 141.
2. The best introduction to the ready-made is the catalog of a Duchamp exhibition at the Galleria Schwarz, Milan: *Marcel Duchamp: Ready-Mades, etc.* (1913-1964), texts by Walter Hopps, Arturo Schwarz, and Ulf Linde.

zontal thread one meter in length falls from a height of one meter onto a horizontal plane, twisting *as it pleases,* and gives a new appearance to the unit of length."[3] Certainly, the parallel is very noticeable between the importance the Inventor attaches to his notion of gratuitous time and Lebel's interpretation of *Trois Stoppages-Étalon,* in *Sur Marcel Duchamp* (p. 29).

Robert Lebel's volume *La Double Vue* was awarded a book prize in France, the Prix du fantastique. It is not, though, as an expression of the escapist impulse through literature that his *L'Inventeur du temps gratuit* bears witness to the attraction of the fantastic. In order to measure its worth in the perspective of surrealism, we should be best advised to assess this story in the light of Breton's declaration, in a footnote to his *Manifeste du surréalisme,* "What is admirable in the fantastic is that there is no fantastic any more: there is only the real" (p. 28).

---

3. See Marcel Duchamp, *Boîte verte* (*Green Box*), published in 1934. *Sur Marcel Duchamp* reproduces *Trois Stoppages-Étalon* (plates 67 and 67a). In William S. Rubin's *Dada and Surrealist Art (n.d.), Trois Stoppages-Étalon* is reproduced on page 28. For a full description, illustrated, see Arturo Schwarz, *The Complete Works of Marcel Duchamp* (1969), pp. 443-444. Schwarz describes "La Pendule de profil" and reproduces a photograph of it (p. 545). A more interesting photograph appears in the 1973 New York Museum of Modern Art catalog *Marcel Duchamp* (p. 314).

ROBERT LEBEL

The Inventor
of Gratuitous Time

As soon as it left behind, in the direction of the tip of the island, the already mutilated silhouette of the terminal, the Elevated penetrated narrow streets, brushing against their iron-stepped façades. Front Street, Pearl Street, which it covered and shut in like tunnels, led beneath, in the pauses between its rattling, only the illusory and silent existence of an old stage set. Impregnably sealed with shutters or blinded by grime, one after the other windows had stopped opening. There, between the East River docks and the skyscrapers of Wall Street, was the strange dead town where all that was menacing in New York City went to ground and lay in wait.

That section attracted me and I wanted to live there, but its houses were so uninhabited that a possible tenant at once looked suspicious. Nobody was willing to believe one was seriously considering taking up residence in those tumbledown ramshackle houses, set apart from everything that city-planning zeal proposed by way of dignity and comfort. I offered in vain the excuse I am apt to give, that of being an artist. This argument, which is often greeted with indulgence, provoked here only more mistrust and hostility.

All the same, I went on making inquiries from door to door. The disappointment I felt at inevitably meeting failure, time and again, was amply compensated by the discoveries I made inside houses that I inspected from top to bottom. I sometimes wandered about for two or three hours without meeting a living soul. It was while exploring an apartment house that seemed to me completely empty that I read on a door the following inscription in French: *A. Loride, Inventor of Gratuitous Time.*— This was written in ink on a sheet of paper affixed with two nails.

I had already been able, on the other floors, to go through the offices of a steamship company, a printer's shop, and public baths, all equally deserted. And so I entered without hesitation. It was three in the afternoon on a working day.

In the center of a vast extraordinarily cluttered warehouse, a completely nude man was going through physical fitness exercises. He turned around and I noted that he must be over fifty, although his body was still fairly trim. He was hairless and his appearance of meticulous cleanliness was surprising in such a setting. However, I was struck above all by his lack of embarrassment. Without thinking to cover himself, show his astonishment, or justify his nakedness, he was looking at me calmly and waiting for an explanation from me.

At first I could find only this rather foolish thing to say: "Are you French?" adding after a silence, "I've come about your invention."

With a gesture, he permitted me to sit down but, except for a bed on which a very young woman was lying, no seat could be seen and I leaned against a packing case, politely. "Go ahead," he said. At that moment, the Elevated came into view level with the window and everything began to shake around us.

"Sir," I responded at last, as soon as we could hear one another, "I'll not conceal from you that I am enormously interested in your discoveries and it's because I am anxious to discuss them with you that I neglected to take the customary precautions before coming in here."

"I see people by appointment only," he replied abruptly. "Leave your name and address (he pointed to a wall covered with notes and numbers), "I will call you in," and, turning his back on me, he returned to his gymnastics.

His letter did not reach me until three weeks later. It came on *A. Loride & Co.* letterhead. "I warn you," he wrote, "I am neither a fool nor a philosopher, nor a mystic, nor a poet. I am engaged in positive research and my activity corresponds to a large degree to the perhaps too affirmative title I have claimed for myself. Engaged in a real enterprise, I was obliged by practical necessity to give it social justification. Others, after all, call themselves oil kings or first class pharmacists. However that may be, our eventual relationship, allow me to stipulate, cannot be other than strictly commercial. I do not want new friends, my eccentricity is my own affair and it was not without precise intentions that I elected to withdraw to a place where only your curiosity and total lack of discretion could lead you to find me." And he set an appointment for a day or two later.

I made the trip by Elevated. Several times already, since our first interview, I had tried the experiment of passing his windows, hoping to catch him in some significant attitude, but, from the coach, if all it would have taken to rap on his window pane was to lean forward, nothing was distinguishable that gave a hint of his presence.

He received me with the impassiveness I had noticed before. He displayed neither reticence nor warmth. It was armed with a somewhat distant good grace that he came to this meeting, obviously neither expecting nor fearing anything. Dressed not without affectation, he guided me courteously through a remarkable disarray of machinery, workbenches, beams, clocks, and safes to the bed that was not occupied. "You have plenty of stock," I said to start the conversation rolling.

"Everything you see in this room, or better still this warehouse, was left here by previous tenants," he replied, "So you will not see much that belongs to me, but I prefer these instruments of chance origin. Their diverse nature prevents me from confining myself to a single mode of thought and, in this laboratory whose resources I am inventorying systematically and, of course, in reverse order, my imagination is in less danger of marking time."[4]

----

4. In his *The Savage Mind* Claude Lévi-Strauss defines a *bricoleur* as "one who works with 'whatever is at hand,' with a set of tools and materials which is always finite and is also heterogeneous because what it contains bears no relation to the current project but is the contingent result of all the occasions there have been to review or enrich the stock" ([Chicago: University of Chicago Press, 1966], p. 17). Clearly, Lebel's inventer is a gifted *bricoleur*, his activities by no means confined in significance to the interpretation surrealism gives to them.

"But what about time?" I asked.

"I was coming to that, since I perfected my theory thanks to the quite providential encounter before me of those three clocks, one of which keeps perfect time, another runs erratically, and the third not at all. Similarly, those scales have led me to revise my views on isotopes and I am indebted to that electric dryer for unexpected revelations on Pyrrhonic suspension," but, meeting my eyes, he added sharply, "Whatever you do, do not take me for some kind of thinker. My only ambition is to bring together scattered notions, I gather up the crumbs of great ideas. I hate abstractions. All these machines, in the main lacking some part or other, bring me back all the time to details, to fragmentary verification and tie me down to a fortunately incoherent form of mental puttering. These impose on my inquiry its concrete form, while their eminently nominal character keeps me from giving in, as physicians do, and as, unfortunately, so many alchemists have done, to deadly concern for results. Here I learn to turn everything uselessly to account. Thus for me the inevitable passing of the Elevated takes on a function as basic as the cycle of the tides. It indicates with just as much perfection that man is marking time; moreover it has the immense advantage of keeping the system in a state of latent exasperation. The ebb and flow of the tide never incites us to anything but resignation, while the Elevated directly impels us to revolt against what people insist upon presenting to us as our situation."

"But what about time?" I insisted.

"We have come to that. Each one of us aspires to the intensity of a dog's life, to those well-filled days that traditionally are a prelude to well-earned rest. It makes no difference that our period pairs liberty with leisure in a ridiculous cult. The most satisfied people are still the busiest, hence the ones most enslaved. Now, it is clear that no progress is within our reach if we do not first master the compulsion to useful activity. And yet it is this compulsion, and this alone, that continues to govern our concept of time. Look," he said, picking up a stick to point at the clocks, "each of these faces represents time in one of its three aspects. For almost all men, only one of them exists. So-called developed individuals have an inkling of two perhaps, but I am one of the rare people to define the third explicitly, so that I can, without too much imposture, presume myself to be its inventor. My purpose, at all events, is less to formulate it theoretically than to give it some consistency. My ambition is to make it a real product, a mere consumer commodity, on a par with those remedies the components of which only chemists know, but which are sold over counters everywhere. This is why I flatter myself I am a tradesman and not a philosopher."

He fell silent, went to stand in front of a machine placed close to the clocks and, with his foot, set a pedal in motion. Some slender wooden wands began to shoot out of an exhaust pipe. "Excuse me," he said, "I have a rush order to meet."

"Would those be your time tablets?" I cried, "I'd have imagined them in crystal form, looking like jujubes from the outside."

"The symbol matters little," he said, continuing to pedal. "It so happens that, without its having anything to do with me, I have at my disposal this machine that saws up dowels for which the hardware merchants in the neighborhood, my clients, have shown themselves greedy. A surrealist sculptor, so I am told, acquires them in large bundles.[5] The fact remains that this activity scarcely demands of me the amount of attention I am capable of devoting to earning my daily bread. I can devote myself to it without taking my eyes off that first clock and, just as easily as, from this same spot, I can see the Elevated come, pass, and disappear on that clock face, time without interruption, the time that has a market value. Those already rusty hands go round with a regularity that can only have something prodigious about it. It seems to be their destiny to go round, whatever happens. For them happiness lies in being neither fast nor slow, and above all not motionless. One can discern in their precise, resolute, self-assured movement the chauvinistic satisfaction resplendent on the face of the honest servant, the diligent housewife, the conscientious worker, the methodical official, the enterprising businessman, of all those people I see jostling one another in the mornings on the Elevated to get to their place of work, and who crowd in once again in the evening to go back home. Now, their time unfolds before me like a film. I

---

5. The allusion is to the Swiss surrealist Isabelle Waldberg, whose earliest sculptures were made of metal rods and doweling.

know, I feel I am a stranger to it. Literally I escape it, but could this be by virtue of my schedule that can be regarded as whimsical? I do not think so. Compare the faces I have described to you with those that replace them during the time so accurately called the slack hours, when the almost empty compartments have become more or less comfortable. The privileged ones who, for generally very doubtful reasons, have benefited from a release, far from showing themselves to be delighted, seem, on the contrary, for the most part anxious and tormented. They glance idly through their newspapers, they screw themselves up nervously in their seats, the slowness of the train aggravates them. In short, their symptoms are those of morbid rumination."

Suddenly breaking off, he kicked away the dowels that had accumulated in front of the exhaust and resumed work. "Do not worry," he continued, "my slack-hour travelers are by no means consumed by remorse. Besides, the reaction of the privileged before the others' enslavement tends to take the form of cynical contentment. No, the explanation lies elsewhere. If, like me, you were to spend several hours a day with your opera glasses trained on the Elevated, from up in this Anglican priest's pulpit (which makes it possible for me to see everything without any danger of being seen), you would be able to note that these travelers break down into two very distinct categories. It is a mere question of interpretation that I had to settle after the fashion of the ethnographer or the anthropologist by an exhaustive confrontation of individual characters. Certain travelers whom one catches smiling during slack hours, or even relaxing, are in reality members temporarily separated from the big ant heap. According to office language, they are out on business or, as the military puts it more loftily, on special assignment. Their serenity, their free-and-easy manner, which differentiates them at once from their closest neighbors have no other origin. For them this could not be a slack hour since society *which does not lose sight of them* hallows its intensity. Time where custom has minted its money remains the very link that binds them inseparably to their restlessness."

While he was once again releasing the products of his machine, I took the liberty of protesting, "And yet, so far as the other slack-hour travelers are concerned, those whom upon further examination you always categorize with the truly idle, how can you explain their melancholy if you reject the hypothesis that they have qualms of conscience? Could it be that we are to avail ourselves of banal exploitation of the distress by which our travelers are supposed to be gripped, at the prospect of being free to do what they like?"

"Not at all," he replied rather testily. "That would mean giving in to the most specious argument of all, the one generally used to justify social iniquities and prove the merits of servitude, by exaggerating at the same time the responsibilities of the lazy and the dangers a free man would run. If individuals who achieve relative independence are, as a matter of fact, the ones in most trouble and the quickest to take offense, this is because, physically emancipated, they remain mentally enslaved. They do not correct their conception of time, whereas the latter modifies its rhythm for them. From that moment a disequilibrium comes into their lives which the hands on that second clock mimic well enough. These hands are set in motion, now, only by an erratic, disordered movement, feverish, so to speak, interrupted by long moments of weighty immobility. All the time they are ahead or behind, but ahead of or behind what, one might ask, since, precisely, these hands are situated beyond the circuit of punctuality? What causes this inconsequentiality, if not the very keen awareness they still retain of social time? In short, their regret at being excluded from it counts more than their relief at being exempt from it. An out-of-order clock, hence a free one, never forgets the clock it used to be, one that kept time. The time it gives is never released absolutely from the other, of which the previous timbre obstinately goes on ringing out the memory."

Without leaving his machine, he began to laugh noiselessly. "Do you see," he went on, "I would never accept the title of thinker except preceded by the epithet *comic*, but in the painful sense of the term and as Stendhal considered becoming 'the comic bard.' In opposition to Molière and his wretched following of vaudevillists, I laugh less at man himself than at the abstractions with which he is imbued. The comedy of thought is much more irresistible than that of character. It is high time we finished with classical comedy and its arsenal of never-fading types, and substituted a comedy of cognition that would end in a fine massacre of ideas, instead of concluding systematically with the defeat of the 'funny man.' I can imagine with no trouble, for example, a comedy about the notion of time, that old coquette with sordid simpering ways, tirelessly counting her gold over and over, as it slips through her fingers. She would be the one that would be discomfited and beaten, while, as it should be, her ideographic configuration would be spared. I often like to believe that the surprising shapes modern art has produced lavishly have assumed bodily form and are preparing for the stage of the future, where they will receive a thrashing. These are the characters in our new comedy and their appearance, sometimes repulsive at first sight, only confirms their mythical significance and foretells the farcical sacrifice for which they are destined."

The piles of dowels had reached a considerable height and, no doubt judging the result of his effort sufficient, the man with whom I was speaking stopped pedaling, got up, pointed once again to the second clock and resumed, "This time that has ceased to be social and has not yet begun to be individual, this amorphous, colorless, insipid time constitutes an intolerable dead weight upon what people agree to call human evolution. Either the latter is only imaginary and, among the eternally primitive masses, we represent but a negligible foam of dissidence, or else, from the outset, this evolution has been heading for a dead end and it is running up against an obstacle that is putting it irrevocably in reverse. But people had better take care, the desire for liberty itself will not resist indefinitely the terrible contradiction that the facts inflict upon it. Between the words we pronounce and our well-known behavior the scandalous gap widens each day. All about us people's failure to do their duty is precipitated and the most rebellious often make one think of those emancipated women who secretly wish for a strong male. All they ever need is a cause to devote themselves to 'with all their soul.' Let us recognize that this social time knows how to maintain in those who, momentarily, have departed from it, a particularly sickening nostalgia. Some are at the mercy of the first ambiguity to present itself, others, proud of their steadfastness, with morose refinement draft the codes of their new constraints. Even those, so few in number, who thrive on being alone pay their tribute in the form of sighs. They become bored, despondent, and, even more ridiculous, they work. Each scrap of that time they are so painfully conscious of purloining from society takes on, in their eyes, exorbitant value. They set themselves up personally as time-lenders, and so as to place their sad savings to better advantage, they calculate, they invent, they build, they paint, they write with dreary passion. No doubt they engage in a sort of transfer: they convert their paper-time into gold-time, they consolidate it, and for this mental operation the language of finance is instinctively used. All we hear about is investment for retirement or, the supreme ambition of the philanthropic banker, a long-term investor, a means of self-perpetuation."

"You see," he remarked with a smile, "I in my turn allow myself to be carried away by satire. I stigmatize modern man, free man, the one who, like the duelist of old, considers himself fortunate indeed as soon as he is allowed to choose the weapons that will kill him. Watch his little game when he hesitates triumphantly between newspapers, professions, churches. Listen to him express himself at his own convenience in languages that confuse time with cadence, like the English *time* or the Italian *tempo*. Watch him go off confidently, convinced that he could, if it pleased him, never return again, whereas he carries within, more compelling than a love potion, the pledge of his submission. In the very forest where he sometimes ventures, fairies, witches, anonymous voices are so many metaphorical clocks, having the function of reminding him what time it is. Under his glance, every surface is a clock face to be read, every shadow a watch lying in ambush. The death agony of the minute bells in every echo and, even in the transport of his dizziness, the traveler listens to himself growing old, for it is *time* that his pulse beats, the inexorable orchestra leader within. To retrace his steps, to recover 'lost time,' what a temptation for anyone who, having thought he too has fled the old earth, takes up the disenchanted exclamation of a well-known author, 'It is nothing, I am nothing, I am always in it.' "

For the last few minutes, my eyes had been glued to the face of the third clock whose unchangeable aspect was beginning to fascinate me. "Do not let that inertia summon up in you facile images of the void or eternity," said my host in a sardonic tone. "Instead, imagine in this stopped clock a mechanism more sensitive than the others, too *perfect* to register the crude vibrations of social time. Somewhere else, in some carefully concealed part of its works, imperceptible oscillations would reveal the almost impalpable passage of gratuitous time. True, the frozen face of this clock, as though dead, is perfectly suited to alienating those who recoil naturally from a possible mutation. Everything shows that a crossing needs to be made, a break effected. Between this world and the other, there is no legendary transition, no discursive communication. We are not being offered the key to another nirvana, since it even seems that, where we are going, ecstasy has no more reason to exist. We link up with nothing and perhaps we will at last have broken with everything. No ceremonial, no incantation, no rites, but attainment of the state of lucidity in which the notion of time becomes a fruit one can peel," and he made nimble little movements with his fingers.

I was dying to ask a question but, forestalling me, he added, "Do I need to specify that, cutting ourselves off from useful time, we do not in the least intend to confine ourselves to the spectator's neutral quietude, to that skeptical or contemplative transcendence which I, for my part, find absolutely repugnant. The domain of gratuitous time is that of extreme risk; of the most sustained exaltation, for it is both the only one in which we knowingly lose time, and therefore our lives, and the only one in which any dramatic effect or any pomposity is inadmissible. Play itself is stripped of verbal compensations or those pertaining to the passions, bequeathed to it by social time, in which no act is justified unless it brings a dividend. Aristocrats in ancient times would take the precaution of calling their guests together before throwing their silverware into the water and in modern literature ritual murders often retain this vulgar style. To us, time-wasting is of necessity not open to all and we will try primarily to put people off the scent. We will be neither magi nor heroes, nor judges, nor prophets but we will apply ourselves to playing indifferent roles with a false air of seriousness that is capable of deceiving. It is within social time itself, and not at a distance from it, which would be edifying in itself, that we shall create, without necessarily allowing this to be known, zones of denial and levity."

At that moment a young woman entered. She was not the

one I had already seen. She merely nodded and went to sit down on the bed without saying a word. I was preparing to continue the discussion when I perceived that my interlocutor's thoughts had clearly taken another course.

"May I ask you never to come back?" he said to me after a few minutes' silence. "Spare me the disgrace of resuming these oral demonstrations which never reflect anything but our tergiversations. The sound of words that pretend to convince is all that social time, momentarily conjured up, needs to find its arrogance once again," and pushing me in a friendly way toward the door he concluded, "Gratuitousness is never without a certain disinclination to speak. No doubt I have said too much already."

MARCEL LECOMTE

1900—1966

One of the most persistent fallacies concerning surrealism is the belief that it cannot survive when and where one views the world squarely: that to be a surrealist, in other words, means forever resorting to some form of distortion, apparently always necessary to surrealists in their dealings with reality. The inference is that reality has no intrinsic interest for any surrealist. To say the least, such a misconception betrays insensitivity to the etymological force of the word "surrealism," borrowed by André Breton and Philippe Soupault from Guillaume Apollinaire, who had subtitled his play *Les Mamelles de Tirésias*— almost entirely written in 1903 and completed in 1916—"drame surréaliste."

Breton, we should remember, insisted in his *Manifeste du surréalisme* that Apollinaire possessed "only the *letter*, still imperfect, of surrealism" (p. 39), implying that its spirit was not to be sought in *Les Mamelles de Tirésias* more than anywhere else in Apollinaire's writings. The prefix added to *réalisme* denotes "super" and points not to a distaste for reality so much as a heightened awareness of it. And so we find Herbert Read, who made an unsuccessful attempt to launch the word "superrealism" in English, commenting, "It follows that superrealism must be dissociated from all those forms of art which under the guise of fantasy or imagination are merely attempts to avoid reality, to take refuge in an illusion"[1]

In his story *Le Rite du billet de chemin de fer* (1936), Marcel Lecomte, born in Brussels in 1900, goes further, refusing to subscribe to the expression of doubt in Read's remark, "I am not sure, however, that one can poeticize the whole of life." In a deceptively simple yet enlightening way, Lecomte questions the habits that reduce existence to drab routine. These are habits that generally have as one of their most dreary effects reinforcement of our sense of reality as endlessly unchanging. As reflected in *Le Rite du billet de chemin de fer*, his is an attitude that takes issue with the "enemy" cited by Breton in the *Arcane 17* (1944): "The great enemy of man is opacity. This opacity is outside him and it is above all within him, where it is maintained by conventional opinions and all sorts of suspect interdictions" (p. 52). From Lecomte's standpoint, habit and routine are agents of stultification. Their effect, he suggests, can be reversed most easily when we deliberately challenge the hypnosis by which they keep us eternally prisoner to the reality principle, conceived as inertly resistant to all aspirations toward something that can satisfy our sense of wonder.

While Georges Hénein ends *Le Guetteur* upon the suggestion that even an everyday gesture may be part of a rite having supposedly hidden significance, Marcel Lecomte's *Le Rite du billet de chemin de fer* closes with the implication that whenever and wherever routine lays a patina of indifference upon human gestures, it falls to us to renew their freshness. We have only to recognize our obligation to find in all that surrounds us a fascination to which we have been sadly insensitive. As Louis Aragon put it, in one of the most celebrated essays on surrealist painting: "The marvelous opposes what exists mechanically, what *is* so much that it isn't noticed any more, and so it is commonly believed that the marvelous is the negation of reality. This rather summary idea is conditionally acceptable. It is certain that the marvelous is born of the refusal of *one* reality,

---

1. Herbert Read, "A Further Note on Superrealism," in his *A Coat of Many Colours*, 1945.

but also of the development of a new relationship, of a new reality which this refusal has liberated."[2]

*

On November 17, 1966, shortly before eight in the evening, a man left his favorite café on the Place Saint-Jean in Brussels, to go to a restaurant on the Grand-Place where it was his custom to take dinner. As the weather was mild, he left his coat at the café, intending to return for it later. Arriving at the restaurant, he died of a heart attack. For several months his coat contiued to hang from a peg at the Petit Rouge, as though to demonstrate that, just as a gesture may give an object special meaning, so the absence of a gesture, a gesture interrupted or uncompleted, may have the same result. Thirty years before, that man had written a story entitled *Le Rite du billet de chemin de fer.*

---

2. From a text published under the title *La Peinture au défi (Painting Defied)* to introduce an exhibition of collages, held in Paris is 1929-1930 at the Galerie Goemans; reprinted in Aragon's *Les Collages* (1965), pp. 35-71.

MARCEL LECOMTE

The Railroad Ticket Rite

I happen to go two or three times a week to a big market town in Walloon Brabant. Early in the morning's the time I have to catch the train that takes me there and carries me through vast plains; they awake slowly in the first glimmer of dawn.

This journey, among merchants, office workers, and numerous workmen, isn't distasteful to me. To tell the truth, I like traveling this way, without baggage, over short distances, and, what is more, making the same little trip in identical circumstances.

Why is that? Well, because I like to see things; and so there are many features of the countryside or certain aspects of towns that, after escaping me for a long time, abruptly appear to me, reveal themselves to me in all their authenticity. And I subsist on the surprises they give me. But it isn't possible for me to reach the station every day in such a way that I don't have to run for the train. It's true enough that most often, when I arrive on the platform, I catch sight of it very far away, traveling at low speed, but sometimes I've barely time to hoist myself into a compartment at the very moment when it's starting off again. All this obviously depends on small details.

So it was that quite recently I really had to sprint, coming off the streetcar, to get to that old train. And I had no time even to buy a ticket at the station ticket office. No, I dashed through the waiting room, came upon the booking clerk, shouted to him that I'd buy a ticket on the way, and, leaving him flabbergasted, climbed onto the step of a coach as the train was moving off. I settled down, a little out of breath, in the middle of a group of workmen, smoking, playing cards, and talking politics.

I thought that, during the trip, the conductor would pass through the compartment where I was and I could pay him the money for the distance I was going, as sometimes happens at that time of day, on that line. I had in fact witnessed on two or three occasions an incident of that kind: the latecomer would explain his case to the employee, the latter would settle down beside him, take out of his pocket a book of tickets, and the exchange of the ticket for the price of a seat would take place in the most ordinary way in the world.

But things were not to develop so simply for me. In fact, that morning there was no visit from the conductor to the coach where chance, in my run, had cast me and, when I got down on the platform of the little station in the market town in question, I didn't quite know what the consequence of my misadventure would be.

I resolved to go explain myself straight off at the station. In this connection, I'd better report a somewhat strange detail concerning the arrangement of the room I went into; indeed, in a corner, but partly hidden by a greasy worn topcoat, hanging from a nail in the wall, I noticed, standing on a small board, a samovar, yes, an old wrought-iron samovar, that no one there could be using, I imagine, but the presence of which was exciting, nevertheless. It seemed to me the employee who was there caught the glance I cast into a certain corner of the room. All the same, he didn't turn a hair. And everything happened on that score as if he'd been completely ignorant of the presence of that object in the room, or had forgotten it.

In other respects, this employee seemed to me very polite. After listening patiently to my speech, he gave me to understand that no great harm had been done and that all I'd have to do was pay for my seat, on the spot, to be in the clear.

And for this purpose, the employee went and withdrew a ticket from one of the pigeonholes on the wall and put it down in front of me on the table.

I on my side handed him the price of the distance I'd just come. But, as I was about to take the ticket with which he'd just presented me, with a gesture he detained my arm as it reached out and pronounced these words, "Excuse me, Sir, from now on that ticket belongs to me."

To which I reacted at once. For he had less surprised than amused me; it was in fact apparent that he hadn't been able to realize what was unexpected about his declaration. I understood at once that I could, in my turn, provoke a surprise in him, a much bigger one. This is why I answered, "Not right away, though, Sir, before it can belong to you I still have to give it to you." And this time taking firm hold of it, I put it in his hand with a certain slowness.

In so doing, I managed to show him I was deliberately *isolating* my gesture so as to make it particularly perceptible to him, as if it had been a question of making him see, but really *see*, the gesture taking place, a human movement in all its sensient acuity.

He remained for a brief moment motionless, nonplussed by the unexpected intervention, but he soon turned away, for he was already allowing himself to be caught up again in the thread of his daily work.

GEORGES LIMBOUR

1900—1970

While completing his military service, Georges Limbour, born in Courbevoie, France, met the future surrealists Roger Vitrac and René Crevel. He was to be associated with them in launching the magazine *Aventure* in 1921. This was the period during which he wrote his story *L'Enfant polaire*, published for the first time in the third number of *Aventure*, on January 10, 1922.

In the 1924 *Manifeste du surréalisme*, Limbour's name figures next to those of eighteen other men, cited as having embraced "ABSOLUTE SURREALISM." Like those of his friends Vitrac, Michel Leiris, and André Masson, Limbour's name appears also in the appendix to the 1930 edition of the *Second Manifeste du surréalisme*, where Breton lists a few choice quotations from letters and publications by former members of the surrealist movement who by now had left the Paris group, or had been expelled from it. Limbour was still only twenty-nine when he wrote in a letter to Breton, dated December 1929, "It would give me pleasure to see your nose bleed" and contributed to the violent attack upon the surrealist leader that appeared in the form of a pamphlet called *Un Cadavre* (*A Cadaver* [1930])

Of Georges Limbour's publications very few were written while he was in contact with the surrealists: the poems *Soleils bas* (1924), two of the tales in *L'Illustre Cheval blanc* (*The Famous*

White Horse [1930], and one other story, printed in his posthumous collection, *Contes et Récits* (1973).

In the second manifesto of surrealism Breton criticized Limbour for his skepticism and for "literary coquetry in the worst sense of the word" (p. 164). Of course, this condemnation of literary pretentiousness accords fully with the general principles of surrealism. But if Breton had in mind Limbour's concern to polish his phrases, his formal tone and mode of presentation, when attacking him in 1930, then one can only wonder why Limbour, who had displayed these very characteristics in *L'Enfant polaire,* had been admitted to the surrealist movement in the first place. Obviously, these were not preoccupations that developed in him only when he had become estranged from surrealism. Whether or not they can be said to detract from his power as a surrealist storyteller, they do not weaken the imaginative force from which his early stories take direction. And this is as true of *Le Cheval de Venise,* written in 1924, as of *Histoire de famille* (1930), and of the story that lends its name to the volume in which all three appeared, *L'Illustre Cheval blanc* (1923). In fact, what is special about the early stories of Georges Limbour, including those written while he was involved in surrealism, is that the imagination is allowed to run free while, denied the undisciplined expression that this freedom might lead us to anticipate, the material furnished by imagination is submitted to the demands imposed by an instinct for stylistic control of a severely demanding nature.

If we wish to aim at summing up Georges Limbour's contribution to surrealism, we could do worse than begin by listening to his comments upon the drawings of a lifelong friend, Masson, illustrator of *Soleils bas,* In his book *Masson: Dessins* (1951), Limbour, who had already written *André Masson et son univers* (1947) in collaboration with Michel Leiris, remarks, "André Masson's drawings offer themselves . . . as an elegant handwriting, sometimes graceful, violent often and impassioned, that, going beyond concern for form alone, although this concern is a constant one, allows him to express a complex and refined view of the universe" (p. 5).

GEORGES LIMBOUR

The Horse of Venice

How could he join together again the fragments of his mind,
dispersed as much as the torn sunlight on the walls and paving
stones, in the alleys of Venice? More free in his wandering than,
a short time before dawn, a man walking in the middle of a
roadway in Paris, separated by a century from the day before
and from age to age from the day after, *he* walks these streets in
the middle of the morning. He goes off without danger, among
a population of pedestrians, on the tortuous route without
sidewalks, calling up at the intersections only the accidents of
his dreams. The monstrous Wheel with its felly of blood, with
splinters of terror and perturbation, passing violently and
pushing the panic-stricken people against the houses, has never
turned on these stones. The one that lames has carried no lazy
masters, its victims from above, with big bellies and the lackluster eyes of somnolence. Mathias follows the whims of his mind,
less crazy than the whims of the streets, goes up and down, and
up again, sometimes sniffing a vague scent of swamp, on those
small staircases from which maliciousness had banned the
wheel. Thanks to the charming peace of the alleys reserved for
man's pleasure, conversations ring out freely, laughter bursts
forth in a fresh smell of fish roaming like a fish in water and
indiscreet Mathias gathers these echoes. From their coiled

marine shell, the alleys allow a murmur of shells to rise, that is so natural since the sea was perhaps singing yesterday in their labyrinth and in their mouth it dozes still. At the invitation of this intimacy, Mathias chooses his path without a qualm, goes side by side with that girl, her gait unhampered, slave to no tramway, so crazy that she distributes her laughter like a fistful of handbills carried off by the wind. Laugh, then, charming girl in the salty tang, and give the air your mouth with all its pink palate as the swimmer does his body, a swimmer yourself in the salt of the air. Let your mockery claw delightfully at its face, touched with emotion by the bite of your laughter, for it is ashamed of its silence when sunkissed hair, rising suddenly from a corner, changes into different hair in the whirlwind of passersby and when, going around some, carried away by others, he finds once again, now turned brown, the blond hair he had been following.

In a shady street, violet algae have grown on the walls: Mathias watches in the air the bright glitter of fish, the surface of the water where bubbles become iridescent and burst, the colored transparency of jellyfish, then his glance drops again to the open shells of shop windows where sleep a pearl and a drowned piece of fabric.

Suddenly, he stops to contemplate, with particular desire and the voraciousness of a cat, a stretch of sunlight hanging from the top of a wall like a piece of meat. He keeps it in sight with that steady gaze which makes objects fall, that lover's torment with which he could be filled by the night descent of a beloved woman clinging to some balcony.

Will he buy those products made only by the sea: silks gathered in distant fishing-grounds, shawls woven by the amorous sea for the shoulders it made quiver one evening, curled shells in which fish have sounded the trumpet, precious stones secreted by illness in the liver of sea animals? Men, why does your purulence not have these whimsies worthy of the harpoon, and why do your abcesses not harbor those marvels with precious incrustations? At least the death of a father would be doubly profitable to you, beautiful, beautiful, too beautiful prostitutes who, in the gondolas, yellow the lacework of your nights in the sunlight.

Wounded animals have been seen running, their twitching

guts dragging to the ground; then they have been seen to lie down and cast their dying eyes about, a saddened tongue on the inside of their bellies, spread in this way about them. That is how, on the perfumed intestines of the sea, Venice has squatted, but the sea laughs and sings and its whole body trembles and spreads throughout the city the fury of its senses.

*

Mathias is never lost, for the path he follows is always toward what he does not know. Also finding his bearings causes him momentary vertigo, when the shock that puts the different parts of the city back into place topples, at the same time, the fabulous attraction given them by distance, running them together, jumbling the spaces between them. Then regret over so much pettiness has soon extinguished the first enchantment and the monuments that fall into place in the mind will no longer be counted except once. The man is going to walk in an immobile city, instead of feeling it shift position about him. At this moment when the abrupt apparition of the known tatters a dream in his head, at this terrifying flash of lightning in which man FINDS HIMSELF AND HIS BEARINGS, himself and the ridiculous purpose of his passing through this place, his vain hope of pleasure, and the desire, always disappointed, for enchantment, the stones utter a cry terrible as when the woman solidifies as a pillar of salt. As soon as the cry has rung out of a city falling into place and solidifying, Mathias usually packs his bags, when the immutability of the plan of the town presents itself to his mind.

But this time what absurd demon of art whispers to him that he will perhaps derive pleasure from submitting to the reality of this city, from permitting it to impose itself upon his imagination? He will turn it over in his mind, as he would a precious vase in his hand, to follow very carefully each contour and every line, for, having passed numerous canals like so many blindfolds passing before his eyes, like so many perfumes blindly breathed in and cheating memory with their diversity, he has a presentiment of that moment when a well-behaved compass points in the senses. Turning it over in his dazzled mind, as a gambler cannot distinguish the meaning of a card on which the Queen is reflected in a perfect wave, not knowing yet if he will enter by the right or the left, from the front or from the side, he feels himself drawn toward this luminous abyss that is a square in a city, but this is a very immortal one, and gathers the bouquet of its clamorings.

For the city reaches completion and fruition at the moment when, suddenly finding his direction, he enters, in secret solitary triumph, a square where he tramples on a carpet of pigeons, leaving on the paving stones bloody footsteps, imprints to which feathers adhere, and multiplying in his absentmindedness the massacre of those winged creatures Latin soothsayers at one time used to kill with tiny knives of gold. This child who at one time threw plenty of bread to the swans, nevertheless a cruel child who wanted to feed his imaginings, watches his soles become colored with a little pagan blood. Then before his eyes tremble the hands of an old despotic priest in his robes and insignia of gold, a ridiculous soothsayer, an exsanguine prophet, who squeezes with paltry solemnity and a cruelty worthy of a child a human chest from which bursts a drop too trifling to give color to his senile face. A whole imperial purple robe, spreading wider than a Caesar's cloak, broad as nations and oceans, was held in check however and now is fading in these drops that roll under the fat of the feathers. Dead Prophesies, unrevealed auguries revolve in the blood of these animals bringing behind them in their flight victories by fleets drowned today, fires resting like big birds on the sea. But while a beggar come from afar enjoys on the square infinite ecstasy, satisfies age-old hungers at a royal table erected in the shadow of so many wings, Mathias, who feels the majestic cold of marble passing over his soul, serious as the touch of a sword, is already near the sea.

For it is there that, too sumptuous perhaps and too clever, she stretches to full length her outline, chiseled in the arabesques traced in the white incandescence of the horizons. Wrought like an oriental palace, she accepts disdainfully to mirror those of the land. The arts of man do not equal hers, the vices of the continent, those in which she finds secret enjoyment. It is there that she is pleased to turn in a thousand directions on her finger the sparkle of her rings, those gems, precious sweetmeats of death, that could, into subjugated lips, pour a final liqueur. In the intoxicating odor you are breathing,

Mathias, and in which your nerves undulate like marine plants, already a head of wet hair is outlined, beneath which such eyes roll, such eyes! One would not believe that to right and left the pupil could make so much movement, to the point of half disappearing in the corner of the eyelid, beautiful eyes about which one does not know if they are human, eyes into which sinks a gold needle, eyes you follow, Mathias, enamored of a woman who emerged before your eyes from a column of shining light, on the staircases once again, once again through the alleys where the trapdoors of love open.

"With the clothes," he says, "in which you are decked out, this luxury in which you veil yourself, what can I recognize in you? The insatiable voluptuousness fermenting in your heart lifts these waves of material on your body, this storm of silk. Your nakedness would leave me calmer, your nakedness would dissipate perhaps the agitation into which your finery has thrown me."

In the narrow alleys where he is led by the woman he is following, passersby jostle him and thrust him aside, tear up his desire, slash into his dream. But She! now he can see her no more, for already it is nighttime, the darkness he recognizes only in the moment of his despair, as if that woman had exhaled it from her very chest to conceal her flight, as if night were only the ink discharged by that octopus in full flight, and twice the spectral light of a motionless Chinese lantern languishes, on a canal where perhaps the fairy has alighted. But it is enough in the shadow of a heavier shadow for him to recognize that body of darkness whose veils he wishes to strip away, for his life all at once to revive and his body to thrust forward. This is only the final disappointing tremor of hope, for a door closes above the steps that have raised the beloved body toward memory. He remains on the threshold, until from inside the palace resounds something like the noise of a torrent in a dark grotto. But we cannot be deceived by the echo within us of those sounds heard in houses encircled by our own passions, even when Mathias hears all night some cascade of gold rolling along the staircases, of a less pure gold though, he thinks, than that of which are made your bones and unbreakable spine, you precious fascinating woman resplendent in the void of a vertiginous brightness. On the distant steps, there is the sound of laughter when it falls from the crystalline throat of death. "The eyes I train on a dagger can go down on a blade deep into your flesh and gaze at the jellyfish with fins of crepe, the octopuses with inky secretions that populate the depths of your pleasurable sensations and spread a great dark sheet on which your kiss is displayed. That is why on their black and purple lips the dawns carry your poisoned tinctures which one wishes to taste again, and nothing, afterward, being able to exist again, to drink a second time, so as to die of it."

For a long time he remained with his forehead against a door with the strength of a sluice gate that held back the torrential fall of a body ready to carry everything away. For a long time he dreamed of his death, at the bottom of an ocean in which the purple spat out by jellyfish in suspense spread like smoke, in curtains, funnels, whirlpools. Slowly, in the bursting of black animals whose liquid fell little by little in parachute curves, the masterly tincture rose above him, unrolling on its edges quivering fringes, unheard-of eyelashes that beat the water, then, hesitant, dropped to encircle, then cover, bodies whose frenzy no doubt was moderated by the water's shackles cooling their fire and permitting them to last as long as those slow metamorphoses.

Why does he suddenly tear himself away from the boards to which, tomorrow, will be seen nailed not owls but sea animals, hung by their elongated dried tentacles as after the ebb of a terrible overpopulated sea, attesting that all one evening a man has invoked love here? Why from this frenetic despair does he seem to rise up in an unforeseen joy he had perhaps only forgotten?

The voluptuous City, the singular lover, the City that sleeps with the Ocean still does not know that a more miraculous seducer has hidden in its bed? No one but Mathias knows why women this evening have carried their uneasy ardor with them so long, why the Ocean had crouched in bitter jealousy, why night had hesitated so long to come down, suspended in the high clouds of a delightful evening. Not a sacrilegious hooter, not an automobile with its raucous horn breaks this silence in which night can be heard softly gliding over itself. If only a sharp ear will give its attention to the stone, it will grasp a secret: Venice on the paving stones of which no horse ever made its hoofs ring out, no gold carriage ever ran, transmits from islet to islet, by the chain of its bridges, the echo of a horse rearing. A quadruped shadow slips through the crooked streets the zig-zags of a storm, ambles along serenely above the city. With what passion Mathias listens, on the lookout like a criminal, to the voices, to the whisperings, that trouble the water, to everything that can make the night turn on the hinges of a ramshackle house, door, porch, roof, weathervane, all driven by the hand of the dream, the vigilance of love: he hears furniture moving in the houses. But stronger than this fragile life, as if the walls of shadow sheltered as many coiners' nocturnal forges, more than one pair of bellows lighting up instruments of torture made red hot in silence, he comes everywhere, stirring up the shadows, upon the breathing of his hidden Horse.

*

The people are feeding. The bread given to the pigeons that the people did not eat is, in that measure, taken out of the mouths of their children. They can absorb everything but, accustomed as they are to seeing every day chimeras in stone and pigeons in flesh and blood, they would prefer to satisfy their hunger on cheap lion meat, on cheaper dragon meat. What am I saying? I have seen some eating dragon, sitting on a boundary stone, and the smell of the Virgin came from their nostrils. They would leave in the evening, their viscera intoxicated with a strange effervescence, singing in their gondolas, and probing the black waters with an oar or a trident.

Mathias too has eaten some. He has slipped on its scales, still sticky with the spume of its infuriation, in the vicinity of certain markets where its blood meandered through the gutters. Then what a victory was celebrated by that joy shining in every eye, making fruit and vegetables roll, glittering, and as a result all glances shifted from the exciting freshness of the merchandise to everything that was invisible on the rooftops, flaming, dancing, exulting no doubt after prodigious combats, revels which from the sloping roof tiles of the big market sent a splendor with divine splashes flowing down onto the sidewalks?

Mathias' teeth bit into the fable and so cruelly that he felt it to be only a dream.

Every time Mathias (how well he remembers!) went through a town, two powerful horses would be drawing a cart full of bottles of beer, and it was rare for one of them not to slip on the peel of an orange fallen from the hair of a washerwoman and not break its knees. Always, then, a man dripping with blood, a cutlass in his hand, would cut through the crowd, ready to buy the unfortunate victim, to chop it up, to sell the meat, meat, meat, he cried out, displaying four, ten, twenty rows of teeth, as if he had his mouth full of mirrors, meat, good people who need, your sleeves rolled up, to fashion your appetites.

It never failed, in all the working-class districts, where the cannibals stood ready to devour anyone who weakened, and to lick up off the pavement every drop of his blood, beast, man, or god.

However, the plebe of Venice do not transport their beer in that fashion. One does not hear in the streets the harness bells mingling with the clink of bottles in the light cart. Mathias thinks of it simply because a little girl is slipping along the barrels, cheeses, fruit on display, gracefully holding in her hands a horseshoe as rare here as the edelweiss and ready to grant her a happiness just as virginal. The legacy of a deceased aunt, an exchange between children of a little dried-up crocodile for the mythological imprint; or else, Mathias thinks in anguish, could someone have inspected his secret?

He followed the child, for he wanted to identify the fetish, all in iron, from one he knew well, being able to bring to mind only the crossbred foot of a mule. He followed the child with ecstatic glance carrying the exceedingly rare horseshoe under her pinafore, against her heart, like a blessed diamond crucifix and a pledge of happiness, until she went into a stinking courtyard where all the fish in the Adriatic had just been scaled. On strings stretched out from one window to another were drying women's colored cotton underwear enough to make you feel nausea at the body that went into it. The child disappeared miraculously into that odor as into a great mystic cloud and *he* had to escape from the courtyard like a fish from a rotten shell.

But you will not get out as quickly as that from this labyrinth, for Misfortune lies in wait for you. In the vicinity of the palaces, what nauseating mysteries! and as the abortionists hide in the shadow of the angels of love, come over here, there is little light, there are these specters of odors the size of doors, there are the merchants with soiled white aprons, there are, I am going to show them to you, the butchers. You who were looking everywhere, in this city, for a horse and would have wished it to be in marble at the palace doors, grazing on the impassible meadow of the sea; you who asked the imaginative well-informed sea, the fruitful sea, to send you at least some of its sea horses, what a rending laugh you gave when you saw in those streets the gilded sign of a horse butcher's, so learning that horses came into this city only when dead. They were eaten by people, whose children had never seen that animal except in pictures.

The fine head was superbly raised above the bloody door of the shop. One could hear it sniffing the smell of the sea and lamenting. Thanks to it, Mathias, who was thinking of his marvelous horse, and that behind this neck the sea served as crupper, recalled furious storms, great fights on the sands. He would have said to the housewives, "Don't eat that flesh; it burns more than alcohol, is more poisonous than belladonna, has more poisons than the flowers of tropical forests and, like minds too intelligent, it is studded with fluorescences set with diamonds and spangled with agonizing silver. It can make those who have tasted it sickly with melancholy or carry them away with rage. Their faces will no longer have the color of healthy men.

"Are you not ashamed to feed on the gods you have killed?"

Disgusted by the sight of the street, Mathias fled, passing the waters in which so many corpses are washed, toward the luxurious beach where the sun, as it went down, brought back to life magnificent bodies stretched out on the sand.

In the morning, his nightmares had not yet gone. Having bathed, he made a tour of the square, not daring to venture into the alleys. He could sense everywhere a taste of the macabre and suspected the marble, then he attempted a few paces in the direction of the house belonging to his love.

He could do nothing against the mortuary cavalcades of

black horses he met, with coats glossy and soft like wolf's velvet, some carapaced in crepe. They disappeared quickly with the lightness of butterflies in mourning.

A distant clamor sent a shudder through him. A crowd was invading the alleys, filling them to the point of pushing the walls back, sending up a thousand laughs like pikes, tinged at once with blood by cries full of menace. Mathias watched it advance, trying to understand what that mob wanted: from the joy the faces expressed he took this to be a carnival. But, suddenly rising above the crowd, carried at the end of a pole by a band of villains, was that not the butcher's shop sign, the pitiable gilded horse advancing with the elegant disdain of a swan swimming above the shouts of the people.

The Golden Horse scaled the bridges, turning its neck with slowness and dignity to both sides of the street and led to martyrdom by the perverted crowd of gondoliers, thieves, and loggia graybeards. The only horse ever to have been through these streets, it had been compelled to draw a pitiable carriage in which women fruit sellers sat in state, with necklaces of running olives, in the arms of gondoliers pestiferous from the water of their canals and bearing on their faces the greenish glimmer of midnight Chinese lanterns. Sellers of spun glass ran behind, blowing up bladders still wet with urine, fresh viscera upon which was expended the most touching side of their art, and some who were spitting blood and sending it down in thin trickles to become iridescent on the transparency of fabric. Then, coughing joltingly interrupting their imbecile laughter, they threw their wonders into the carriage where those balls fell on the knees of sticky gorgons who burst them with the tridents of their combs and threw them back, deflated, to those who had made them and who were swallowing their saliva and blood. The carriage suddenly fell to pieces and all those fashionable people were rolling together in the mud in obscene attitudes and those following behind prevented them from getting up. But ugh! another carriage was giving way before the carnival-esque triumph, contrasting through the sound of suction rather than kisses that filled it, with the silence of a light hearse, full of murdered whores, and connected to the golden horse's mouth by thin reins of death-agony foam.

The masquerade passed by Mathias, stiffened against a

wall, and some time went by before, having recovered his senses, he began to follow it. Cutting across town he even overtook and walked a long way ahead of it like an hallucinated drum major. Then he enjoyed the preparations in the street where that fine dream was to pass: balconies overloaded with impatient spectators over carefully closed shops. He admired the faces debased by this mid-Lent joy, he sought out their eyes in which, behind a thin layer of skin, flourished their taste for pleasure, their soul of joy.

Now, at the moment when his contempt designated them most harshly for his sarcasm, she appeared, the ideal Queen for one evening, her elbows resting on a balcony, no longer nonchalantly, but her body taut with impatience and quivering.

All of a sudden in the sunlight the splendors of the street attained the strange intensity in which, powerless, the eye sees darkness coming down instead. He saw the overloaded balconies sway on the invisible waves of heat sent up by the paving stones. As in an insolation storm, he saw the streets breaking up until, master of these whirlwinds that had just carried away the bad dream and capsized the scorned boats, he plunged into a stairway that must twist down into the street.

Where, while he was speaking to the street and persuading it, did the people take their sad trophy, along the path followed many times by procession flags, by madonnas and crosses? Did it fall to some pestilential wave, was it thrown on a charnel heap, where the sadness of that gilded head perished? Perhaps someone walking alone has caught sight of it shining in the mud of a canal and has thought it to have been an adornment on the fronton of a building at present under water; thought of the passing of the centuries, of the ruins of palaces, of splendors done away with, of terrible revolutions? At night, he will have seen a strange gleam in the mud and perhaps a naked arm reaching down from a gondola will have tried, around midnight, to fish up a treasure.

Excited by the cries of joy with which the city resounded and the pleasures she had promised herself, for a long time the Beautiful Woman resisted Mathias' invitation. Did he not beg her for silence and solitude? But the dream he was inviting her to share, the wonder he was proposing to show her were so strange that soon she was able to resist no longer. He claimed, indeed, to have brought back from an oriental city, in a ship laden with precious fabrics and material worked by incredible hands, a ship now anchored within call of the palaces, its scarcely furled sails still aquiver and beating with the fervor of the voyage, a horse whose impetuous hoofs had in several places made holes in the deck. The foam when the wind ripped it angrily from his mouth and carried it off over the sea gave birth, when mingled with that of the waves, to untamed birds that fought and tore at one another until their blood momentarily colored the waves, and this perpetual carnage had been a constant accompaniment to the voyage.

Not being able to give up his desire to visit a city so unfit for horses, he had imprisoned his own in a little palace, to keep it under supervision.

When they arrived at the marble pavilion where the animal lived, the horse that had just broken a few vases and ancient statues, reduced to the fine powder of an arduous road, seemed particularly interested in a vast painting representing some nude women lying on a beach of magnificent draperies and the sea at their feet was not more vast, or deep, or terrible, than their neglected sashes. Perhaps even, at the hour when sensual pleasure is fatigued, distracted by their exchange of tender glances, they will dress in the sea itself, instead of those draperies capable of creating over again on the abandoned shore an ocean of another color.

Distracted from his contemplation by the visitors' arrival, the horse majestically came down a little staircase to meet them. His pride seemed to make a new space rise about him. He champed his pride like a diamond bit.

No doubt he recognized that this man and woman made a perfect couple, worthy of his attention, worthy of receiving on their faces the fire of his nostrils. The woman could not bear his glance, mysterious and terrible like that of children, because it uses a language other than our own, because of its awful stubbornness: but she raised her hand to the savage neck; her whole flesh hung from the strong mane until she pressed her apprehensive mouth to the quivering flesh of the nostrils.

*

Disposed to every excess, she now recognized in the sky of

her own life nothing but that wonderful body. But the Platonic admiration of its beauty, reduced, because space had been abolished, to what was ideal and chimerical in her, was not enough for her: she tried to derive pleasurable sensations from it, and feeling it was impossible for him to love her really and to have herself loved by him, she was assailed by despair, pressed against his neck; and later finding his pure image in the whiteness of a cloud, in spirit she gave him his liberty again, pursued him through the blue sky and on the horizon heard the fall of their exhausted tangled bodies. In the shining of the sea and stones, the splendor of the light, she could see only the radiance of his beloved body.

Everything was becoming pure in her at that time! Never had she seen the sun resplendent with a more sonorous brightness, the squares more free and glorious, the beaches more spacious, undulating on their border with the movement of the sea, touched with emotion to every depth, to each shadow in the sky, prepared for a mad and terrifying ride.

With the imperiousness of her passion, the conviction of her tone, the gentleness, the fury of her caresses, she was trying to subjugate him, surprised there was no echoing response to her voice other than the absurd "I love you" with which she invoked the human behind that impassive forehead, the desperate appeal of which, it seemed to her, the fury must bring loves lost far from the implacable law of bodies back within the circle of possible passions.

The worst of it was that she could not ride the horse, despotically command his movements, guide his torso between her legs, make of herself and of him a single body. She was tortured by the desire to hoist herself onto the superb back and direct a vertigo of incredible speed in which her will power would no longer exist, totally abandoned to the runaway animal, free to save or smash her to pieces.

The Horse remained insensitive as one sees indifferent rivers flow under a rain of stars. She cried out to him: "Horror! You express neither contempt nor friendship. But why does one of your hoofs sometimes strike the ground in an impatient gesture?

"Don't turn away, for you are my love. I have only one of your eyes for my suffering to be mirrored in, and I am afraid

when appearing to myself so uncomely in that indifferent orb.
What do you want me to do for you? What rug, what cushions
do you desire, to tear up with your shoes? Do you want me to
give you back your liberty? What countries do you prefer, where
the grass is more springy, the meadow stretches wider? Isn't the
sea your desire, where the waves striking against your breast
would cover you with foam like a curly pelisse? They say that
queens of old . . . Oh no, no one has loved his horse as I love
you, for I have sacrificed all lovers to you; I have devoted myself
for you to the horror, to the torments of chastity. Some lose
themselves in the contemplation of numberless stars, others are
drawn by the attraction of unknown countries; but you are my
star and my impetuous river and in you I lose myself. You are
the force by which I want to be dominated, the superb intoxication that cannot, alas! intoxicate me."

As she held the horse, he raised his head and inhaled her
hair deeply, then he ate the flower on her corsage; now she
bared her chest and he licked her breasts. She closed her eyes;
she would have liked him to bite her chest. In her hands she
lifted up the heavy head, pressed her lips to the nostrils, parted
them, crushed her burning mouth against the clenched teeth of
the horse.

She thought him responsive to her love.

*

Having a key to the garden, she would come alone to visit
the horse and would see Mathias only on the beach or in town.
She hid her love from him very carefully, but he discerned in
her glance the majesty of a grief the depth or cause of which he
never suspected. How noble she was then! All beauty inflamed
her. She released herself from the overflow of her passions by
the Dionysiac use of her body. In vain, she tried to exhaust in
the sea that triumphant strength gathered by love, which she
could not expend. She would roll in the waves, swim with
temerity, plunge into the water as into joyous heavenly flesh,
look for solitude far from the coastline and the imbecile cries of
bathers, return exhausted and find strength in drying herself on
the sun-kissed sand; for it was stretched out on the sand that
they had their most passionate moments. Then, not suspected
from what love came that beauty of hers, that pride, Mathias

would feel the adoration he had devoted to her from the first evening, and knowing however that nothing in himself brought that admirable woman to life, he felt gnawing at him a confused jealousy, to which he could not admit, of everything that gave her joy and about which she made the sea, the light, and the sand her silent confidants, and his desire, although entirely human, was no smaller and less painful than that with which the Amazon Beauty burned.

*

Like a white and gold pope shut away in his palace, an emperor secluded in his majesty, for a long time the horse could have reigned in his stable, shut up on a little islet, like the rarest one in Venice where the paving stones were not meant for his footsteps. He would have been its secret glory and beauty, at once the mark of its imperfection and the sign of an impossible dream, of a desperate thought in the direction of Beauty. He would have been its most tragic prisoner, victim of no plot, of no infamy, except of the pettiness of a God.

What hand then gave him back a conspicuous liberty and showed him the way to a fatal triumph? Did his lover's despair designate death to him as a grandiose end in which to reduce his love to nothing or, out of all patience with her still perfection, maddened by all those caresses lavished upon him without his ever being able to reciprocate, did he himself escape, seeking to satisfy the delirium of his senses, ready to tear to pieces the woman who had reduced him to this state? Of course, it was love that made him walk through the streets, and whoever met him could not believe him to be "animal" since, because of the absurdity of his presence, in those places and of his noble disposition as happens only in a dream, he seemed a work of art and stranger than a dragon, more chimerical than a chimera because he *imitated the real so well*; and the real, contaminated from then on, in its turn lost all its reality. He caused doubt to fall upon palaces, water, churches, History. He transformed the period and was understood by gondoliers who no longer felt the deck of their gondolas, by sacristans who feared the marble statues might escape, and by some ridiculous attendant fearing he might take a place again in his museum.

He entered the square.

Some gazed at him in ecstasy, believing him to be made of the same spiritual matter as stones and time. They heard the collision of the sea and the still sky; they heard the voice of the Sun, at the moment when, prodigiously, he disappeared.

As mysterious as that of the horse was the Amazon's flight, at the moment when Mathias, caught in the play of his senses, was beginning to believe in her reality, and even, his imagination having let itself be dethroned, to submit to it. The upward flight of a horse from such a city did not astonish him any more than the escape of the hours struck by the big clock, waves enlarged in a melancholy way, after the fashion of an embrace relaxing, of collars around the heart slackening. But that she, unfaithful woman, should have climbed into the saddle on that supernatural animal, at the moment when it was going to disappear in the evaporation of the sea, left Mathias doubly at a loss on the paving stones above which overweight mosquitoes were losing their strength, close to death and loosened from the evening by a strong wind, like the sad flower of the dandelion.

He visited dark prisons where he saw the roof bent toward the sky by the effort of the prisoners, blocks of granite translucent to hope, to crazy dreams. He saw his torture sweat a shadowy sweat, condemned to shake heavy carnal chains in the dark, while they, the fugitives, passed through the rock, on wings, and reached the sky.

Prey to every love, he took with him through the city his frustrated love, revived incessantly by the scent of the sea. For her first appearance was, in front of him, the rise of a tide, and the salt odor now tormented him and he found in it the same sensual memory as in breathing, in tearing up the underwear she had left behind. And so everywhere, as if the city had been an immense closet, and every alleyway an unusual drawer opened in spite of him by a terrifying hand, in the air dresses spread, without bodies, voluptuous near the sea; more intimate and perverse near the motionless canals. His thoughts followed the fugitives, from afar confusing the swelling sails with the firm crupper of a horse, while he searched among the women stretched out on the sand for a form he had coveted more than any other.

*

Unfurl your sails, ships, for it is dawn. The nascent light

will stream over the swelling of the badly set sails, like the transparent water of springs in the hollow of hands pressed against the rock.

No one will see abandoned love go off in the silence of dawn; no one will know to which horizon it furrows its ephemeral wake, if it fled at night like a guilty person, or spread its sails like broad flowers of disdain.

How far away and empty the palaces are already: calm Adonises could be seen there and vigorous women, tireless porters, bearing the heavy architecture above the triumphal route of the centuries; missing at present is a marble statue, radiant with glory, for which no horseman has been found and which held up the whole sky.

When the migratory birds, when the cranes pass over Venice and from the height at which they fly catch sight of the humble rooftops of red tile, not suspecting which stones support them, which waters divide them, they continue on their way and go further to look toward the North for a humble peaceful village, leaving behind them the city where they have not lived.

JOYCE MANSOUR

1928–

Born in England of Egyptian parents, educated in Egypt, Joyce Mansour attracted the surrealists' notice with her first volume of verse, *Cris* (*Cries* [1953]), which closes on a poem beginning, "The Vices of Men / Are my domain / Their wounds are my sweetmeats." From the first, the writings of Joyce Mansour have celebrated, to borrow the phrase heading a section of her poetic collection *Carré blanc* (*White Square* [1965]), "the Erogenic Hour."

Like *Carré blanc*, Joyce Mansour's prose narratives *Jules César* (1958), *Les Gisants satisfaits* (*The Satisfied Recumbent Figures* [1958]), and *Ça* (*That* [1970]) are dedicated to André Breton. Her work challenges the opinions and flouts the interdictions that, according to Breton's *Arcane 17*, maintain "opacity" in man. It is marked by a distinctive approach that gives mood and color to the stories by which she is represented here. Prudishness, we soon discover, has no meaning for Joyce Mansour. And yet it is not by concentrating upon realistic details that we enter most easily and penetrate most rewardingly into the erotic universe where her characters breathe a rarefied atmosphere. Naturalistic elements are by no means the ones that set her signature upon her writing. What impresses most is the juxtaposition of unsentimentalized signs of passion and imaginative detail—at once absurd and shocking, and above all humorous—which creates not only a distinctive narrative tone but also an atmosphere conducive to uninhibited response to sexual drive as the most important and the most meaningful impetus in human life.

In one way, we soon come to understand that for Joyce Mansour the erotic experience defies communication in its fullest intensity unless narration is permitted to overspill the limitations of the rational, carrying author and reader, in their pursuit of the characters who interest them, into a world beyond the confines of the reasonable. In another way—and this is perhaps more important still—we learn that the special value of the erotic, so far as Joyce Mansour is concerned, lies in its power to entice us beyond the boundaries of reason and common sense.

The people who appeal to Mme Mansour and command her exclusive attention in the stories she relates come to life only in situations occurring at the very limits of credible experience, beyond the literary conventions of the grotesque. Characteristically, one of the tales in *Les Gisants satisfaits*, called *Marie, ou l'honneur de servir* (*Mary, or The Honor of Service*), show us a murderer, who has been watching Marie bathe, rowing toward her, "his eyes globular with pleasure, his mouth full of an animal plashing sound, a heavy black serpent hanging out from his navel."Reading stories such as this one, we find ourselves in a twilight zone where we are torn between laughter and horror.

The horror to which Joyce Mansour introduces us is double-edged, so to speak. It involves feeling the shock administered by the spectacle of behavior that defies the norm. But, more than this, it is horror born of her disgust for modes of conduct that we are accustomed to consider normal. Specifically, Joyce Mansour confronts us with her own contempt for the confining influences of bourgeois life, no less readily set aside in *Infiniment . . . sur le gazon* than in her play *Le Bleu des fonds*, first published in the magazine *Le Surréalisme, même* in 1959. Consistently, the erotic battles with those "rancid vapors exhaled by daily life," to which Joyce Mansour refers in her *Déchirures* (*Tearing* [1955]).

The scabrous, the scandalous, the humorous: these are the elements brought into unlikely alliance by a woman who has described herself in *Rapaces* (*Raptores* [1960]) as "Awaiting the arrival of the uncertain / Sumptuously dressed in soap bubbles and shit."

Le Cancer appeared in the third number of *Le Surréalisme, même* (Autumn 1957). As the text reprinted in *Les Gisants satis-faits* is defective, the version below follows the original. *Infini-ment . . . sur le gazon* was published originally in the fourth issue of *La Brèche: action surréaliste*, in February 1963. The version that appears here is based on the text as revised by the author for inclusion in *Ça*. In both cases the English text incorporates additional changes, made by Joyce Mansour on the manuscript of the translation.

JOYCE MANSOUR

The Cancer

For years on end I didn't understand that woman was dying. Everything in her vibrated with pent-up sickness and under her flowing robe her skin itself was flowing: old, she was beautiful with emotions only hinted at but, when she tore her eyes away from mine and turned away her head swathed in cotton, all I could see was her hump.

Alone with her monstrous hump, Clara lived in the largest house in the village; her father, the Count of Deauville, was dead, as was her mother, so that the house and the grounds, the trees and the mahogany furniture, everything belonged to her. I, a mute little boy, was her only flunky. Women always find someone or something to keep them going and Clara, mysterious Clara who never went out and saw no one, would lean on my thin shoulders and console herself with me.

I worked conscientiously all day; I'd half-open the shutters, heavy with dust, creaking with discomfort like everything else in the house where even the rats wore mittens; I'd clean the frayed pathways, I'd tend the canary. Clara would busy herself too. She'd get dressed. I'll always remember the first time I saw her naked, my mistress Clara, the only woman I've known. I was drinking my milk, one hand resting on the door jamb, my foot already raised for the first step backward, my eye to the

keyhole of her bedroom. I was twelve years old. She was looking at herself in the mirror and I had no doubt she could feel my
inquisitorial eye lingering innocently over her body; fortunately
her everyday clothes lay on a chair, it was the sight of these that
saved me from fainting; they were the only inert and normal
objects in the room. As for the hump, it stood up, pink, over-
shadowing the body on its spidery legs, enthroned above the
oblong breasts and the hollow buttocks: a fortress. The hump. I
had eyes only for that, really; although I got to know the rest in
the mad weeks following that first vision, the hump was my
great discovery.

Clara left the mirror and slowly dressed in front of me; she
wasn't shy; she smiled, her head nodding against her chest; she
found pleasure in the evident justification for her indecency and
my fear.

I didn't leave the house again from that memorable day on-
ward, despite the strong smell of sulphur that permeated it: I
was in love with the hump and alive only in its presence.

Clara discovered love at the same time as I; I'd caress her
timidly and she'd look with pride at the evidence of my frenzy.
She'd listen to the muffled voice that cried out in me, unaccustomed to expressing its sad confession; she'd understand me
without words and, ready for anything to please her, idolizing,
I'd wriggle around that hump.

One day, she questioned me, "Are you afraid, little one?"
Blackmail! I stroked her forehead and the soft hairline, I touched
her breasts that bruised slightly under my fingers, I kissed the
pout of her swollen mouth, but wept with vexation: she denied
me her hump. "Why are you punishing me? I was so happy, so
happy." Reading my despair through my tears, she, cruel thing,
ordered, "Well then, be a man," and, eyes closed, offered herself. Mortified, I threw myself on the bed, teeth chattering, my
glance fleeing through the galleries; I was now only a planet that
had cooled.

The most unbearable pains are aphonous. I reproached
myself with my cowardice, I tortured myself, I ate all day in the
vain hope of consoling myself; gripped by anguish, I didn't dare
come near my mistress any more. I knew that body was
stretched out on the divan with all that meat on its back, and I

suffered, knowing myself to be incapable of mastering that meat.

The house was full of the burning scent of decay and death burst from every side at once, without, for all that, finding itself a choice nest. Clara was dying, eaten up by her hump, and the house was sliding in her wake into the mire of afterlife without even trying to cling to the ground. *I* was dreaming of marking the gigantic dome with my teeth, of rubbing myself against its polished surface, of going off, my arms full of the immobile tumulus, toward the city where life begins: Babylon. In the evening, before bedtime, Clara would describe to me life in Babylon and I had no sooner closed my eyes than the smoky streets, the icy virgin wind, the prostitutes, all beautiful and of course humpbacked, would take form. She had lived for several years in the city of my dreams with her father and an old aunt, until the death of the former and the disappearance of the latter. Then, when she was alone, with the young bud of a hump in the region of her shoulder, she went into voluntary exile in the country to devote herself to the treatment and cultivation of her disease. That was when the hump began to grow in earnest. At first, Clara would try to conceal it, ashamed of the furious mushroom of flesh, concerned for her health; then she began to love the shifting sand, knowing that beneath her skin a mystery was silently budding, feeding on her blood, sedentary.

Before I made the discovery of women, if I found in Clara only an undemanding, rather crazy and aggressively ugly mistress, it's because I still earned my daily bread draped in the blind shawl of childhood, insensitive to the beauty blossoming before my eyes; I suppose I lacked imagination.

Around thirteen, still unable to satisfy Clara, although tortured by desire for the hump, I awoke one morning to find my body bathed in a sort of granular sweat; my torso seemed badly adjusted to my neck, I squinted, my penis stretched alongside me, stone dead. Clara understood the nature of my ailment at once and was delighted that at last my desire, like a fish coming up to the surface, finally had broken through to daylight. "Breathe deeply," she said to me, "don't worry, I'll warn you when the moment comes." The hump contemplated my betrayal from the height of its pulpit. Clara, a thin and wan gleam of skin beneath the concupiscent enormity of her hump, took me like a bird between her cicada's limbs and gobbled me up. This is how, choking in happiness, I became the Perfect Proprietor.

*

There's no doubt that desire exists independently of persons; now that I'm old and no longer hope to see the object of my adolescent love again, I live and relive each instant of my idyll, continuing my erotic explorations on my own. Nobody can understand the feeling of adoration to which that lead-covered box, that parasite gave birth in me: if destiny placed it in my path once again, I don't know what folly I'd be capable of. Clara yielded to my passion, a bit surprised at the violence of my ardor, a bit jealous of that part of herself I preferred to any other. She got thinner from day to day and the hump swelled at the same rate: her hands, long and delicate like lianas, lashed the air with jerky movements of madness, her face was always hidden, for her neck bowed beneath the additional weight, and her eyes, turned upward in an effort to see what was happening in front of her, awakened in me the rage of a stallion before the wild expanse of a crupper.

We lived every instant together. I slept in her bed, one hand crowning the hump; I ate with her at the big table; I broke the water of her bath with my boyish puny body, incompletely decorticated. Clara was happy; she'd dress in bright colors; smiling—she who never used to smile—her head carefully tilted, without being urged she'd offer me my share of pleasure. But that didn't last very long, either: despite her happiness, Clara was dying. She was one of those creatures meant to live in the dark, without air, without satisfaction of any kind, in a vault at a bank, a cold room, or a glass jar. If, temperamental and unhappy, she was able to live because she braced herself, thinking only of the struggle, once she had found happiness, all that was left was for her to disappear.

As for the hump, it was in full flower. The very hot weather suited it so well that Clara let herself be eaten up without noticing. All-powerful, immovable as a rock, the hump was for me the symbol of eternal life: that rock was alive, depriving me of all sense of direction. It made no difference that I could see death on my mistress' diaphanous face, almost brush against it, I was very much too obsessed with the frantic hump to think about saving the woman. A selfish person, I couldn't believe that with Clara's death the word END would be inscribed at any point along the route I was taking: the hump was my life and if Clara's, a pale shadow, faded as she groped her way along, I didn't miss her, for my priapic love was sufficient unto itself. But disaster came. Death described its capricious arabesques closer and closer until one day when I found Clara lying on her belly, on the bed with velvet curtains, her face buried in a plush teddy bear. I felt no fear, for the hump seemed even more alive than ordinarily; I felt a heart beating beneath its membrane, virgin of all other mortal contact than that of my hand. Clara was scarcely breathing. The light swayed to the rhythm of a boat; the woman looked like a ridiculous puppet under her frizzy hair and her slow myopic eye rasped my face. Without pity, I threw her nightgown over her head. Naked, the hump wriggled in the lamplight, my hand pressed with all its sleepy weight on its crest; it was burning hot.

Clara died around four in the morning. The memory I have of that night is one of a fullness I've never found again; banks of fog hovered around me; insecurely anchored to my skin, I went mad.

The hump triumphed without proffering a gesture: a wave of shadow passed over the body, the death-rattle suddenly stopped; Clara was gone. Tenderly, I uncovered the face of the deceased: I didn't close her eyes, for their expression pleased me, but I put on her head the hat of crow feathers and Parma velvet she wore to town and I stretched out the sheet over her legs. A mute can't utter a cry of distress, so I didn't weep, but my heart thumped in my chest and my hands were trembling. The hump was cooling and its magnetic power was wobbling on its base. I laid my palms on it, I kissed it, I licked its wounds, but it was leaving, in the fatal indifference of excrement. I jumped on the bed to battle with the enemy. During this struggle, sweaty body to sweaty body, I tore my throat hollow, wishing to engrave my despair on the walls of its soul; the complete possession, hoped for so much, was but dust in my mouth: the hump no longer knew me.

Under a curse, hiccupping with vexation, I wandered through the house all day. Fat Satan was getting drunk near the bed, the clock added the triviality of its voice to the pains of mine, the hump sighed like a fat woman after exertion. Toward evening my timid rancorous nature carried the day: I took the Count's knife and, without thinking, attacked the parasite. The blade sank in with a sucking noise; outlined in red, still holding onto the shoulder of its victim like a monstrous leech, it fascinated me, sweeping me into vertigo. I had had the taste for it that certain men have for women of lighthearted vice. I had felt myself irresistible; disappointed, I cut the sucker to ribbons, astonished at its majestic appearance under the rain of blood, but in no way worried about the consequences of my gesture. Finally I had to lay off. A transparent mist floated between my eyes and the form lying on the bed, and I had no other ambition, now, than to sleep, for my body, too, was but a corpse, a voiceless corpse still breathing. I lay down in that swamp that had once been the rug and slept heavily.

The police woke me. The doctor was examining Clara: he was probing her poor belly with his tweezers, ignoring the collapsed hump, ignoring me too. The newspapers declared that my mistress had died of cancer: no one paid attention to me, despite Satan's unfavorable deposition; the house was sold, the hump buried.

Since then I live quietly with my own hump, my tongue— at last loosened—and the little crab incomprehensibly found near the body; some days I have the impression he looks like me.

Sumatra
holding a
sword

7663240
poste 328

Joyce M

JOYCE MANSOUR

Infinitely . . . on the Grass

Often four, sometimes three, never alone; the siesta hour was the best of the day. In heat, I suppose, my mother would go to and fro on her commode with the well-placed hole; an embarrassment but not embarrassed, she would linger, though not invited. Arnaud smoked cigarette after cigarette. The couch, love's cinder track, would collapse beneath our bodies. Arnaud couldn't stand boredom.

*

It was almost always in the afternoon.

*

"One of these days, I'll beat that old owl's head in," exclaimed Arnaud, speaking of my mother. Her pursed lips got on his nerves. "You look like her," he'd say to me, without unzipping, and I had to climax just like that, in front of her, upon command, without tenderness or trombone. She'd go off with dignity, then, toward her commode, to wait for dusk by the kitchen window.

Arnaud's friends smoked almost as much as he. They were dirty, good sports under their rolled collars, and without respect for the furniture. "Why grieve? Let your mother do the work, with the mouth she has, she must *like* housework." Arnaud couldn't put his cigarette out anyplace but on the rug, and his friends, imitating him in everything, followed his example. My mother would have liked to be able to ignore the true tenor of my relationship with Arnaud: she'd have preferred to rest peacefully on the green couch, her eyes blurred by the tears of the woman announcer in mourning, her feet up, her soul at peace.

*

"You could have waited to see me under the ground before defying me, every day at siesta hour. *I* never looked at any man but your father," she'd caterwaul if I got up in a rush, without touching dessert, to call the elevator, answer the phone, close the window, dress, undress, anything to keep moving about as I waited for my lover's noisy arrival. The old woman complained but, when the moment came, she was always the one who opened the door to Arnaud. Stammering, her tongue heavy with a thick coating of shame, her toad's legs flapping and her wide-mesh sex gaping, my mother couldn't refrain from greeting him with the ceremonial due a king. "She's outdoing herself, your old woman is," Arnaud laughed the day that, there in the hallway, under the wrought-iron lamp and the general's portrait, she voluntarily presented him with my father's pipe and slippers. A gesture that didn't keep him for a moment from walking about, dressed only in the hairy thighs of his dark mate, artistically draped around his neck, and his perpetual cigarette, quickly lit, extinguished in dirty fashion, never put down without the intention of doing harm, naked before my mother's horrified eyes.

"Invite him to lunch with the super-nuncio," the old woman proposed the day Arnaud forced me in front of her, on my knees on the rug. My happy mother, who thought an official lunch could transform my friend!

"You'll see," she growled, her hands clasped to her sunken bosom, "he'll learn good manners in the end."

*

One of his old mistresses, on the Quai de Béthune, saw to Arnaud's needs. Guided by self-interest, he consented to go

visit her once a month and, in spite of my disgust with everything that had to do with his old ways, I'd go along with him
regularly to his benefactress' home. Mme S—— lived alone,
certainly not because she liked to, or even from force of habit,
but rather by force of circumstance: no man could tolerate for
long the sight of her diseased skin next to his own, without
thinking of death. "A blind gravedigger, that's what you need,"
Arnaud used to say to her as he left her, disconsolate, on the
threshold of her dusty apartment, eternally in her velvet dressing gown, marked, like her skin, with innumerable shallow
wounds.

"Come back," she'd plead, looking me full in the face . . .
but Arnaud's thoughts were already someplace else. At the bird
market, for instance.

"I'm not a blackbird," cries the blackbird, stamping its foot
on the bottom of its cage, and a woman's hand seems to soften
the air around all that marble. Arnaud becomes more human
among birds. Maybe I'll be happy for a few moments without
explosions of fury or needlework. There's a smell of flowers and
the infernal magic of children's dreams. "Goodby, you easy
woman." Arnaud has disappeared already.

"There's nothing more we can do," Mother threw at me
after one of those outings. "I don't even dare face the concierge,
anymore."

War. Mother was in love with Arnaud. From then on I
knew she was dangerous. Like a smelly pitiable blind alley, she
was going to finish up, of course, on a doorstep, a stairway,
Arnaud's stearic lair. I wasn't afraid of losing my friend between
her thighs, I feared (I had my reasons) that she'd lose face, yes, I
dreaded my mother's final humiliation when confronted with
Arnaud's porcine teeth and enormous laugh. What a mockery,
that wrinkled pubis under its scrap-iron curls. Those dugs,
turned blue, that hesitant gait couldn't satisfy him. She set my
teeth on edge.

In the evening I'd watch out for that furtive shadow. She'd
bedeck herself in borrowed plumage, in front of her dressing-
room's scalloped mirror. She'd rub her body with tumultuous
creams, try on hats, prepare herself imaginatively for the
moment when smoke from the masculine lamp would blacken
her fine makeup. She bored me.

At my request, Arnaud no longer came to take his siesta with us. "I'll go someplace else," he growled, slamming the elevator door without giving me time to finish my sentence. "I don't give a damn for your reasons," he yelled from the elevator shaft.

"Where's Arnaud going?" Mother, dripping with lace, perfumed and impure, was getting ready to pity me. "He'll be back," she added, confident in my power.

"Don't count on it."

"*That's* a surprise."

"Excuse me, Mother, I'm only his friend now, a woman like so many others."

"I don't understand what you're talking about" (she wasn't smiling anymore). "Invite him," she insisted anxiously. "Invite him for tomorrow."

*

Then came days of regret upholstered in gray silk. I twisted my ring frantically around my finger. I drank too much coffee. I was a bag of nerves and Mother, driven by the craziest illusions, prowled around me like a crow in the festooned vines. She was hoping I'd leave. I didn't dare leave her alone. With my head on her knees, I'd listen to time falling, drop by drop, into the sink. There wasn't much left for us to say to each other.

*

Astonished by so much mystery and indifference, Arnaud went on the offensive.

"Here I am!" (He seemed to have lost weight.)

"Yes," Mother acknowledged, pushing me to the back of the hallway.

"I'm alone," he said mistrustfully.

"Yes," she answered, following him into the drawing room without throwing me even a glance.

*

She locked the door.

"Oh, I get it," said Arnaud with a laugh. Then silence.

*

He's kissing the breast that gave me life! What an inheritance!

An hour went by, then two. My blood flowed slowly along the sidewalks. How far does she want to push happiness? I couldn't even appreciate the bitter taste of waiting. Exhausted, beyond suffering, I ate nervously, with my cat for company.

*

"And that's that," declared Arnaud, closing the door behind him, "now she'll spare us her impertinence. See you tomorrow," he shouted back, as he rushed downstairs. "See you tomorrow!"

"See you tomorrow." In my mind, I was already following my mother's hearse.

*

"The police? You can't be serious, little girl." Mme S—— clutched her dressing gown about her thin shoulders connected by numerous little bones with badly fitting joints. "Take my word for it, one has to learn to live with one's misfortunes." I could see the colors decomposing on the walls. I knew her refrigerator was empty. With what irreproachable memory was she building a nest?

*

"Otherwise make little cookies out of your bad luck, gossip, little packages, envelopes . . . What do *I* know? You have to learn how to economize, to use up left-overs . . ."

"I'll not forget," I said as I left. Thank God, I've got other friends.

*

I made so much noise with my ax that they put me in a cell.

*

You could have gone about it some other way," grated Arnaud in hostility. (He'll never forgive me for my family spirit.) I tried to kiss him, to shut his mouth. "I'll be back," he said, "make sure you're alone."

"To Sainte-Anne," cried the cabby, and the wind took the rest . . .[1]

---

1. Sainte-Anne is an asylum for the insane mentioned in André Breton's *Nadja*, where an attack is leveled at those who presume to treat the mentally ill. Breton's remarks (see *Nadja*, trans. Richard Howard [New York: Grove Press; London: Evergreen Books, 1960], pp. 136-142) brought protest from medico-psychological circles (see the documents published with Breton's *Second Manifesto of Surrealism*, in André Breton, *Manifestoes of Surrealism*, trans. Richard Seaver and Helen R. Lane [Ann Arbor: University of Michigan Press, 1969], pp. 119-123).

MARCEL MARIËN

1920–

Born in Antwerp, Marcel Mariën was seventeen when he met the surrealists of the Brussels group, René Magritte, Paul Nougé, and Louis Scutenaire. He first participated in a surrealist group show in London, the year after the International Surrealist Exhibition held there in 1936.

In 1946 Mariën edited the special number of the New York magazine *View* devoted to surrealism in Belgium. Eight years later he was to found his own magazine, *Les Lèvres Nues* (*Naked Lips*). He produced and directed, in 1959, the film *L'Imitation du cinéma*, a short subject about a young man's crucifixion complex.[1] Since 1967 Mariën has frequently exhibited his collages, drawings, paintings, sculpture, and objects, his creative productivity justifying the title given the catalog of one of his shows, *Homogeneous Heterogeneity* (1972).[2]

Under the imprint Les Lèvres Nues, Marcel Mariën has published an important collection of texts (two volumes of the writings of Paul Nougé, for instance), without which writing the

---

1. Space does not permit discussion of the wider implications of this film. See, for additional information, J. H. Matthews, *Surrealism and Film* (1971), pp. 122–129.
2. See also Mariën's *Trattato della pittura ad olio e aceto* (1972) and his *Crystal Blinkers* (1973).

history of surrealism in Belgium—something Mariën, by the
way, regards as a futile undertaking— would be impossible.
And yet Mariën has banished "surrealism" from his own voca-
bulary. He has his reasons for doing this, with such thorough-
ness that throughout the first series of *Les Lèvres Nues* (1954-
1960) the word occurs only twice—once used ironically, incidentally: Mariën believes the word "surrealism" lends itself to
such confusion as to be an impediment, when one is defend-
ing "the rigorous complex principles characteristic of the surrealist spirit." Hence his deeply felt need to dissociate surrealism as "an attitude of mind" from the "official" surrealism
centered on André Breton.[3]

Mariën's refusal to take a place beside those led by Breton
certainly shows him to be no respecter of persons. So does the
second series of *Les Lèvres Nues*, launched in 1969, which grants
no mercy to anyone falling victim to its editor's ferocious sense
of humor. But devastating word play, sarcasm, and calculated
provocation are but the outward signs of a point of view that
gives weight to the title of a volume of Mariën poems published
in 1973 as *L'Ancre jetée dans le doute* (*The Anchor Cast into Doubt*).

It is easy, no doubt, to see that the man who, calling it *Le
Marquis de Sade raconté aux enfants*, wrote a humorous version of
Sade's *Juliette ou Les Prospérités du vice* for the fifth number of *Les
Lèvres Nues* (June 1955) is the same man who, in 1970, entitled
one of his collage-paintings *Trois Spermatozoïdes allemands tra-
versant l'Atlantique* (*Three German Spermatozoa Crossing the At-
lantic*). It is more difficult, perhaps, to recognize in the author of
Le Cœur sur la main (dated October 30, 1953), published in René
Magritte's magazine *La Carte d'après nature* (*The Map from Life*
[January 1954]), the artist whose collage *La Tendresse aussi*
(*Tenderness once again*[4] [1972]) shows the contents of a box of
fancy cookies, numbered for identification, the numbers referring us to various parts of the female genital organs.

---

3. Mariën made his position clear during a radio inteіview conducted by
Christian Bussy. See the catalog *Marcel Mariën: Rétrospective & Nouveautés 1937-
1967*.

4. This is the translation given in *Homogeneous Heterogeneity*.

MARCEL MARIËN

The Children's Marquis de Sade

There once was a fairy whose name was Juliette. She was gentle, graceful, and beautiful, and they called her also the Apple Fairy, after the two apples she always wore on her chest. These apples were round and smelled good and she offered them to all who asked to be able to roll them over their tongues. Now, although everyone bit into them, they were nevertheless always full and whole and of perfect shape.

In the same country where the fairy lived, there was also an ogre who was called Saint-Fond. He was a horrible nasty, who sowed desolation wherever he happened to go. He was armed with a big dagger fourteen and a half inches long that he wore attached to his body and this was the instrument with which he perpetrated his horrible heinous crimes. This dagger was magic. The ogre by the way had been good, and would have remained so if, when he was seven, while he was still only a little boy, a wicked fairy who had the name of Nature had not cast a spell over him in the form of this dagger, which she had joined so skillfully to his lower abdomen that it was no longer possible to detach it. And so, inseparable from this treacherous weapon, the little boy grew and became in spite of himself the terrible ogre who brought sadness to the countryside.

But many other marvels were told of this dagger. How, for

example, when it was not in use it was limp and soft, as if it were nothing but the sheath of skin enclosing it. But every time a victim came before the ogre, the terrible dagger would swell hugely, until it burst through the end of the sheath, and then it stood up with such energy that it irresistibly carried along the ogre, born good, who thus had to participate willy-nilly in the evil deeds his magic weapon compelled him to carry out.

One fine summer's afternoon, the sweet fairy Juliette was out gathering flowers in a meadow when, suddenly, she found herself face to face with the horrible Saint-Fond. No sooner had they caught sight of one another than the dagger swelled beyond measure, leveled at the fairy. It was thick and red, and you'd have thought it was from perpetually gorging itself on blood that it took that fine scarlet shade making it only the more terrible to see. But Juliette was not afraid and, instead of running away, she approached the monster and started to laugh. "Look, your lordship," she then said, pulling up her dress. And by a magic effect she made a fresh wound appear on her body. "Why then would you wish to wound me, since I am wounded already?" And with her delicate fingers, Juliette separated the edges of the wound just a little, as if to show that it was indeed real. And the ogre could see that the inside of the wound was pink and very deep. But the magic dagger was not the least bit abashed. It charged at Juliette, carrying the poor ogre along with it, and it had no sooner thrown the good fairy down on the grass than it began to dig into the marvelous wound furiously, plunging in up to the hilt.

After a moment the dagger came out again but as it wanted to drive itself elsewhere into the fairy's flesh, immediately at that very spot, anticipating its penetration, a new wound appeared, into which the sightless weapon thrust in a frenzy. During this time Juliette, who was staring into the eyes of the ogre bending over her, recognized deep in them the gentle glance of the man who had been born good and she felt great compassion for him. She held out to him one after the other the apples she wore on her chest and forced the ogre to taste them. He nibbled them gently, so that the fairy was moved to tears. With a lithe, adroit movement she rid herself of the dagger bruising her and knelt at the ogre's feet, forcing him to get up. Courageously, then, she brought her little mouth to the terrible dagger and although the latter was of enormous proportions, she succeeded in taking it in, letting it slide gently between her lips. After a moment, and without her attitude giving any warning of this, while the dagger was thrust so far into the back of her throat that she almost gagged, Juliette, suddenly bringing her teeth together, bit off the magic dagger level with the belly and briskly spat it out on the ground. At once the monstrous weapon could be seen, as though taken with convulsions, wriggling the way a snake does, growing quiet, and finally changing to stone.

Freed of his abominable instrument, Saint-Fond was no longer an ogre. He had become a good man once more. And so he was able to marry the fairy, but, a curious thing, they had no children.

MARCEL MARIËN

Wearing One's Heart on One's Sleeve

> You can see very well that, when
> you write to someone, it is for him
> and not for you: you must therefore
> less seek to tell him what you think
> than what pleases him the more.
> —Laclos, *Les Liaisons dangereuses*

> These things have to be done.
> —Chaplin, *Monsieur Verdoux*

Isabelle was a coquette. She hardly ever showed herself with
her hands bare. As a result, this sometimes became something
of an obsession with her. She had no patience with the fashionable world in general. She liked to appear in it, though, to show
herself off. But without touching, without dirtying her hands.
She lived alone with herself in her apartment of mirrors.

   I must tell you also that her hands disappointed her a bit.
She could have wished for more beautiful ones.

*

I don't remember too well what prompted me that day. I think I wanted to protect Isabelle from the mortification she might feel when I reported to her that the show we had intended to see together had closed the night before. She had her heart set on it. To the point where she owed it to herself no doubt to blame me for not having taken her in good time. I was grieved at her disappointment, about which I felt a bit guilty and was thinking about some fortunate compensation that would release me from that burden, from those unstated recriminations I would surely imprint on her face, in the evening, when I saw her again.

Chance happenings in the street are full of traps. Just as I had stopped in front of a shop selling gloves, it began to rain.

I went in.

*

Inside, I found myself a bit perplexed. But I didn't think I ought to walk out. I consulted the saleslady. She didn't know Isabelle's hands, or her tastes. I knew the latter to be fairly hermetic in these matters, very unforeseeable despite my being used to them. To add to my difficulty, I couldn't remember her hands, how big they were, what size glove should be selected. So as to put an end to the saleslady's somewhat aggravating solicitude, I abruptly decided in favor of some black gloves, of delicate transparent mesh. It seemed to me they would look well on Isabelle's hands, of which I could imagine only the softness and not the disgrace she attributed to them, unjustly in my opinion. This way, they could be seen a little, even so, as one can see a joyous pure sky through frosted glass.

*

Evening came and I met Isabelle.

Now, she valued her nontransparent gloves, and insisted upon keeping her hands secret. The transparency that had appealed to me seemed to her in questionable taste. Long before, she had made a study of its defects, condemned the very idea of it. However, at my insistence, she agreed to try them on.

The matter was settled like that, all at once: her hands were small, the gloves were not.

*

Then, by fits and starts, a sort of drama got under way.

I no longer knew what to do with those gloves she had no use for. They weighed me down; their transparency, their size, everything conspired to make Isabelle begin taking umbrage. All that was needed, now, was to add fuel to the fire. And so I hastened on to my own destruction.

I can't say I had to ration out my money. That would have been difficult. I had to reckon with Isabelle, but also with my funds. I did try to save the situation, however. I suggested Isabelle accompany me to the shop, the next day, to try to exchange her pair for one more to her taste, more expensive if need be, but with which she could be delighted. That way, I'd not lose the benefit of my first purchase; I'd only have to pay the difference.

At those words, the smoldering fire became a bright flame. Isabelle couldn't conceive of taking such a singular step. She pointed out, not without acrimony, that she had asked me for nothing. She informed me next that I was even less a judge of glove shops, if that were possible. There, too, one found shades of quality. The one to which my steps had taken me was naturally at the bottom of the ladder. Thieves, trash. They'd make fools of us, as they'd already made a fool of me. No; I ought instead to take back the gloves she had no use for and get a refund. After, we'd go together to a good place. There at least we'd get satisfaction.

Here I displayed my timidity. I dreaded just as much as their obsequiousness when one is making a purchase the icy contempt shopkeepers reserve for dissatisfied customers. I'd just as soon jump in the river. (It's possible too that I began to feel a little weariness.)

Isabelle, maybe more experienced than I in the subtleties of these transactions, set about losing herself in the labyrinth of my embarrassment. Not without a touch of sarcasm, she asked me if she had better take the gloves back for me. I protested, but the question had been enough to revive the flame and make room for it. Isabelle then considered my making a gift of my present to a lady she knew and to whom I owed a kindness. It even seemed to her that I couldn't decently shirk the gesture.

She didn't know however that, rankling in my mind, where that lady was concerned, was an old sordid business of pots and pans, of bread doled out in stingy fashion in hard times. I said nothing about it, but my silence anchored me to refusal of this unforeseen action, all the more firmly because it provided the occasion for my displeasure to grow. To the point where the lady was blackened, in my mind, maybe a bit more than she deserved.

The transparency of the gloves nevertheless was being eliminated more and more with each phrase. It was beginning to cut us off from one another strangely.

*

For all that, I didn't give up the idea of saving myself. I knew Isabelle had been dreaming for a long time of special gloves that came up to the elbow, three times the length of ordinary gloves. They were also three times the price.

When the battle was at its height, I made an heroic resolution. I could refuse Isabelle nothing that was in my limited power. I forgave her therefore for being scarcely concerned about the state of my fortune, making it only just possible for me to buy her those gloves, without leaving anything over, in the agreed time.

But at the same time I couldn't accept her innocence, either. Love demands, rather naïvely, a flawless mirror. The contempt she had shown at the beginning seemed to me all the less permissible because the gift was an unfortunate one. This very failure of my effort to please her ought to have touched her, even more than success. Anyway, with her mockery turning to blame, how could I have refrained from regaining the advantage by turning her shafts back against her, by this odd sudden change of roles?

She must have felt the arrow tip coming, sharp and very slow. She raised objections. I insisted. In the end, as though to please me, she accepted. We decided therefore to meet the next day and we tried to talk of other matters.

*

Isabelle proceeded with what was holding her attention: arranging her hair. This took a certain amount of time. The moment came when she had to dry it over the gas flame.

That was when—she and the fire coming together—I managed to turn the latter into a source of intense heat. As I had just crossed my legs, I suddenly remembered there were holes right through the soles of my shoes. I thought of myself, thought I owed it to myself to take them into account sometimes. It was bound to rain for the next few days, and Isabelle, perhaps noticing my difficulty, was bound to bear me a grudge because of it.

Now, that wasn't all. We would see one another again at noon. As Isabelle had to go back to work at two o'clock, she would have little time at her disposal. I was going to take from that time. And so, in addition, it was becoming impossible for me not to invite her to lunch.

I sank back into ominous calculations. Three hand's lengths, to which had just been added the length of the pair for which she had no use, and now the cost of the meals; her gloves would come more or less to her shoulders. It's true that, for my part, if need be I could go without, at the restaurant, and make do with gazing at her. But I knew her generosity would prevent her coming to terms with the injustice of such a pose.

As ill at ease as it was possible to be between that heavy hammer and that all too beautiful anvil, I could find no better way out than to let myself be sucked in further. All at once, Isabelle's thoughtlessness where I was concerned appeared unjustifiable to me. Wasn't it fitting to answer selfishness with selfishness?

At the very first, I hadn't been able to see that no argument from her would have been able, now, to divert me from the plan of imposing on her the gloves she dreamed of. The most convincing argument could only have made my decision firmer. Contrary to these feelings, I caught myself thinking she'd accepted altogether too easily the chance to see a desire fulfilled. I thought I saw pretense in her reticence. But, all in all, what was I up to, if not reproaching her with having placed me, with my full consent, in a thorny situation; just as I was reproaching myself with that curious obstinacy in giving her as a gift something she didn't dream of asking me for? I was getting entangled in the sublime, floundering in the ridiculous. In short, I invited her to put off the purchase until times were better.

Obviously, I said nothing about the lunch or the shoes. We really had enough to do to get out of the tangle over those gloves.

*

Isabelle didn't display too much anger over this about-face. It was enough for her to feel angry. Who could have suspected that, buying a pair of gloves with the purpose of giving her a pleasant surprise, I would end up in a curiously roundabout way giving her nothing but a slap? That was the point my gesture had reached. The flames, rising to the ceiling, had invaded the whole room.

Isabelle's hair having dried meanwhile, it seemed fitting that I should take my leave. I made to kiss her, she evaded my lips. We settled for a handshake, limp and anonymous, and we parted. She, very cold, cheated of something she hadn't counted on at all, boiling with contempt—I, crestfallen, very displeased with her and with myself, with my capsized intentions.

*

But the gloves did not only weigh on my conscience. They remained with me in the flesh, strangely stripped of all affectation. I didn't know which hands to dedicate them to.

I tried all the same to get something out of them, since, anyway, I was their owner. Throw them away? That would have been an insult to the world's misery. I paused for a moment over an elegant solution: to lose them deliberately in some public place.

A restaurant for example.

*

I was already thinking over how I would do it when, all at once, I thought of Elisabeth's birthday. She loved me; I hardly loved her at all, being entirely preoccupied—as you've seen—with Isabelle.

All the same I sometimes thought of Elisabeth tenderly, of our long life together, shot through with joys and storms, broken off some years earlier thanks to her faults and mine.

Her birthday, in happy times, had always been a sort of cult for me. I showered her with gifts as best I could.

I looked at the gloves, I thought of her hands. I knew her to be unhappy. I imagined her joy at receiving something from me while it cost me so little. I arranged it so that the pair of gloves reached her through a third party. But without thinking for a moment that, overloaded with so many signs, weighed down with so many feelings already, she was not, all the same, rendered speechless, unable once again to clear herself an unauthorized path.

As it was, a while later as a result of those gloves I received a visit from Elisabeth, beaming and happy.

She didn't omit to thank me at once, to describe in detail her joy upon receiving the gloves. So much so that it seemed to me she exaggerated a bit. She didn't allow herself to wear them to go out, for fear she'd spoil them, or maybe that with their use, through a touching superstition of which she kept alive just the caress, the renewal of her hope would be brought to ruin. On the other hand, every night before falling asleep, she'd take plesure in trying them on, then running her hands gloved in black, and visible through the mesh, over the whiteness of the sheets.

Of course, they suited her to perfection.

"How nice of you," she said again, "to have thought of me! And how well you know my taste, how well you read me!"

*

A month later Isabelle and I split up. Without any fuss, what is more. We both felt it, all the same. But I knew the gloves had had some bearing on the maneuvers to which she'd been impelled so that things ended in our parting company. The gloves had been like a nasty glimmer cast on the face of a self she didn't know I had, of which I had no idea, that no doubt didn't exist, but that she was no longer able to efface. She got married without enthusiasm.

I followed her example, a little later. To Elisabeth, who had given me no respite since those too-beautiful gloves that went straight to her heart. She's completely won me back today. So much so that all I've left, for Elisabeth just as much as for Isabelle, is this hope that, with the help of chance, they don't happen to read this. Elisabeth could find here reasons perhaps to love me less, to imagine herself less happy; Isabelle, not to hold back on the downward path of a regret or of an indignation with no way out—in short, both to become confused even more.

*

Many years later, I found the gloves again, forgotten at the back of a drawer, soiled, no longer in use.

Only then did I think of Cinderella.

JEAN MARKALE

1928–

In his own words, Paris-born Jean Markale's *Dans la chambre d'Arianrod* was inspired by "a collage of drawings," These drawings presumably provoked verbalization of a theme in which Markale has identified an obsession. The latter has to do with an inquiry, focused upon the Welsh goddess Arianrod, relating to two of the books he has published, *Épopée celtique en Bretagne* (*The Celtic Epic in Britain*) and *La Femme celte* (*Celtic Woman*). In contrast with the formal character of these seriously researched volumes, *Dans la chambre d'Arianrod* typifies one form of response to myth engendered and fostered in surrealism.

At one extreme stands the probing and enlightening interpretation of myth patterns such as we find illuminating the surrealist mentality and sensibility in André Breton's *Arcane 17*. At the other extreme is imaginative transposition of similar thematic material, as in Maurice Fourré's use of the figure of Merlin in his novel *Tête-de Nègre* (*Black-Man's Head* [1960]) and Markale's text.

Citing as his source the thirteenth-century Welsh poem *The Book of Taliesin*, Markale concentrates on Arianrod, who, like others among the Children of Don, left her name to a constellation. While Llys Don ("The Court of Don") was Cassiopeia, and Caer Gwydian was the Milky Way (called Caer Wydian in modern Welsh), Caer Arianrod ("Arianrod's Fort") was Corona Borealis, the Northern Crown to which Markale alludes in his narrative.

In 1956 Jean Markale published a book devoted to the great Welsh bards, introduced by André Breton. Breton's preface to *Les Grands Bardes gallois* is particularly useful to us in that, incidentally, it helps situate the contribution made to surrealist narrative practice by writers such as Jean-Louis Bédouin and Jean Markale. Commenting on exegetal practice, Breton remarked: "It is amusing and disconcerting, according to the observer's turn of mind—when all those who understand anything about the matter agree in proclaiming that the quality of a poem depends as incompletely upon what it 'signifies' literally or seems to signify as that of a painting upon what it 'represents'—that textbooks, compelled by the trend in *feeling* to give more space from day to day to more or less hermetic works, increasingly overburden themselves with glosses aiming, at any price, at establishing once again the primacy of intelligibility over sensibility." Breton went on to insist that there could be no more deliberate way than this of resisting the movement of poetry during the last hundred years and more. He emphasized that "long before being reduced thenceforth to a means of utilitarian exchange between men," language meant "breaching the unknown," and "making a hole in the blue sky."

For André Breton, the poetic revolution culminating in our time has the consequence of demonstrating "the fallacious character of—I repeat—'literal' modes of apprehending language that have not yet abdicated or aspired to reconquest of the purpose for which it was originally destined." He announced in *Les Grands Bardes gallois* his conviction that these modes of apprehension must be opposed by "everything that can be developed in the direction of greater permeability" to what emanates from language "by virtue of intuition and analogical perception." In short, Breton as a surrealist appreciates that the writings of Aneurin, Llywarch-Hen, Myrddin, and Taliesin have a lesson to teach that may be learned, too, from Markale's *Dans la chambre d'Arianrod:* "From affective communication much more is expected—now and henceforth—than from total comprehension."

Dans la Chambre d'Arianrod first appeared in the second number of *La Brèche: action surréaliste,* in May 1962.

JEAN MARKALE

In Arianrod's Room

Arianrod, beautiful in appearance,
dawn of serenity,
will dispense about her city the
current of a rainbow,
a current that will drive out
violence from the earth
and destroy it. Over the world,
there will subsist . . .

—*Taliesin*

I pushed open a door and was in Arianrod's Room. It was a dark room and I did not know toward which latent ray of light beneath the battens of the floor I was headed. I stopped close to a darker mass and heard a voice saying, from very far off, as though stifled by clay and ashes, a voice saying, "Come closer, come further forward toward me, I will reveal to you the Circle of Silver . . . " I approached and discovered that, from the darkness, a very white light was slowly streaming in seven coronas about my face. And from those seven coronas emanated a fragrance of sandalwood. And from the fragrance of sandalwood sprang a sort of chimney of white stone, leaning as if it were going to collapse. Then I saw with amazement that from this chimney, in the wafting sandalwood, an imprecise form was coming into view: as a matter of fact, it was a pair of long legs raised toward me, with a hardly veiled rump. And the voice, inside the chimney, was saying, "Come and give me pleasure! . . ."I was far from inclined to refuse and, knowing that for a woman there is no more noble pleasure than being caught up in the workings of destiny, I took hold of those legs, of those thighs, of those buttocks, exciting them with my nails, squeezing them with my palms, gripping them with my iron fingers. The voice came to me with a more raucous, a warmer tone: "I was waiting for you; I am not disappointed with your caresses." This was an encouragement: I slipped my finger inside the flimsy underwear and could tell by touch that my caresses had not been without effect. Thus I sent this woman of whom I knew nothing, except the very essence, into a state bordering on the frenzy of a prophetess. I heard her cry out, "Take me! take me! but let the fruit of your enjoyment not run within me, for I am barren. All around you is where you should sow your seed if you want to know the Citadel of the Circle of Silver!" I took her and did as she had asked. Springing forth from her hot crowning distress, I spattered all the horizon about me. And the horizon became indented. A vast curtain drew back, showing a universe of stars and constellations, and in the silvery night pouring over me from that moment, each squall in that storm swirled like a star about the sun I had become. The light took on reality and the wind began to vibrate with all the power of fire. I saw a sleeping woman reclining on a rain of asteroids: the calm of her body petrified in the dust clouds of the unknown hurt me and I turned my eyes further toward a woman in a black coat, with bare breasts, the flower of immortality in her left hand, undulating along the folds of the great curtain. On a nameless planet, a smiling bearded king was smoking a French excise cigarette. Above, in an astonishingly subtle giratory movement, a luminary indicated to all the blessed hour when the secret beauties of the universe can be discovered. It was ten-ten, but I no longer remember whether in the evening or in the morning. Higher still, on Saturn, wearing gray diamonds on her head, dressed in a beach hat to ward off the ultraviolet rays, a woman was reading the latest Françoise Sagan novel with delight. On the orbit of Jupiter, an old man was sadly pacing the solitude of space. He carried over his shoulder a long curved scythe, in his right hand a lantern that shed a few pearls of red light every time a gust of wind came disturbing it. His beard was of hammered zinc, his eyes of bronze crystal. Above, I recognized it at once in the very heart of the Northern Crown constellation, was the City of the Circle of Silver, mysterious and shining like the thunderstorm's fiery sphere through the spring snows. My eyes were dazzled by it. The cold froze me, then the heat took me by surprise and became enjoyable to me. My pleasure and joy had reached their high point. And in my wonder I saw, in the very center of the City of the Circle of Silver, a woman whose torso emerged from a wave of sparkling lights. This woman was covering her long hair with dark silver. When she saw me, she smiled at me and said, "See my face. Rare are they who can boast of having glimpsed it. My legs and sex are on earth, under your legs, mastered by your sex. My face and bust are in my citadel. For I am Arianrod, the Circle of Silver, and one cannot mount to my face except from my sex. See, I am beautiful and strange. Take care not to lose yourself if you come pursuing me!" At that moment, I heard a noise and perceived high above the Northern Crown, on the orbit of a planet, an automobile of decrepit style that evidently had broken down. One of the car's doors opened; a man sprang out, throwing himself toward the space surrounding the machine with its thick fog. A few seconds later, a white shape swelled and the man, with his parachute, began to float interminably through a labyrinth of stars of all sizes and colors. I could make out this man's features easily and noticed that he had a long nose. There was no doubt about it, this was Cyrano de Bergerac. But while a furious wind began to shake all the pendants in my sky, like fruit on a tree, I heard crackling above my head. There, suspended from the distant ceiling, was a resplendent crystal chandelier. But from second to second it was becoming more and more brilliant, more and more blinding, so that I could not keep my eyes open. After a moment, however, I wanted to know how things stood: I discovered I was in Arianrod's room, dark, very dark, and that only a few dusty rays of light filtered in under the door through which I had entered.

PAUL NOUGÉ

1895-1967

Born in Brussels a year before André Breton, Paul Nougé
outlived the leader of surrealist activities in France by one year.

In collaboration with Camille Goemans and Marcel Lecomte, Nougé launched a series of tracts under the heading
Correspondance. The following year, 1925, he and his associates
made contact with Aragon, Breton, and Éluard, co-signing the
surrealist broadside *La Révolution d'abord et toujours* (*Revolution
First and Last*).

"I am terribly, wretchedly perhaps—an intellectual." This
confession in Nougé's diary[1] established a fundamental difference between his approach to surrealism and Breton's. It is a
distinction that may well have contributed significantly to giving
surrealism an orientation in Brussels markedly dissimilar from
its development in Paris. During a radio interview in which
Nougé was discussed, Lecomte was to remark: "At the beginning there was already in him the notion of intelligence, considered as a means of exploration and explosion: intelligence
conceived as capable of provoking a strong backwash, subversion."[2] As Nougé himself put it in 1928, speaking of intelli-

---

1. Paul Nougé, *Journal 1941-1950* (1968), p. 26, entry dated June 19, 1941.
2. See Christian Bussy, *L'Accent grave* (1969), no pagination.

gence, "I can't honestly trust in anything belonging to any other level of the mind."[3]

Nougé's *Journal* lets us see him defining his essential intellectual characteristic as "never losing control, never letting myself go, no spontaneity."[4] Far from sharing Breton's enthusiasm for automatic writing, then, Nougé was, in Lecomte's phrase, "a sort of Monsieur Teste," possessed of the kind of intelligence we associate with Teste's creator, Paul Valéry. Indeed, asked by Christian Bussy during a radio interview printed in *L'Accent grave*, why he wrote, Nougé replied without equivocation, "In the Valéryan sense of the word, to 'charm,' that is to say influence, hence to act upon the possible reader." On another occasion, he noted, "I write, I've always written for someone who is much more intelligent than I, much more sensitive than I, much more . . . Of whom I'm afraid. And who doesn't exist."[5]

Between February and April of the year 1928 three issues plus a supplement of the magazine called *Distances* appeared in Brussels under Nougé's editorship, its name derived from the phrase meaning "to keep one's distance." Asked later, "In the surrealist mind are liberty and revolt the same thing?" Nougé responded to Bussy's question with the one word "Necessarily." It was not, therefore, in his ultimate ambitions that Nougé kept his distance from Breton, but in his idea of the methods most suitable for attaining them. To him, distance implied intellectual detachment above all. As he wrote no later than 1927, "Surprise does not always come to us from the revelation of something quite unforeseeable, but also from the distance noted later between the thing we had imagined and the object presenting itself to us."[6]

Now the intellectual bent of Nougé's mind is clearly discernible, as are the reasons underlying his mistrust of literary devices and his opposition to the possibly haphazard nature of automatic techniques: "What it pleases me to give you, what really concerns you, I intend this to be the very thing I direct at

---

3. Paul Nougé, "La grande question," in his collection of theoretical writings *Histore de ne pas rire* (1956), p. 65.
4. *Journal*, entry dated June 18, 1941, p. 25.
5. Paul Nougé, *Fragments*, Second Series (1926-1941) (1969), no pagination.
6. "L'Occasion des sortilèges," *Histoire de ne pas rire*, p. 291.

you, *against you*, on which I count to lead you where I should like to see you and I am headed with you."[7] Stating his position slightly differently, he wrote in 1941, "Why do I happen to write, why do I imagine one writes with some degree of pertinence? Well, to disturb one's reader, to upset his habits, big and small, to *turn him over to himself.*"[8] Drawing an analogy with chess, he commented elsewhere, "But the supposed reader should be above all an opponent. An opponent before being beaten."[9] Hence he could assert in 1941, in an entry in his *Journal* dated June 18, "The circumstances, the mediocre circumstances of my life, have been such that all I've done of value has always been presided over by subversion, by offensive action" (p. 25).

Yet again in *Histoire de ne pas rire* Nougé admits to being dedicated to "that fairly exclusive cult of subversive intent, of traps, of machination" (p. 130). So as to remain true to his purpose, he proposes to "keep, once and for all, to what he does not know."[10] Such a declaration disposes of any illusions we may have regarding Nougé's use of intelligence as merely a means of anticipating the predictable. As he puts it in a statement that illuminates his *Hommage à Seurat*, "The *reality* of an object will depend closely on the attributes with which our imagination will have endowed it, on the number, the complexity of these attributes and the manner in which the invented complex fits in with all that pre-exists in us and exists in the minds of those like us."[11]

Hommage à Seurat ou Les Rayons divergents first appeared in Marcel Mariën's magazine *Les Lèvres Nues* (no. 9, November 1956). It was reprinted in a collection of texts by Nougé, *L'Expérience continue* (the title means both *The Continuous Experience* and *The Experience Continues* as well as *The Continuous Experiment* and *The Experiment Continues*), published under the imprint Les Lèvres Nues in 1966. The story dates from 1929.

---

7. Paul Nougé, *Fragments*, First Series (1923-1929) (1968), no pagination.
8. *Histoire de ne pas rire*, p. 127.
9. Paul Nougé, *Notes sur les échecs* (1968), p. 85.
10. Paul Nougé, *René Magritte ou les images défendues*, extracts published in the fifth issue of *Le Surréalisme au service de la Révolution* (May 15, 1933), published in book form in 1943; full text in *Histoire de ne pas rire*.
11. "La Lumiére, l'ombre et la proie" (1930), in *Histoire de ne pas rire*, p. 87.

PAUL NOUGÉ

Homage to Seurat
or
The Divergent Rays

1. *The Elegant Devotee's Story*

MacIggins is curious and sensitive. He dresses with care and
here he is entering a circus. No sooner is the canvas enclosure
behind him than a lemonade vendor offers him a full glass. He
drinks, pays, and walks on. A charming hand appears between
two pieces of canvas. He gallantly kisses this hand, very
touched by this fortunate portent. An enormous elephant
appears at the entrance to a tent. MacIggins is very surprised.
He turns away a moment, no doubt the better to savor and
soothe this overlively emotion. Sure of himself now, he wants to
see the bewildering object once again. But a tiny elephant stands
in place of the monster. MacIggins wonders if he is in his right
mind. Could he have been so mistaken? He leaps toward the
lemonade vendor. What do you see there? MacIggins keeps a
watchful eye on the lemonade vendor's face. The man looks
carefully: I see an enormous elephant, he says. Rather than
believe himself mad, MacIggins strikes the lemonade vendor in
the face and walks on.

Using an enormous brush, a man is putting up a poster.
The brush handle bars MacIggins' way. He stoops, the handle
comes down. He straightens up, the handle comes up. He takes

a step. The handle is level with his face. MacIggins decides to
crawl, and in fact gets by while the handle, raised to full extent
by the man putting up the poster, would not be in the way of a
giant. Straightening up, MacIggins, very satisfied with having
passed the obstacle, slips and crushes his top hat. He hesitates,
furious, puts the flattened hat on his head and goes off with
becoming dignity. And how little that trivial misadventure would
count, if a bigger concern had not been disturbing MacIggin's
pleasure. Now here he is again in front of the elephant's tent.
Everything is deserted in this remote part of the circus. A slight
noise: MacIggins jumps, but it is only a man—perhaps the bill
sticker—come from somewhere or other and sitting down on a
sack. You have to be pretty nervous or obsessed to take fright so
much in advance. But MacIggins will not let the chance go by
to clear the matter up. What is there in this tent?—An enormous
elephant. Oh no, a very little one.—An enormous elephant, I
assure you; anyway, I'm going to bring it to you.

This is something, all right, that would put an end to
doubts and restore calm and joy in MacIggins, if it were not the
man himself shooting out of the tent to fall at his feet, propelled
by some unknown force. Will the matter rest there? No, fortunately, since at the entrance appear side by side a big and a little
elephant.

MacIggins sighs with contentment. He is now free to taste
unadulterated pleasure. Why is it that once again he must turn
his eyes in the direction of the entrance of the tent, somewhat as
one turns with a certain feeling of pleasure to the memory of
some past misfortune. He has cause to rue it, for at once he is
obliged to take to his heels, howling in terror. He has, without a
doubt, seen a goose coming in the most natural way possible,
sheltering from the sun beneath a little parasol. MacIggins
begins to mistrust himself once more. Now he is face to face
again with the lemonade vendor. The vendor is careful; he now
has his face covered with a mask which he raises scarcely at all
to reply to the person questioning him. And this time MacIggins
will employ a ruse. The first time, the brutality of his questions
compromised everything, maybe. He gives a glance to the rear:
it is indeed a goose with a parasol—My friend, what do you see
coming over there? Could it not be . . . a horse in pants. (Let's
make a false allegation, they say, to get at the truth). The lemonade vendor too has sworn to be prudent. He looks carefully. The

goose has gone back into the tent and that really is a horse in pants coming out, for the moment. No doubt about it. My word, it's true, he says. A horse in pants. His mask affords him little protection from MacIggin's punch. MacIggins runs off terror-stricken by the others and by himself. He gives up his attempt to know. He will live, will come to terms with his uneasiness. What is going on inside him? What is happening to him? He goes back to his room to think things over and guard against everything.

II. *The Lemonade Vendor's Story*

Marcus' soul is as simple as his trade. His stand set up, guile plays a small part in his dealings with visitors. He counts more on surprise. No sooner is this elegant devotee within range than he holds out to him a full glass, without lingering over any canvassing that would risk compromising everything. Here's an empty glass. Marcus is not without psychology. But his psychology does not take the exceptional into account and will not fail one day to show its deficiencies. This visitor is strange; why oppose his idiosyncrasy? There is without any doubt an enormous elephant over there. And now Marcus, who is rubbing his cheek to reduce the burn from the slap, abandons any attempt to discover what offense he can have given his distinguished customer. One must know how to live with the inexplicable and to be content with a few precautions. Marcus leaves his wares for a moment; he returns, his face covered with a leather mask. He has, incidentally, no reason to regret this and perhaps it is curiosity that is pushing up the number of customers this way.

But here is the strange devotee. He seems calm, he even has a smile. Beyond a doubt, that's a horse in pants. Why not say so?

Now, to tell the truth Marcus does not feel the burning on his cheek, so great is his perplexity, no longer allayed by the idea of offense and madness, by all the explanations he can invent at this moment.

III. *The Dancer's Story*

You will see all right, this woman has so much charm she can do without a story. The moments of her life are linked together smoothly like the steps of her dance. And when she dances everything all around joins in her dance, to the point where she could then become motionless, remain suspended without our being granted the means to notice this. But now the dancer is resting, walking about through her kingdom of fine sand, ropes, nickel-plated bars, animals, and men before proving to herself, through her dancing, her dominion over this world. She pushes her bare arm between the two pieces of canvas of the tent to feel if the air is cool yet and she encounters two overhot lips. She quickly withdraws that hand, pulls herself together, and her well-directed dancer's fist strikes the importunate fellow's invisible face. Recovering her equanimity, she would like to go out a little, but a billboard, on which no doubt work is being done, completely obstructs the doorway. The dancer is patient, she is in a good humor, and anyway the billboard is sliding, moving off.

There is a young man in front of her, his face and gestures expressing a form of admiration so naïve and so pure that she really could not take offense or reply, with gestures similar to his, to a feeling she cannot even imagine being able to share. And if she smiles at him in the most gracious way possible, this is because he also has just smiled at her and if he lightly strokes her cheek with a hand trembling a little, why then would she not caress his face tenderly? Why be surprised at that marvelous dance he is doing in front of her, assuredly the most refined homage he could render the queen of dance and the most obvious sign of happiness? Why now refuse his extended hand, why not follow him, if he wants, to the ends of the earth? But for the moment it is only to the door of her dressing room, where he lets her put on traveling clothes suitable for disguising a dancer who is giving up her dominion for a purer triumph.

Now she is ready and slipping to the place of the final rendezvous. The wild animal that suddenly leaps across the passageway might frighten her. But he is there astride that dream bicycle gleaming in the crisscross beams from the spotlights at the pathetic moment during her aerial round dance. Let her go on with him then, the world lies before them. But is it a mere misfortune that causes the animal to get there before her, and the man to take off now with the beast riding behind, and to have just faded into the horizon of the plain, leaving her there, suspended in her prison of glass, in the shimmering empty kingdom of her purposeless dance?

IV. *The Ringmaster's Story*

The ringmaster is tormented by desires for which the circus is no longer enough. He is unlucky, but perhaps this has to do with the weakness of his imagination that has never offered him anything to satisfy them but a means as simple as it is unreliable. His accomplice, the cashier, has been dismissed. The combination of the two of them was not bad but he lacked craftiness. As for his replacement, he does not seem to understand in the least what it would be natural, after all, to expect of him. And so the ringmaster has decided to get rid as soon as possible of an individual he could not reckon with. That isn't easy. He can scarcely conceal his bad humor. And what especially exasperates him is the others' good humor, and most of all the Negro Jocco's. The Negro Jocco is obviously looking forward to lighting that big cigar. So the ringmaster will take it from him—who would dare blame him for this?—and now that he is preparing to light it, he is dreaming, a burning match at the tip of his fingers, of what is going to happen at the pay box where the cashier had innocently put his extinguished butt under the gasoline tank, something that has made it possible for the ringmaster, opening the faucet hardly at all, to soak it in gasoline and to take to his heels without being noticed. But alas! an unforeseen accident suddenly changes the favorable course of his thoughts. Interrupts it, even, for a moment; the explosion, at the moment when he has put to the cigar the match that was going to burn his fingers, was so violent. But the ringmaster is not a weak soul whom misfortune can divert from his designs. Jocco has run away at just the right moment. Left alone, he wipes his face and immediately invents a revenge that he wants to be a resounding one. He is wicked enough not to lack accomplices. Advantage will be taken once again of the constant absentmindedness of the cashier who is too honest. And as it happens that, to talk to Jocco, he has just left the caravan he uses as a pay box, the very similar caravan for wild animals will be substituted for the latter, so adroitly that he will not be able to notice. How could that cashier take notice of anything at all,

absorbed in his accounts and also having to protect himself
against chatter from his friend Jocco. There is nothing surprising
then in his getting quietly into the wild animal's cage, but what
is more so is seeing him run off afterward and, his turn of speed
and the strength of his cries prove it, unscathed. It would be
enough to reduce the deepest-dyed ringmaster to despair, for
ours has not even the consolation of seeing Jocco eaten up. But
as we are aware, he does not know the meaning of despair. He
will use this very terror that the event has revealed to him as the
most palpable defect in those he wants to destroy. It does not
take long, with some fur, to disguise one of his accomplices as a
lion and to give him to understand that this terror, repeated
through his good offices, cannot fail to be followed, after a short
delay, by the intruders' rout. There they are now, apparently
getting their second wind. The ringmaster loses only a minute
watching them. Could he foresee that in such a short time an
escaped lioness would be able to put his disguised confederate
to flight, simply by appearing, and that she is in his place now
and that *she* is the one he orders to hurl herself on his enemies
and that he is surprised at her stillness and silence, and that he
turns around, furious, and that now all his strength and
dexterity are not too much to bring him to a place of safety? This
is a shock that comes close to shaking the ringmaster seriously.
In search of his damned soul, he is strolling about rather
haphazardly. A shadow passes, not yet he, an escaped lion. He
leans for a moment against the canvas, a violent blow sends him
rolling on the sand. Everything is definitely in league against
him, for his accomplice whom he finds once again at this
moment, whom he justly blames for showing so little courage in
this affair, kicks over the traces, throws off his lion skin and
makes as if to go away. The ringmaster has to follow him, which
is humiliating, has to think of the charm of language to convince
him, to win him back. But it is all over. A slight sound, they turn
around—by what horrible prodigy has the lion skin, hopping
along, ambiguous, begun to follow them? The ringmaster this
time has to admit to being beaten; he runs off as fast as his legs
will carry him toward the countryside; he does not see his little
dog shed the lion skin, the better to follow him, and it is only
much further on and much later that he begins his calculations
all over from the beginning, that he casts doubt on the basic

incentives of his enterprise, that he gives up the attempt to get rid by some direct means of a cashier who is too honest, that for the first time arises in his mind the possibility of problems more adroitly posed and of solutions more subtle.

V. *The Negro's Story*

To Jocco, I really believe there is almost no past, I am sure there is no future. He is content, all in all, quite simply with taking the things of the world into favorable consideration. Desire is not so keen that regret draws tears from him, or rather, his desire adopts changing forms that protect him from regrets. Suppose an almost abandoned cigar tempts him, and suppose he denies having so nimbly stolen it, suppose it is stolen from him, he will be capable of laughing as ingenuously at the explosion that suddenly knocks his thief down and gives him a face with its color of dirty ink. And this is why, in a world that offers him only faces tense with joy, trouble, and hope, in a world of which he does not try to catch the faces by surprise—he does very well without understanding—here he is playing the flute for no reason at all and without having to invent any. In this way an inimitable music begins to exist of which the virtues are not slow to manifest themselves in that world, precisely, to which Jocco hardly belongs. And now, and this was not so much, in their cages and without his noticing, the animals are dancing, the mice are dancing, the elephant is dancing. But although living in the world of miracles, how could he not be frightened and run away if some mechanical bird, made simply to give out two or three sad notes without moving its wings, without leaving its small wooden base, starts dancing too, with all its limbs, in the most mysterious way possible?

His friend the cashier would be able to reassure him no doubt, being good and possessing knowledge and no doubt the mysterious power that goes with it. But his friend is completely absorbed in his account book which does not allow him to give particular attention to miracles. There he is, going back into the caravan that serves as his office. But what is happening? Why these cries, this headlong flight? Things shall not happen this way. Jocco is a faithful friend who knows all about the duties that go with friendship. The razor he takes from his pocket is of

sufficient size and sharp enough to allow him in the circumstances to fill, honorably, the role of righter of wrongs. They are
going to have a good laugh. But if he slips stealthily into the
caravan, if at first he catches sight of nothing that could send his
friend running, how will he be able to make himself understood
when he has escaped danger with an unprecedented leap, how
will he make those understand who do not know what one goes
through when one has a narrow razor as one's only weapon,
what one goes through upon suddenly feeling on one's face the
burning breath of a gigantic lion? But what is the use of trying to
translate and give an understanding of the unique or simply the
exceptional? His friend the cashier needs his help. He will do his
best to submit to his desires and to help him realize his plans.
With care he listens to the cashier's explanations and the effort
of his mind consists, as always when he must act, in separating
from a fairly mysterious whole in which are entangled the
reasons and circumstances that would not fail to mislead him if
he did not leave someone else to take care of getting to the truth
of the matter, in separating from all this the elements of a few
simple decisions by which subsequently he will abide stead-
fastly. And little by little he comes to consider it certain that all
the released wild animals he might meet subsequently are only
the cashier's enemies, disguised this way for their evil purposes,
that they are scarcely more formidable than in their human
shape and that, to win them back to better feelings, he has only
to give them a few blows with the club his friend has just
handed him. Jocco moves forward with the joyous tranquillity
that comes from a task well defined which we have made up our
minds to carry out honestly. And now just behind the canvas
there is a shape that touches him lightly, stands out against the
canvas and leans against it. Jocco has struck with all his strength
and the club falls from his hands and his triumphant laugh dries
up as he hears himself cursed by his friend whom he has just
beaten by mistake. Who would have believed a task so well
defined could meet such miscalculation in execution? He returns
to the hunt, swearing he will be prudent. This time, no doubt
remains, he vigorously strikes what is sliding along behind the
canvas and a formidable roar answers which, at the same time it
throws him twenty paces, sends doubt into his soul. If the wild
beasts to be encountered at this hour were not all wild beasts in

disguise and if . . . But Jocco has faith in his friend's word. He quickly pulls himself together and smiles at this coincidence that has made him lean his back against the inoffensive picture of a lion that a circus poster for the moment is pressing against his shoulder. This even cheers him up so much he would gladly linger tickling this high-colored snout if two horribly really alive paws, terrible lion's paws, did not suddenly burst through the paper to close about his shoulders. Where does Jocco find the strength to break loose, to run off? And who would blame him for not turning his head and for not seeing that the poster concealed the bars of a cage? And that he should drop exhausted onto a bench, how could one not understand this? But that he should at once recover all his energy to run off once again, leave the circus, disappear forever into the countryside, sobbing, pleading, pleading with the wild animal that has just planted its jaws in his flesh and that is unyielding before his leaps and cries. It is not known how Jocco perceived his error and how he had let himself fall into a wolf trap, left there by accident. That is a pity. He would have been curious to know the lasting strange effects an adventure of this kind was to have had upon him.

VI. *The Cashier's Story*

A certain simplicity, a certain clarity, a certain guilelessness that honesty confers and which gives it away to the least practiced eye is not without advantages. This is how Peter has suddenly found himself attributed that which another was denied and how he has become cashier in place of Emile, convicted of dishonesty and no doubt of dubious underhand deals with the ringmaster. And we have to believe the circus owner was not wrong, since the possibility of such curious deals Peter is forever incapable of conceiving. The only difficulties he meets in his new profession do not come to him from the more or less strongly marked incompatibility between some desire and certain conditions ill suited to serving it, but come solely from certain difficulties inherent in his job and which at first it is difficult to suspect. Thus, how to go about stamping out the impatience of that rather brutal crowd? He cannot count on habit (and anyway he has no habit that can serve him here) but instead on the resources of an ingenious imagination. And the fact is that measuring by the length of your arm rolls of tickets you are distributing to the public treating you violently is, indeed, the right way to disperse that crowd while giving it satisfaction. Peter derives special pleasure from his first minutes alone and voluptuously sniffs a big cigar he has put off lighting, only too often. But how short-lived pleasure is. Now a late spectator is coming up. Peter bends forward a moment over his tickets, but when he holds out to the gentleman the one he intends for him, this strange customer has disappeared. Peter picks up his cigar again and now suddenly the gentleman's head rises directly in front of his face, bumps against his cigar, explodes, a painted balloon hidden and shown again by this facetious child so well concealed against the pay box that Peter could not have caught sight of him. An experienced man does not let himself be caught by such a crude joke. And so when he again sees at his own height a painted balloon, quicker than lightning Peter stubs out his cigar on it and does not have time to be astonished at his mistake, for the old gentleman, burned in the face, does not understand this story very well and, despite his age, does not take long to drag Peter from his pay box and beat him appropriately. But then, whom can one trust; the ruses of the world are innumerable. It takes luck to make Peter notice, as she is just about to go through the entrance of the tent, something strange in the walk of that honest Negress who has just bought her ticket. And an explanation for this comes incidentally when he suddenly sees emerging from under her skirts five youngsters too nimble for him to be able to stop them taking seats in the circus they have not paid for. And how can one swear not to be caught again, since this other Negress whose skirt presents an unusual outline slaps Peter and raises a real scandal leaving him with but one recourse, to run off as quickly as he can, a scandal having to do solely with a discreet gesture from Peter, who emerged from his pay box to check, by lifting the woman's dress a little, if some cheat were not hiding there.

Peter has taken refuge in the circus and, mingling with the crowd of spectators, he is beginning to fear the Negress' anger a little less and to be in a good humor again. And, what is more, now a very charming spectacle confronts him. An adorable

woman's hand emerges from a slit in the curtain, sways most
graciously a moment in space, until that elegant young man
kisses it before Peter's eyes, with the greatest distinction. Who
then would blame Peter for wanting to take advantage of such a
windfall? And who could have foreseen the slap he receives?
We really must admit certain of us are unlucky. No indeed, to
Peter this opinion would seem not very well founded. This
charming picture presents itself to him merely, it seems, to
compensate him. And at first this picture is not dangerous, as
was the hand a moment ago. It is a poster recommending to the
public, in the most touching fashion and with a perfection that
would deceive the most demanding eye, the dancer's charms.
Peter, who has long been giving her admiring glances, can no
longer resist the desire to reach out a hand to her, and since with
a long prudent look around he has just made sure no one is
watching him, that the bill stickers have disappeared, how can
he resist the desire to caress tenderly with his hand the faithful
image of that cheek, of that arm, so tender there is something
miraculous about its bloom. And now moreover the miracle
does take place. The picture lights up, very quietly, with a sort
of smile, the eyes in the picture seek out Peter's eyes, the hand
in the picture responds to his caress, and the dancer, leaving the
frame of the doorway, takes a step toward her ardent admirer.
This is where no doubt a man will give, if he can, the measure of
his genius. Peter at once recovers the gestures that suit the
feeling he has and relate to other solemn gestures which are
quietly lost in the night of the world—Peter dances in front of
his idol, with the feeling that he really is freeing himself, that he
is escaping delightfully from something that would have made
him die right away, if he had not been able to give it the
marvelous pabulum of look and gesture that he is weaving
voluptuously about the attentive bewitched woman and that
ends in the throbbing immobility of a kiss from his lips on the
dancer's lips. And that winds up and is prolonged in limpid
happiness: Peter accompanies the dancer, with regular steps, as
far as the entrance to the ring where she is awaited by the
anonymous homage of a thousand eyes, hands, and mouths.

   It is appropriate here to admire Peter's nobility. Another,
perhaps, would have shut himself up and lost himself in the
universe of a love so marvelous. But he knows how to retain

among prodigies the sense of his being. He returns to the task
he has freely accepted and wants to see through successfully.
He ignores the chatter of his friend Jocco and puts off until later
being enraptured by the stories, such touching ones, he is
accustomed to telling him. Here is his account book. He goes up
the steps of his caravan. But Jocco has followed him, no doubt,
since, to attract his attention and take him from his work,
someone is touching his shoulder. Come now, have they not
understood he demanded to be left in peace? He turns toward
the nuisance and takes flight, giving the most piercing cry he
has uttered in his life. This is not without consequence, if you
find yourself suddenly facing the most bloodthirsty. lion in the
whole menagerie.

Out of breath, Peter lets himself fall onto a coil of rope, that
promises a certain amount of rest and the reflections imposed
on him by the circumstances. But now the elegant young man
whose happiness, in relation to a charming hand, Peter not so
long ago had occasion to appreciate, now this young man who
seems singularly troubled, comes to distract Peter from his most
urgent thoughts. How difficult existence is! Could he foresee
anyway where he would end up, listening this way with his
habitual complaisance to that young man's misgivings? And
that by wanting to show him the little elephant, while he
ignored the presence of the big one, he would mistreat him so
severely? But Peter has a sense of sequence in ideas. He comes
back to the story of the lion that is simply the result of an
unfortunate coincidence. Anyway those voices, only too well
known, that come to him through the canvas wall assume
responsibility, in spite of themselves, for making him understand. And everyone is going to have a good laugh if the
ringmaster imagines he will frighten him with that old bedside
rug. Here anyway is Jocco who will be of great help to him. And
both of them, armed with clubs, go off looking for favorable
encounters, Jocco in one direction, Peter in the other; they will
meet again in the triumph of a victory already assured.

But Peter alas! has not yet drained his cup of misery. It is
true he has not quite taken into account Jocco's silliness. By
mistake, as he was resting a little against the canvas wall, Jocco
has given him the blow from a club intended for the imitation
lion. And who knows if, this time, he was not going to give

himself over to despair, if the ineffable dancer had not just at that very moment appeared in traveling clothes, lost to the dance, won over by the man who is going to run off with her. Let us, then, get on the fine bicycle he will propel with a vigor increased a hundredfold by love. Already the soothing calm of the pure countryside is beginning to take effect. All Peter needed, to know at that moment the greatest number of delights it has been given man to bear without dying of them, was a kiss from the dancer. He turns toward her just a little, enough to discover the horrible snout of the wild animal that, without realizing, he has taken on behind. There is no reason to talk any more about Peter, who disappears in a scene of carnage in which our thought that has created him becomes diluted, loses its way, intervenes no longer.

BENJAMIN PÉRET

1899-1959

One of the founders of the surrealist movement in France and for a time (December 1924-July 1925) coeditor of the first French surrealist magazine, *La Révolution surréaliste*, Benjamin Péret, born in Rézé, near Nantes, remained faithful to surrealist principles right up to his death.

Péret brought to the practice of storytelling the same distinctive imaginative freedom that marks his verse collections. His qualities as a narrator are displayed in a "novel," *Mort aux Vaches et au champ d'honneur* (*Death to Cops and the Field of Honor*) written during the winter of 1922-1923, in a novella called *La Brebis galante* (*The Gallant Sheep*), and in a collection of tales published in 1957 under the title *Le Gigot, sa vie et son œuvre* (*The Leg of Mutton, Its Life and Works*).

Benjamin Péret's total dedication to the surrealist code made him the best exponent of verbal automatism, ruling out the possibility of compromise with literature, as surrealists condemn its practice. In consequence, while being ignored or misrepresented by literary critics who think they can confine surrealism within limits that give them confidence, Péret enjoys in surrealist circles an unrivaled reputation as a great poet, in that special sense with which the word "poet" is invested in surrealism.

In an important theoretical article called "La Pensée est UNE et indivisible,"[1] Péret claimed it to be no mere chance that, in France, the eighteenth century produced but one poet, the Marquis de Sade, who stood for violent protest against the essential postulations of an age that had deposed religion, it is true, but only to set up in its place another deity: reason. In the same context, Péret advocated the overthrow of "the values of conscious reality, seen through the deforming prism of rationalist education." In his *Anthologie des Mythes* he intimated that taking such a step is essential to the poetic process, "For the poet—I'm not speaking of amusers of all sorts—cannot be recognized as such if he does not oppose, by way of complete nonconformity, the world in which he lives" (p. 30).

Such a conception of the role of the poet takes its origin in a specifically surrealist interpretation of poetry to which reference is made in Péret's *Le Déshonneur des poètes* (1945): "Its innumerable detractors . . . accuse it of being a means of evasion, of retreating before reality, as if it were not reality itself, its essence and exaltation" (p. 72). His *Anthologie des Mythes* expresses Péret's conviction that "the poet with the active and passive collaboration of everyone will create exciting marvelous myths that will throw the whole world into an assault upon the unknown" (p. 31). In his long preface to this anthology Péret sought to show that "the marvelous is everywhere, hidden from the eyes of the vulgar, but ready to explode like a time bomb" (p. 15). While the same text tells us that "the flesh and blood" of poetry is magic, in "La Pensée est UNE et indivisible" Péret declared "the heart and nervous system of all poetry" to be the marvelous.

In Péret's short stories, irrationality is not a device to be exploited to literary purposes. It is, instead, essentially a viewpoint upon reality, the pathway to the marvelous. It stands, in other words, not for the distortion of reality but as a corrective to the distortion for which Péret held rationality responsible. And so humor assumes a central role in discrediting reason as the means by which we bring the world into focus. Humor represents at one and the same time rejection and affirmation: refusal

---

1. *VVV*, no. 4 (February 1944), pp. 9-13, translated as "Thought is *ONE* and indivisible" in the English surrealist magazine *Free UNIONS libres* (1946).

to be bound by the restrictions Péret associated with common sense; assertion of an imaginative liberation that shows the world as the projection of desire, not as the sterile reflection of the drearily familiar. Expressive of his opposition to the compartmentalization of experience, Péret's humor mounts an attack upon what Breton's *Anthologie de l'Humour noir* calls "the zone of opacity that alienates man from nature and from himself" (p. 505).

Une Vie pleine d'intérêt dates from 1922. *Un Plaisir bien passager* was written two years later. *Le Dégel* is dated 1942 and appeared for the first time, in a version by Ralph Manheim, in the June 1942 issue (no. 1) of *VVV*.

BENJAMIN PÉRET

A Life Full of Interest

Coming out of her house early in the morning, as usual, Mrs. Lannor saw that her cherry trees, still covered with fine red fruit the day before, had been replaced during the night by stuffed giraffes. A silly joke! Why did Mrs. Lannor think to accuse a couple of lovers who, the evening before, at nightfall, had come to sit at the foot of one of those trees? To leave there a souvenir of their love, they had engraved their entwined initials in the bark. But Mrs. Lannor had spotted them and, seizing a sucking pig, she had thrown it at the couple, shouting, "What are you doing there, artichoke children! Would you like a begonia, by any chance?

To her great astonishment the two lovers slid along the trunk of the cherry tree as if a pulley were hoisting them above ground. When they had reached the top, they flew off like swallows, describing ever-widening circles in soaring flight, then they fell into a neighboring pond. At once there was a terrifying racket comparable to that of 3,000 trombones, cornets, saxaphones, bass drums, bugles, etc., playing all at once. Mrs. Lannor was, with every right, stupefied at this, but did not want to show, and said, "I've been making pocket mirrors for a long time."

And she had stopped thinking of that incident. But this

morning, seeing stuffed giraffes in place of her cherry trees, she
could not refrain from making a connection between the event
of the evening before and that of today.

To clear the matter up, she decided to go to the pond where
the lovers had disappeared. The pond was empty and on the
mud carpeting the bottom—mud already dried—she saw hun-
dreds of dead marmoset bodies laid out, holding hunting horns.
In the middle of the pond rose an obelisk more than ninety feet
high, surmounted by a hat in musketeer style. At the foot of the
monument, holding hands, were the two lovers from the evening before. His head bent toward her, he was saying, "Gertrude!" and, she, in the same attitude, replied, "Francis!" And
so on, indefinitely.

Seeing this spectacle, Mrs. Lannor did not doubt she was in
the presence of the guilty parties. Already she was rejoicing at
having guessed so quickly and so well. She was rejoicing too
soon, even, for one of the marmosets sat up and shouted to her
with the purest Provençal accent, "Cast the first stone." An
excellent idea. Mrs. Lannor seized an enormous stone and
threw it in the direction of the lovers, but, having come within a
yard of Francis' head, the stone stopped in flight, a spark shot
from the stone to Francis' head, while a formidable sound of
broken glass could be heard. The sound had scarcely subsided
when from the base of the obelisk emerged a band of naked girls
holding hands and linked together by an ivy stalk wrapped
around their bodies like alpinists on a rope. They went off singing the *Brabançonne*, to dance around the obelisk. One by one
the monkeys got up to dance with them, some singing, others
accompanying these on their hunting horns. Mrs. Lannor felt
herself become very light indeed, and danced like everyone
else. If that poor Mrs. Lannor, instead of dancing, had looked at
what was happening at the top of the obelisk, she would have
no doubt died of terror.

The obelisk had opened like the two points of a pair of scissors. Between the two points separated in this way rose a thin
column of smoke in which all the colors of the spectrum were
represented. Above the column of smoke hovered a bicycle on
which a couple like Gertrude and Francis were making love. At
the very moment when the smoke was starting to form spirals,

the front wheel of the bicycle came away from the machine and slowly ran all along down one of the sides of the obelisk, coming to rest delicately on the head of one of the girls. The effect was immediate. All of a sudden every one of the girls burst into flame and in their place a little blue flame could be seen for a few seconds, a few centimeters high, then the girls were replaced by a cherry tree, half of which was in blossom while the other half was covered with ripe cherries.

Mrs. Lannor was so excited by this she forgot her age, so disturbed she forgot the imminent arrival of her nephew who so advantageously took the place of an eiderdown. "My cherry trees," she said, "So they were the ones!"

She ran toward the obelisk at the foot of which Francis and Gertrude were still kneeling and repeating their names endlessly. She was about to pass the line of cherry trees that formed a circle about the obelisk when she saw with stupefaction two of those trees between which she wanted to pass move closer together and block her way. She wanted to go around them, but if she edged to the right a cherry tree placed itself in front of her · and the same was true on the left. She wanted to run: the cherry trees did so too. All that was left to do was fly. She did this. Alas! the cherry trees followed her example. This game of catch could have gone on for a long time if suddenly Mrs. Lannor had not had an idea: "I'm going to dig an underground tunnel that will end up at the obelisk."

At once she alighted on the ground and strode home to fetch a pick and shovel. A moment later, she was at work. The cherry trees, to show her that her mettle did not impress them, dropped a rotten cherry on her head, from minute to minute. Mrs. Lannor raved and worked with increasing rage. Came the moment when the hole was deep enough for her to disappear into. Satisfied, she felt like a moment's rest and stretched out on the grass, her face to the sky. Scarcely had she stretched out when she saw a strange cloud assuming the form of a sausage equipped at each end with an enormous ear moving slowly like a fan.

"There they are again," grumbled Mrs. Lannor.

She was getting ready to go back to work when she saw that sausage was splitting longitudinally and something was being released from it: a cherry ten times bigger than a pumpkin that fell on the obelisk and remained stuck on it. Mrs. Lannor saw in this an act of defiance and got up.

"Oh! the gangsters! We shall see!"

And she seized her pick which she brandished above her head, but remained frozen in that position. She had just seen in the hole she had dug 7 or 8 jaws, opening and closing regularly. That was not enough though to frighten Mrs. Lannor. She pulled a carrot that she threw into one of the jaws, and this made a stream of yellow smoke come from all the jaws, spreading a sickening odor of incense. All the jaws disappeared and when the smoke had cleared away, Mrs. Lannor saw, seated at the bottom of a hole, a little girl holding a leek between her legs. The leek was growing visibly, so rapidly even that the little girl was ashamed and her stomach, soon followed by her heart and liver, left her body and went off with slow steps as though regretfully, while the little girl discovered that her back was covered with scales.

"And yet I'm not a mermaid," she whispered.

When she wanted to withdraw the leek, what was not her fright at seeing that henceforth it formed part of her body. After efforts long and painful, she succeeded however in uprooting it, but beneath the leek lay an iris bulb which was only waiting for that moment to blossom. Scarcely had the flower opened up when the little girl felt labor pains and vomited a prayer book that opened on its own to the page with the invocation to Joan of Arc. The little girl saw in this an order from heaven and at once vowed to take the veil. She got up and left the hole without bothering any more with Mrs. Lannor who, in her turn, was feeling labor pains and bringing into the world a ridiculous Louis XV clock that struck the hour ceaselessly. This time, Mrs. Lannor did not feel reassured. Her uneasiness gave way to distress beyond measure, when she felt invisible hands putting on her feet sewerman's boots that were soon full of sweat. Mrs. Lannor fainted.

She came to herself again hearing the sea breaking close by. She opened her eyes and saw herself in an immense metallic box with holes pierced in all its sides. She was in the company of shoals of sardines which, when she sat up, rose on their tails and, politely, bade her welcome, then disappeared all in the same direction as if they had been sucked up by a gigantic pump. Mrs. Lannor moistened her finger with a little saliva and raised it above her head to find the direction of the wind.

"East-north-east," said a flying fish who had approached without her noticing. And she set about undressing, but she was to take off only her boots, for, scarcely had she reached this decision when a human spinal column was coming down from the ceiling to upbraid her over her attitude and abuse her. Conscious of her humiliation, Mrs. Lannor kept silent. The spinal column covered itself in pink phosphorescence and disappeared with the loud noise of a slammed door.

Mrs. Lannor was in despair, for she had understood she would never see her cherry trees again and she was about to make up her mind to go home, sick at heart, when she was taken with violent pains in the feet.

"It's nothing," her limbs told her, "It's springtime."

Mrs. Lannor's feet became covered with cherry tree leaves and blossoms appeared a few seconds later. From each of these fell a wax vesta which burst into flames upon contact with the ground. The blossoms disappeared, replaced immediately by cherries. A current of air passed, laden with sulphurous vapors, the cherries lost their color and their stones appeared. In the time it took her to reach out an arm the stones became shrubs. Mrs. Lannor saw lightning followed immediately by a dreadful roll of thunder. When she opened her eyes again she was suspended by the feet from the top of the obelisk on the Place de la Concorde and all around her head floated thousands of cherries, bursting like puffballs. Then Mrs. Lannor realized her final hour had come and died as mushrooms die.

BENJAMIN PÉRET

A Very Fleeting Pleasure

It happened one day that I owned a dog, a magnificent New-foundland, clean, strong, and lithe: a new motor.

Satisfied or displeased, never did he bark. On the other hand, he displayed in all things an admirable decisiveness. If a woman wearing a green hat passed close by him, he fell into a wild rage. With one bound, he would jump on the woman, the hat was torn off, and the woman scalped. A real live Sioux would not have done better. This was not, of course, without certain disadvantages—for me only—since my dog would take off at top speed and return only the following morning, carrying a bunch of leeks in his jaws.

That a dog should go off carrying a woman's green hat and her hair, we can let that go; but that he should return with a bunch of leeks, there was something mysterious about *that*. For a long time, I looked for an explanation for this strange pheno-menon, without finding one. Chance—a unique chance—was to set me on the right track.

One morning, I had gone to the La Villette market to buy a sheep necessary for my experiments in vivisection. I wanted a very special sheep, a sheep with thick black wool, with the head and two right feet white. After examining more than two thousand sheep, I found the one I needed, a superb animal, big as a horse and with a bleat so powerful that all the slaughtermen in La Villette—who nevertheless had seen a thing or two—stopped working and were murmuring in astonishment, "You'd think it was Marshall Joffre or Clemenceau!"

I was going to buy it when my dog began to bark in rage (I've said he never barked), running around me; then, all at once, he sped like an arrow toward a corner of the room.

I called him, but to no avail. Reaching the corner of the room, my dog disappeared. I saw at that spot a blue circular hole, of the most beautiful azure blue, as when one looks at a very pure sky through a broken roof. It was surprising enough to attract the attention of a spectator less curious than I. I moved toward the hole and, at the moment when I was going to thrust my arm inside, an enormous oyster ready to be swallowed was presented me on a silver platter around the edges of which could be read: "Mobilization is not war." Naturally I was not foolish enough to refuse so pleasant an hors d'oeuvre, especially when a glass of excellent Pouilly followed. Next came a turbot blown up with I know not what, turkeys with chestnuts, then some tempting vegetables, which I am incapable of naming and which I had to refuse, then a peach and, finally, fruit with ice cream; all this accompanied by admirable wines, worthy of a place on a millionaire's table. At last the hole closed and left showing only a delicate woman's hand with fingers weighed down with rings enriched with sapphires and brilliants.

I took hold of the hand and kissed it respectfully, then, as I drew it toward me, I found myself in a narrow alleyway, tortuous and dark, lined with low walls over which hung branches of olive trees. From the gutter taking up the middle of the street rose a dreadful smell of rotten eggs and in front of me the sheep I had chosen at La Villette was walking slowly. I was thinking of the beautiful hand weighed down with rings and grieving over its disappearance when, in the light of a winking street lamp, I perceived a fountain where the water flowed into a little basin. From this basin emerged a hand moving feebly over the water. I recognized the hand with fingers covered in rings. I rushed forward and pulled at the hand, not without first having kissed it devotedly. Alas! the hand was not followed by an arm and a charming body as I had supposed. It was attached to a bunch of carrots being eaten by an enormous pike. I retained the hand *which was warm* and pink and not at all cold and livid like a lifeless hand, and put it in my pocket, postponing all explanations until later.

However, since the hand was *warm*, it was necessarily alive. It did not take me long to put this to the test, a fairly pleasant test by the way. Ten minutes had not elapsed when I felt the hand stirring in my pocket (no doubt it felt a little stiff). The movements grew stronger, then suddenly the hand tore a hole in my pocket and took off like an arrow, drawing me after it without my having time to think about what was happening to me. Need I say that, all the same, I did not display undue surprise?

A few minutes later, I found myself sitting on a bench on the Boulevard Sébastopol with, by my side, the prettiest young woman imaginable, dressed only in her stockings and a transparent chemise. This occasioned cries and sighs that in the end excited the infrequent passersby. Then people paired off and here, there, and everywhere cries testified to what everyone was feeling at that moment.

Suddenly there was a loud noise of horses and weapons and, above the houses, in the dazzling sunshine, famous Napoleonic regiments could be seen marching past, led by military bands.

After they had gone by, all movement had ceased. Near the Rue Turbigo, only three sheep were grazing on sparse grass coming up between the shining paving-stones.

BENJAMIN PÉRET

The Thaw

A road set with blue trees was plunging into a well. A fine rain
of red wine condensed on the fleecy ground. A man, who
seemed invertebrate—his body gave such a feeling of softness
when one saw him advancing with eiderdown steps on the
spongy road—came out of the well wearing on his head a milky
way. As he came forward, one found oneself noticing he did not
have a milky way on his head but his skull was sweating stars
that rose in the air red and burst white.

At the side of the road a young woman with conflagration
eyes was watching the man coming, from the window of a
house just like a sabot. It seemed, even, that she was waiting for
him, so much emotion animated her translucent face, from
which emanated waves of rainbows. However this was not the
case at all and she left her window when this man was no more
than a few paces from the sabot. He then seemed to hesitate a
moment before rounding the point of the sabot and draining
away like a barrel of oil in a copse of bottles that bordered the
strange edifice, murmuring, "Léoparde! Léoparde!" in a harrowing tone. At the window of the sabot appeared a delicate hand
with nails of crystal, holding an almond tree in blossom that
gave off fitful swirls of moiré smoke. The almond tree was put
down on the cloudy road where its roots attached it at once and

a great cry of surprise rang out from inside the sabot: "Monaco! Oh! my Monaco!"

The rain of red wine was coming down heavily and hastened the arrival of the blood-colored night. Black winged shapes, which seemed to be condensations of fog, moved about heavily in the moist air, sometimes giving off a brief phosphorescent flash. The sabot seemed to be the center of a strange, disquieting life one did not dare look in the face, for fear of finding oneself involved. Muffled sounds of sacks falling on beaten earth alternated with the sharp cracking sounds of broken windowpanes and long, scarcely human groans like the slow tearing of thick material. Through the still-open window the hand would appear momentarily, in movement, as if to emphasize a speech one could not hear. But the hand alone appeared, the rest of the body remained invisible, either because it did not exist, or because the heavy shadow that reigned inside did not make it possible to pick out.

Meanwhile the heavy winged shapes were gathering above the house, which they wreathed with big soft circles streaked with pale lightning and these circles were slowly shrinking, as if they had wanted to fascinate the house. And, indeed, the uneasiness, the horrible distress obviously prevailing there left no doubt that such was their aim. An extreme agitation filled it with a buzzing of various sounds, sometimes dominated by a long, harrowing moan. At moments, the sabot was even taken with a convulsive trembling and innumerable black balls, big as a fist, sprang from the roof to fall in a cluster on the ground where they broke into pieces, at once blending with the soil. The trembling became more frequent and more accentuated, and more dense, too, the spray of black balls, until the sabot appeared shaken in all directions by uninterrupted shudders, so violent that they inevitably had to bring about its collapse. The latter was so brutal and so sudden that one might wonder if it had really taken place, it was so complete. The earth shook, seemed to rise like a milk soup, a long, dark flame of aquarium glints shot out from under the sabot which was thrown up into the cavernous air, danced a moment in the flame, and burst like a puffball into moths that, in fright, flitted in all directions, colliding with one another and forming a mass so dense that the light, already diffuse like that which reigns during eclipses of the sun, darkened still further to become daylight shadowy as though woven with dusty spider webs.

The reddish shadows, as one became accustomed to them, made it possible to pick out, in place of the sabot, a white human form which one soon guessed to be a woman whose long hair prolonged her reclining body. Her respiration, that of a contraption for killing, the spasmodic movements shaking her whole body, uncovering long perfect legs resembling a branch of camellia, showed she was alive. Suddenly poisonous lightning shot out through the thick layer of moths and the woman disappeared, covered up again, absorbed by the big black shapes whose beating wings loosened a heavy wet storm. Cries and moans pierced the pile of wings which was becoming a sort of sieve that sometimes provided a glimpse of an arm, a breast, or the pure gleam of hair.

Suddenly a new flash of lightning shot through the cloud of moths in the opposite direction and the woman appeared, nude, her two arms raised toward the invisible sky in a gesture of ecstasy and crying at the top of her lungs, "I want all of life, all of life! Men, birds that pass through the flowering clouds, flowers that conceal wild animals similar to the beating of an outraged heart, the sea that can be held, altogether, in the palm of my hand and the sulphurous night, that is summed up in one drop of deadly perfume, slide like a locomotive in delirium over the rails of my veins without paying attention to the thousand signals from my nerves. I want all of life, for I am the whole world, all nature, even to the stones that sparkle in the inviolable coffers of mountains that do not echo."

And daylight reappeared, triumphant like a forest in flames. The cloud of moths vanished, dissolved like a pinch of sugar in a glass of clear water and settled as drops of milky dew on the body of the motionless woman, quiet as a buried city that, suddenly, reappears in the light of day invaded by clusters of pellitory and flights of sparrows. The woman was this way. A honeysuckle had slipped along her legs and was getting ready to entwine her in a long flowering branch and a little bird was moving aside her thick hair to make a nest in it.

A multitude of stars of all colors were sparkling in the lusterless air, like the gleam given off by fish leaping from sunny water. Still motionless in her ecstatic pose, the nude woman was changing visibly. The veins in her arms, in her temples, in her whole body were rapidly turning a delicate green, while her skin took on opaline transparencies and it was soon evident that the woman was dead, that no more was left of her than a light shell, similar to a soap bubble. And this empty shape began to move slowly with solemn steps, scarcely touching the grass that lost its color under her feet, leaving behind her a wake of heavy shadow like the one stirred up by the flight of bats at nightfall. She had soon reached the road where the birds were losing their multicolored plumage to provide her with a path of glory. And yet the shadow was opening out behind her shoulders, giving her two half-open wings that stretched to infinity. This shadow, more and more dense, was peopled by impalpable, moving, changing shapes that seemed to be absorbing one another. Scarcely was one able to make out a gigantic lion's head when this head unfolded, opened up and became an orchid a hundred times life size. In its turn, this orchid was in movement, dividing up, and, from the black pool of shadow, arose a Hindoo god with a thousand flaming eyes: the firing of a machine gun at night. The eyes blinked and went out, replaced by telegraph wires, along which telegrams could be seen running. There were strange ones: "The black poppy is invading the bride's gown. Where are the swallows' beaks?" simple ones: "Tomorrow morning, early, color the bread," touching ones: "My two arms are useless without you," sinister ones: "Blood is stirring," and many more still that passed by, in a hurry, jostling one another to get to their destination more quickly. But rapidly the telegrams became illegible and the wires became entangled in an immense head of hair in which a diadem shone.

And the woman, or rather her transparent ghost, was still walking toward a gilded lake that shone in the distance like the eye of a wild animal in a dark copse. Before her, everything crystallized, lost volume and opaqueness, vanished in Prince Rupert's drops to condense behind her head in heavy soft mingled shadows, seeking their life and form. But in the distance, very far behind her shone bright spangles.

. . . .

A crawfish stopped the stone that was rolling in the torrent and covered it with a long gray veil.

JOSÉ PIERRE

1927–

One of the most articulate critics of painting to emerge from the surrealist movement, José Pierre, born in Bénisse-Maremne, joined the Paris group in 1952. He contributed the volume on Futurism and Dadaism to the general history of painting published in Lausanne by Éditions Rencontre. His *Le Surréalisme* (1966) in the same series shares with André Breton's *Le Surréalisme et la peinture* the distinction of offering the most reliable guide to surrealist painting. The three plays in his *Théâtre* (1969) bring noteworthy innovations to the surrealist theater. The texts presented here as reflecting his approach to the short story are all taken from his collection of brief narratives and short plays, *D'Autres Chats à fouetter* (*Other Fish to Fry* [1968]).

As *Cyprien de belle humeur* shows, the stories of José Pierre testify to the potent influence of Benjamin Péret upon surrealists coming after him.[1] And yet it would be unjust to say Pierre's tales are derivative in nature. The wry story called *Dreams that Money Can Buy*,[2] for instance, has no antecedent in the writings

---

1. José Pierre dedicated the texts of his *Le Ça ira* (1967) to Benjamin Péret.
2. The French text bears this title in English, apparently borrowed from a film in several sequences made by Hans Richter according to suggestions by a number of artists: Man Ray, Marcel Duchamp, and Max Ernst. For details on this movie, completed during the mid-forties, see Ado Kyrou, *Le Surréalisme au cinéma* (1953) (rev. ed. 1963), pp. 198-200.

of Péret. José Pierre dedicated it to the surrealist Annie Lebrun. It is not unfair to say that, if the point of departure of a Pierre story like *Un Pou sur la montagne*—written for Fernando Arrabal—is as far removed from common sense as one by Péret, the narrative advances, as is the case too with *L'Armoire à l'ange*, less by accumulation of antirational details, such as Péret habitually used, than according to the principle of deduction, proceeding logically from a nonreasonable premise.

Introducing *D'Autres Chats á fouetter*, Robert Benayoun, a fellow-surrealist, described José Pierre in terms less fanciful than at first appears. He spoke of Pierre as secretly slipping saucers for right-handed people onto the assembly line in a factory making teacups for lefties: "a perfidious but efficacious form of sabotage that has a lot to tell me about the nihilist impulses of this character."

Benayoun also alludes in the same context to the role played by eroticism in several of José Pierre's stories, when it comes to giving expression to these impulses. We might add that, in Pierre's writing, erotic elements are complemented by humorous ones, not weakened by these. His special form of humor finds its distinguishing characteristic in a method evidently standing at the opposite extreme from automatism. It is born of an inverted logic. Whether or not we are facing lateral inversion, as Benayoun implies, the end result is the same: reason finds itself implicated, becoming party to its own destruction.

JOSÉ PIERRE

Cyprien in Good Humor (a Neapolitan tale)

Cyprien, getting up that morning, rubbed his eyes and, in the mirror of the wardrobe facing his bed, glimpsed a nasty bearded gentleman who said to him in a severe tone, "The pants button salesman will not call Saturday: falling down, he swallowed the rest of his merchandise."

Then, horribly vexed, Cyprien threw at the mirror-wardrobe the tame anvil that always slept at the foot of his bed. Instead of splintering, the mirror turned scarlet and began to laugh so loudly it woke up all those living in town and in the nearby suburbs. Wakened up also, Cyprien's mother came into the room, disguised as a reaper-binder-thresher, as she had the objectionable habit of doing from time to time. As she was opening the door, she trampled on a horrible curé with yellow ears who was none other—but very slightly made up—than the nasty bearded man previously glimpsed by Cyprien.

"I change used sewing machines into barometers, souls in purgatory into false moustaches, and pleasure yachts into chocolate bars!" cried the curé with yellow ears, taking from his pocket a grimy handbill on which could be read:

A good move!
A good deal
  EXCHANGE YOUR MORTAL SINS
                    for:
1. BLUE striped socks;
2. a Cremona violin TUNE;
3. a pint of GOOD blood;
4. a window with a VIEW over the sea;
5. a waist-cincher that belonged to SOPHIA Loren,
   etc.
AND YOUR *soul* WILL KNOW PEACE!
     THE SOCIETY OF THE OPTIMATE
     BROTHERS OF UNIVERSAL LEVITATION
through the intermediary of its representative
kisses your hand
and sends
its sincere wishes.
               Don't miss this CHANCE!

"What would you make of a reaper-binder-thresher that, to tell the truth, could do with a few repairs?" asked Cyprien, carefully putting on his rimmel.

"Four dozen fig leaves for imported Apollos and two or three pots of English mustard," responded the curé with yellow ears.

"Well then, just take it away!" said Cyprien, pushing the whole lot out onto the landing.

And so it was that Cyprien got rid of his old mother who was becoming a bit of a nuisance since she had contracted, reading the complete works of Henri Bordeaux, the annoying habit of disguising herself as a reaper-binder-thresher.

But Cyprien, heartless fellow, went on getting dressed after opening his bedroom window wide. The air outside was so cool that Cyprien sneezed violently and a rain of pale-green butterflies fell onto his work table. The largest one had fallen into the inkwell and, rolling on a sheet of paper, it wrote the following poem:

The night bursts open
the tree catches fire
and forty-seven gumless notaries

cry after the moon
and become square.

C . . .

Reading these words, Cyprien understood that those butterflies were sent him by his adored Caroline. He began to jump so high with joy that, going through the window, he passed over the roofs and found himself driving the horses of a stagecoach at top speed on the Santa Fé Trail.

Carried as if by a whirlwind, he scarcely had time to recognize, by the side of the trail, the mother and the curé with yellow ears, both transformed into a loathsome purée of peas lavishly garnished with croutons rubbed with garlic. To pay them final homage, he fired a few shots into the air, and, at once, two or three bison crashed down on the stagecoach. In place of the latter, when the dust had settled a little, Cyprien perceived a saloon from which came laughter and songs punctuated by the sound of a player piano. One hand negligently resting on his revolver, he entered.

Then Caroline, who was leaning on the bar, turned toward him, threw her cigarette on the floor, ground it with the heel of her boot, and said, unbuttoning her opulent bodice, "You've come too late, Cyprien!"

And then the shoot-out began . . .

SEVENTEEN YEARS AFTER,

We find Cyprien selling soft-centered candy at the foot of Vesuvius.

But now six o'clock strikes and Vesuvius in person comes down the slope on his old secondhand scooter, crying out to Cyprien in a thunderous voice, "The day is over, I'm going for a ride around town. Do you want to come with me, Cyprien?"

And Cyprien, stuffing his soft-centered candy in his pocket, climbs onto the scooter behind Vesuvius and, in no time at all, there they are seated at a table on a café terrace, in front of a very cold vermouth.

"Oh! what a job!" says Vesuvius, "Smoking nonstop: it does the windpipe no good . . ."

"And what about soft-centered candy? It's sugary, it sticks to you, it draws ants, violinists, children, Red Cross nurses, chair menders, and railroad derailments!"

A chestnut vendor in national costume—with that charming helmet of tin over which stands guard the eternal flame that announces from afar, at night, the proximity of one of those brave tradesmen—no doubt identifying Vesuvius thanks to his famous Panama hat jauntily tilted toward the back of his head, called to him, "Isn't it true that this summer the icebergs of Greenland are parting their hair in the middle?"

But Vesuvius had not had time to open his mouth to reply when already Cyprien was shouting, "Caroline! What have you done with my wrist watch of chrome brass and our fourteen children of whom thirteen were girls, the image of your adorable self?"

At these words, Caroline—for it was indeed she—tore off her chestnut vendor's hat and collapsed in a rattan chair, sighing, "What do you expect, Cyprien? I'm so absentminded!"

She had scarcely pronouced these words when the rattan chair gave a bound that unseated Caroline. Then the chair began to take on more and more disturbing bulk: it looked pretty much like a map of Great Britain done on a ball of gold-beater's skin in the form of a washing machine. Soon could be clearly distinguished, at the level of what could be Wales, a vertical zipper.

Motivated by a sudden presentiment, Cyprien opened the zipper with a trembling hand and suddenly fourteen fox terriers, thirteen of them immaculately white and the fourteenth covered with freckles, leaped out, each of them holding in its jaws a piece of the tomb of Jules II.

"My children! Our children!" Cyprien and Caroline cried out as one.

And Vesuvius began to cough into his glass to hide that he shared the emotion of his old comrade Cyprien.

THE NEXT DAY,

Cyprien and Caroline who had had many children, resolved at last to live happily. They left to travel through the world on a new honeymoon and nowhere did their stylish trap drawn by fourteen delightful puppies pass unnoticed.

JOSÉ PIERRE

Dreams That Money Can Buy (a silly tale)

During New Year's Eve, passersby going late to some party without having taken the precaution to provide themselves with a gift for the host were very pleased to meet, on the corner of Waterloo Road and the Boulevard Saint-Germain, the good countenance of the dream vendor.

In exchange for an insignificant sum, they would get from him a sort of little balloon, smothered in down as white as snow, which they could carry off at the end of a length of thin metal. And all the rest of the year the dream vendor would never be seen again.

One was advised to present that little balloon with the words, "May your dearest dreams come true!" The person receiving it then had to tie it to the head of his bed, as close as possible to that of the sleeper. Many people who tried this declared that they had felt themselves weightless during the course of the night, really, really weightless. Apparently, they had thought unconsciously of the shape of the balloon and identified with its tendency to rise. As for those who wanted to know what was going on, they discovered, upon bursting the balloon, only a sort of cheap plush stuck to the inside and to the outside of a very ordinary gold-beater's skin. And the thing was so inexpensive they shrugged and thought no more about it.

Now, one year a scandal took place. All the inhabitants of an apartment block having, by chance, given or received little dream balloons, awoke after a jolly New Year's Eve party in beds not their own. And chance, if so it was, had worked things out pretty well: people who were secretly in love with one another, people in love too shy to admit it to one another, had been brought together as though by a miracle. But just try doing good for people in spite of themselves! The first moment of abandon behind them, a few persons became concerned about what people would say, about respectability, public morality, their concierge's opinion, and other nonsense. The more stupid ones went so far as to lodge a complaint.

There was some problem locating the old fellow who sold dreams. He admitted in the end that, during the year, his only clients were little girls from the elementary school and particularly clumsy burglars. The latter, so it is said, could then bring off fruitful operations.

But, in the course of the trial, the court could grasp only the moral significance of the scandal. And the district attorney declared, "If dreams came true, there would be anarchy!" From extreme right to extreme left, the newspapers all approved this lapidary phrase, as well as the verdict.

The dream vendor found himself denied the right to manufacture and sell anything at all. But, since he had to make a living, he finally was authorized, under strict supervision, to sell rather odd little pictures he painted himself. And every Sunday afternoon he could be seen, with a certain number of canvases laid out around him, at the corner of Waterloo Road and the Boulevard Saint-Germain. But people did not like his pictures, for these were not of hinds in forest clearings, nor of cats on cushions, nor of sunsets over the sea.

He would have died of hunger, that ex-vendor of dreams, if from time to time an old client—a little girl who had become a prostitute, a burglar who had become a banker—had not out of compassion bought one of his canvases. But no doubt, as soon as he got home, the purchaser of that canvas set it aside in a corner, in a closet or in an attic. For who is interested in other people's dreams?

JOSÉ PIERRE

A Louse on the Mountain
(a tourist tale)

There was, on that occasion, a louse on the mountain. And the louse was big enough to be seen from the valley where the town was, full of tourists at that time. The louse caused quite some excitement among those people: some could not suppress a shudder of disgust when they raised their eyes to the peaks or when they heard there was talk of the subject; others, more curious, trained binoculars and telescopes in the direction of the freak, watched the slightest movement of its head or feet, trying to interpret. "He's scratching," they'd say, or again: "He's chewing something."

The mountain, on the other hand, was not at all delighted. "What about my reputation as a tourist attraction?" it grumbled. But what could it do? And the Chamber of Commerce took pleasure in revolting inertia.

As for the louse, it felt very satisfied. "They are admiring me," it thought. However, it soon realized the situation, in the long run, would give rise to monotony and financial difficulty. The tourists were leaving town by the trainload. Some major modification in perspective had to be made, without any loss of advantages already gained.

And the louse began to suck the substance out of the mountain. The latter, taken by surprise at first, sank little by little like a collapsed air chamber. Now enormous, the louse thus found itself on a level with the town. And, in spite of its fantastic corpulence, it began to walk about among the houses, thinking to make itself popular that way.

But a detachment of artillery arrived in the suburbs and demolished the louse with cannon fire.

The louse expired, murmuring, "Mountain air is no good for me."

JOSÉ PIERRE

The Angel Closet
(a spiritual tale)

One Sunday morning, opening the big linen closet where she stored her sheets, Helen discovered a pallid and somewhat shabby individual who seemed cramped in that piece of furniture which had come down to Helen, though, from her grandmother. She was beginning to feel astonished when she recognized what she was dealing with: this was an angel.

The latter, without shaking off his uncomfortable mien, had taken a few steps into the room. He was rubbing his eyes as if he had not had enough sleep or as if the light of day dazzled him, while he ruffled his feathers in a furtive way.

"I must do something," Helen said to herself. And she tried to start up a conversation. "Sir . . . ," she mumbled and at once felt ridiculous, But she had succeeded all the same in catching the attention of the angel who, seeming to discover Helen's presence for the first time, rested his gentle stupid eyes on her.

"Just my luck," thought Helen, "the very time they send me an angel, I have to end up with a simpleminded one." At the same time, she noticed the visitor was afflicted with a slight strabismus that drew his eyes in. "You wouldn't by chance have some milk?" he asked in a hesitant, somewhat hoarse voice.

And he began to stare at a copper crucifix hanging on the wall—another memento from Helen's grandmother. Returning from the kitchen with a glass of milk, Helen almost dropped it: there was the crucifix melting in long rills that ran to the ground. The angel appeared embarrassed. "It wasn't an antique, I assume," he said by way of excuse. And he drank down his glass of milk in one go.

Helen then tried to question him. "By what chance, etc." Her interlocutor very quickly became uncomfortable, coughed, went red in the face, and, judging by how quickly he was managing to contradict himself in the space of scarcely a few minutes, Helen had to bow to this fact: she was dealing with an arrant liar. "I'm on vacation," he admitted in the end, and of all the things he had said, this seemed the closest to the truth.

Despite her highly developed sense of hospitality, Helen ended up with the thought that she must not make herself a slave to this unusual presence. Standing there, in the middle of the bedroom, anyway, with his wings on either side, the angel took up a lot of space. At the moment he offered one of his biggest lies, he had unconsciously stretched his remiges and knocked over a curio on the mantel. The object, a little plaster grotto containing a Saint Bernadette as high as a lead soldier, had been smashed to smithereens.

Helen then tried to make him understand that, if he wanted her to take him in, he could in return devote himself to light housework: she lived alone and her typist's pay did not allow her to avail herself of the services of a cleaning woman. But he proved to be incredibly clumsy, notably in his relations with dishes. What he managed to do best though was sweep up: skimming the floor with all his feathers, he was not without style and, from the point of view of harmony, the silky sound he produced this way was easily better than the throb of a vacuum cleaner.

As night was coming on, Helen at first though to give him the bedside rug but she soon blamed herself for such an uncharitable thought, Anyway, there certainly could be no sin in sleeping beside an angel! And so she invited him to share her bed and turned away, in spite of her curiosity, when he undressed. She tried to imagine what his underwear could look like. And what about when he snagged his bodysuit?

Helen had had a few lovers, merited by the grace of her eighteen years, and, if she lived alone, this was out of taste for peace and quiet rather than from natural coldness. And so she snuggled without prudishness against her guest who in the end took her in his arms. "Alas!" he said, "for thousands and thousands of years we angels haven't known how to make love . . ." They nevertheless achieved some satisfaction and, tenderly enfolded in one another's arms, they dreamed for a moment, having retained as a bed sheet only the wings which, flapping gently, provided a little cool air on that warm spring night. Then the fanning movement ceased: the angel was asleep, his head on Helen's bare breast.

The following morning, when Helen, her hair still undone, moved close to her strange lover to wish him good morning, the angel leapt to his feet, stepping back and cried, "No! no! I'm not what you think, I'm not a heavenly being but a famous criminal sought by the police of several countries! I'm a wretch." And he burst into tears.

Quite surprised, Helen tried to console him. "What about your wings?" she asked, "Untrue, artificial. See for yourself: I'm going to tear them off." And he began to pull at his wings like a madman, tearing out feathers by the handful. But he put forth generous vigor to no avail, the wings held and he had to give up the effort, red with fatigue and shame.

"Another lie!" thought Helen. And with despair in her soul, her heart heavy with sobs, she gently pushed the angel in the direction of the big closet. He submitted, docile, head down, in an attitude full of resignation. And Helen closed the closet doors on him, turned the key, and gave a deep sigh.

Since then she has never opened the angel closet again.

ANDRÉ PIEYRE DE MANDIARGUES

1909–

André Pieyre de Mandiargues, who was born in Paris, published his first book in Monte Carlo, where he had taken refuge
during the German occupation of France. Called *Dans les Années
sordides* (*In the Sordid Years* [1943]), it was a collection of prose
poems and strange stories of surrealist inspiration that foreshadowed his volume of stories *Le Musée noir* (*The Black Museum*
[1946]), from which *Le Passage Pommeraye* is taken, and *Soleil des
loups* (*Wolves' Sun* [1951]).

A number of significant themes favored in surrealism find
development in *Le Passage Pommeraye*. Its epigraph serves to
remind us that surrealists in France have brought a special kind
of wonder, born of their sense of the marvelous, to the description of the urban landscape, never animated by a livelier imagination that that of Louis Aragon in *Le Paysan de Paris*, with its
famous evocation of the Passage de l'Opéra, a Paris arcade
demolished since the time when Aragon wrote his text in 1924.
It seems that Pieyre de Mandiargues felt the influence of Aragon, when writing his story, as, too, he may have drawn
inspiration from the example set by others who preceded him in
surrealism. For instance, it is not difficult to believe that the

illuminating presence in *Le Passage Pommeraye* of a strangely
beautiful, enigmatic woman owes something to André Breton's
account of his meeting with the haunting figure to whom he
devoted his *Nadja*. Pieyre de Mandiargues's story is something
more, however, than testimony to the appeal exercised by two
classic texts of surrealism. *Le Passage Pommeraye* makes a valuable contribution all its own.

In a strange environment that no surrealist would fail to
recognize as a *privileged locale*, Pieyre de Mandiargues shows
beauty drawing someone into a strange adventure. He ela-
borates skillfully upon the idea of *passage* as an initiative experience culminating in metamorphosis. He adds, too, the monstrous and a hint of menace as well as horror, in his description
of the Pommeraye Arcade. For this there is no precedent in *Le
Paysan de Paris*. Furthermore, he enriches his tale of magic
encounter with an erotic note (far less audible in *Nadja*) which
becomes more and more insistent until it dominates *Le Passage
Pommeraye*, finally giving disturbing meaning in one man's life
to the intervention of chance, which has always held irresistible
appeal for surrealists.

It is perhaps a coincidence—but to the surrealist no less
worthy of note for being so—that the one word uttered by the
woman in *Le Passage Pommeraye* is "Echidna," when André
Breton's fetish animal was a tamanoir.[1] But it is no mere
accident that this unsettling story is dedicated to the German-
born surrealist Meret Oppenheim, creator of disturbing objects
like the *Déjeuner en fourrure* (*Breakfast in Fur:* a cup, saucer, and
spoon covered with fur) which attracted attention when it was
shown in the 1936 New York exhibition "Fantastic Art, Dada and
Surrealism." The subject of a remarkable photographic portrait
with compelling erotic overtones, by Man Ray, Meret Oppenheim was later to devise for the 1959 international surrealist
exhibition in Paris *Le Festin* (*The Banquet:* a nude woman lying in

---

1. See the photograph of the tamanoir-object created by Breton in 1962
(*L'Archibras*, no. 1 [April 1967], p. 22). A few hours after Breton's death in 1966,
a tamanoir had to be chased off a Parisian airfield. See George Sadoul,
"L'Homme que j'ai connu," *Les Lettres françaises*, no. 1151 (October 6-12, 1966),
p. 16.

the Galerie Daniel Cordier, her body serving as a table from which one could help oneself to food). This was the Exposition inteRnatiOnale du Surréalisme dedicated to the theme that has never lost its appeal for Pieyre de Mandiargues: EROS.[2]

---

2. Pieyre de Mandiargues's preoccupation with the erotic has none of the vulgarity one might infer from the title *Naked under Leather*, given the film adaptation of his novel *La Motocyclette* (*The Motorcycle* [1963]). See, for instance, his *Le Lis de mer* (1956), trans. Richard Hughes as *The Girl beneath the Lion* (New York: Grove Press, 1958).

Those interested in seeing photographs of *Le Festin* will find them in *La Brèche: action surréaliste*, no. 6 (June 1964), facing p. 16; Sarane Alexandrian, *Surrealist Art* (1970), pp. 227, 228; Robert Benayoun, *Érotique du surréalisme* (1965), p. 191.

ANDRÉ PIEYRE DE MANDIARGUES

The Pommeraye Arcade

In certain renowned
arcades, it is known that
nameless animals sleep
easy.
—André Breton and Philippe Soupault

A free-floating balloon was sailing over Nantes at the end of that
very fine Fourteenth of July day, a balloon that carried, like a
propitiatory victim offered up to the winds and tides in honor of
the national holiday, an octogenarian aeronaut whose kindly
face could be seen in all the evening papers, sad and gentle, eye
limpid, hair white. There is something thrilling in those words
"free-floating balloon," an echo of the youthful popular will to
exercise power that impelled the men of the nineteenth century
to action. I thought of that man from Nantes, Jules Verne, and of
the unforgettable prints embellishing the books we used to read
as children: of the long thin old men, bearded, belted with
cartridges, armed with big Colt revolvers and repeating rifles,
their eyes ablaze under the exceedingly broad brim of a felt hat,
the peak of a jocky cap, the rim of a fuzzy toque; identical,
always, whether they were bound for the equator, the pole, or
the center of the earth. "The horizon," I said aloud, and I saw

the boreal dawn in the dark sky of Terra del Fuego, the edge of the horizon like a reddening line and night about to come down over the town.

Slowly I walked up the Rue Crébillon, surprised to find it almost deserted at that hour when it is usually congested with pedestrians and with the elegant women of Nantes. This emptiness made me notice what, other times, had escaped me: to the left, and a little back from the Rue Crébillon, there is something like a very small square, where the opening of an arcade gapes, surmounted by this inscription in gold lettering on a black background: "Visit the Pommeraye Arcade," while a metal plaque, rising on the outside, provides further information: "Tourists, don't pass through Nantes without seeing Hidalgo of Paris' display, to the right, at the top of the stairs, on the gallery of statues."

How could I not obey this double mysterious injunction, rendered all the more imperative by the big red hand that appears all on its own, index finger raised, in the shadow of the archway? The hand is a shop sign for a glover whose place of business bears the quite curious name "The Well," conjured up perhaps by the aquatic atmosphere common to all these glassed-in galleries, or perhaps because of the peculiar construction of the Pommeraye Arcade, comprised of two floors connected by a very steep staircase, going down deep.

When one comes in from the outside, and from the daylight, it takes one's eyes some time to adjust to the semidarkness of this enclosed place, then one is able to make out that the upper part of the arcade is decorated with some quite nice stucco, in the taste of the end of Louis-Philippe's reign; busts, on which damp is laying a greenish patina, stand out against a background of half-rose-windows; all this is in ruin, crumbling here and there, and these ruins seem to have been invaded by serrated algae, or by fern, or by moss (do we know what?), carpeted with a bluish dust that is like a very fine down. The contours of the arcade, which are hazy, this paludous vegetation, the damp, the opaline glaucous hues, place the Pommeraye Arcade pretty well in the abyssal landscapes of *Twenty Thousand Leagues under the Sea*, where deep-sea divers, led by Captain Nemo, go hunting turtle and shark through the colonnades of submerged Atlantis.

I had stopped close to the entrance, in front of the display case for a press and publicity agent where I was looking at the photograph of a catamite in girl's clothing, his hair arranged in the Andalusian style, smiling, with a rose between his teeth, under the tall comb and mantilla of black lace. Below, a poster announced: "Rosalio? Two dance recitals." Already at that moment, it seemed I really did see in the pane the reflection of a dark silhouette behind me, something fleeting and vaguely menacing like the slow approach of a very large black fish one can hardly make out behind the glass of an aquarium, like the apparition of the glanis, the giant silurus of the Lake of Morat, that used to fill me with terror in my childhood dreams. And what, then, was that cold feeling that took me between the shoulders, that terrible weight like all the weight of time which always came, too, pressing down on me at the end of my dreams? As in a bad dream, it disappeared almost at once, without leaving me feeling in the least ill at ease; and it had had so little reality that I did not turn around, but continued to advance toward the far end of the long vestibule, passing in front of a shop selling smokers' supplies, dedicated to "The Pasha," which displayed majestic meerschaum pipes with lions' heads on them.

Then I saw that enigmatic gallery of statues, the name of which brought to mind a dark necropolis inhabited by still, white shapes. Beneath a roof of glass, from which at that late hour daylight slanted down, there is a big rectangular balcony surrounding and overlooking a steep very wide staircase which can be seen plunging toward the darkest depths of the lower floor. As for the statues, they are morose adolescent figures of both sexes, spaced at short intervals, embellishing the balustrade, their backs to the shop windows.

A nude child, carrying a candelabrum balanced on his chin, in an attitude rendered fairly obviously obscene by the swelling of his cheeks and the stupidly passive expression on his back-tilted face, guards the opening to the stairs. Three lines of allegories decorate the two long balustrades and the smallest one at the far end of the gallery, where you can make out yet another child-candelabrum, matching the first.

It is like a game of riddles: seated beside an anchor on a coil of rope, Navigation stares into the distance with completely blank eyes that gaze off into infinity; Agriculture rests on a sheaf of corn, Commerce on a heap of sacks and packing cases; that somewhat heavy girl, sadly pensive, resting her elbow on the broken torso of a statue of Aphrodite, could just as well represent Fine Arts in general as, in particular, Sculpture or Archaeology, but *he* is Industry, for sure, the boy wielding a blacksmith's hammer, and there is probably Science, that virgin with long braids, a shell in the hollow of her hand, who seems to have been abandoned by an inconstant god, between a globe and a printing press. Others, more fanciful in the choice of attributes, give no clue to their identify. Such figures recur, without one understanding why only they, and not all, do so.

Paltry creatures, a little smaller than life size, pale, bereft of smiles, coated with a dirty yellow-cream color, running to green, from you emanates an affliction no less immense than from a seraglio of old children, sick children, poor half-starved children; at the same time you are nevertheless quite disturbing, beneath the veils half-covering your puny nakedness, through the effect of this curious atmosphere of melancholy, resignation, and repentance in which you are steeped; like a flock of dejected beauties thrown in costume into the fog of a Turkish bath for a Mardi Gras orgy. Here and there, on a cheek, a breast, a leg, damp stains draw the eye like the suspect erosions of flesh, symptoms of some hidden sickness.

I wandered a long time among the sad supernumeraries of this steamy carnival, leaving to chance responsibility for directing my steps. Incessantly, a few words buzzed in my head: "The burden of destiny . . . ," the beginning of a phrase, a vague rhetorical figure, or what? And destiny, sphinx in the grandiose cold desert of existence, what part did *that* play in the gallery of statues in the Pommeraye Arcade, where I found myself at that moment, facing the "Modern Dental Office of Hidalgo of Paris"?

A shop as absurd as it is unusual. A quantity of signs in variegated warm shades, yellow, red, orange, emblazon everywhere that sonorous name, which seems to scoff at geography, "Hidalgo of Paris," and again: "This is Hidalgo of Paris," written in characters arranged vertically as on Chinese signs.

The shop window is a freakish bazaar where perfumery and instruments of dental surgery mingle with the most disparate objects it has ever been possible to bring together in the service of publicity. A little glass-fronted cupboard contains, neatly arranged on the insipid glossiness of a pink silk cushion, wax casts of human teeth eaten away by all the diseases to which they are subject. I noticed too, with imaginable admiration, an ingenious advertising picture for "Hidalgo special antiseptic shampoo—with organic capillary cell base" bringing to the attention of bald men "a few cases of alopecia photographed from among our clients."

As if this were not enough, four showcases set out against the balustrade of the gallery held also many other things one could expect even less to find in a dental office, however modern. I went to lean over them and never in my life did I gaze on a finer collection of dribble glasses, imitation turds, fire-crackers and squibs, heaped there pell-mell with everything imaginable by way of tricks and jokes. Surprising wonders, a list of these is enough to make a fair spangled with images too suggestive for one to resist for long the desire to lose oneself among them, to wander lazily through this disordered, squall-ing, roisterous mob of liberated words: infernal sneeze machine devil's plate raiser, love's centimeter, Satan's fluid, murderer's soap, snake hat, fart cushion, climbing mouse, astounding candies, trick cards, wish-you-happiness cigars and jugs, packs of water-spraying cigarettes, mysterious picture, flying cigar, endless thread, rubber water biscuit, surprise bombs, fulminant speck of silver, invisible body suit, devil's nails, joker's cork-screw, water-throwing cork, amora mustard, comic labels, stars of peace, funny visiting cards, tiny movies, lovers' thermom-eter, rocket-log, squirting badge, key of happiness, electric ring, snow block, digital dynamometer, dismay butter, and the calf's cry and the diversions from Liège, and the naja egg, and the bride's open sesame, and the zouli, and the Senegalese boa.

Who are those formidable exploding cossacks forming an advance guard of honor for the pirouetting troops of fancy sugar candy: Cupid's candy, Don Juan's candy, and the soft-centered Cupid candies "when it comes to making people fall in love, there's nothing like it for a laugh," flower of the fields candy, devil's eye candy, swimming fly candy, cockroach candy, octo-pus candy, sea serpent candy, happy fisherman candy, frog candy and tree-frog candy, academic candy "which contains a very nice collection of female nudes," snow candy, rock candy, pepper candy, snake candy, goldfish candy, cork candy, angora candy, swimming candy, turtle candy, elephant candy, forfeits candy, ribbon candy, photographer candy, nightingale candy, torpedo candy, and devil's candy? An intoxicating list, so long, so lavish that all the little light-colored prisms in their transparent paper wrappers seemed to me in the end to make up a veritable apologia for love and barely left me with the ability to take an interest, also, in a few finds as subtle as harem powder, dog-attracting powder, and powder to make cats miaow.

I no longer had any idea of the time gone by since I entered the Pommeraye Arcade, since Rosalio's smile had fallen under the shadow of the barbels normally found around the glanis' enormous mouth, since I had lost my way in the procession of little sickly allegories, since I had been confronted with the dentist's office of Hidalgo of Paris, where the angel of the bizarre in person could have operated without my being surprised. I recalled perfectly well the order in which these encounters took place, but a feeling of time intervened no more than in an hallucination taking me walking through a world just as absurd, and where the absurdities unfolded in as natural a way as in our world; for nothing, either, gave my reason a shock, if, that is, it was indeed my reason that still governed my being. And when I raised my head, I was not astonished to perceive I was no longer alone. A woman stood beside me, though nothing had warned me of her presence or her approach; a woman who was looking at me without saying a word, whom I had surely never seen before, whom I seemed to recognize, however, as if I had always known her. Of this woman I saw at first only the great head of hair in movement, so black and so lusterless that it was like a plumage of floating soot, above a dome of chalk, in the vague breathing of a night of the full moon, then the face appeared in all the strange beauty of its architecture, ideal while yet of a character indisputably familiar to me.

Where had I been able to gaze at that face, just a little too elongated, delicately molded in white flesh devoid of pink, with shadows between gray and green; the harmonious contour of those concave temples like the frame of a lyre, of those cheeks, as gently rounded as tulip petals, of that chin with its oval projecting a little more than average; the line of that somewhat

aquiline nose, hooked a little at the end over widely scooped
nostrils and at the same time of so fine a texture that I thought of
a convulsive ivory; especially that marvelously drawn mouth,
full, arrogant, half open, voluptuous, and of those thin prominent lips around a double barrier of teeth that wounded me like
offensive words? Why did the slightly oriental aspect of that
entrancing face tell me something more, and what did it tell me
exactly?

I tried to trace the link connecting me, in some way difficult
to understand, to the present phenomenon, tried to go further
back, to come upon whatever could be at the origin of that
unquestionable feeling "I've seen this before" and even at the
same time "I've at last found it again" that had come over me
from the very first contact. I searched my memory—knowing in
advance I would find nothing—and found nothing, indeed, but
a vague resemblance to the face of certain statues on the island
of Cyprus, the statue of the Sindon that is in Turin, and that of
Judith and of a few Botticelli angels. However, I did know that
my thrill came from somewhere else, other times, other envi-
ronments: from regions and situations now forgotten, but which
had held much greater importance for me, and which I felt I was
on the point of discovering once again. At the same instant, it
seemed to me that this proximity of something I desired so
much was dangerous, and that I was on the brink of an abyss.

Her back to the balustrade, the woman remained still,
frozen in the attitude of someone offering herself, or rather of
mute prayer. Her eyes weighed on mine in a glance whose
waves, interrupted by momentary blinking, enveloped me and
sank into me in a continual assault. I read in it a warm feminin-
ity, far from clear, a shy insistence, passivity, sadness too, and
resignation; all shades of feeling that together made up an
expression sometimes read in the eyes of certain herbivorous
animals, of cervidae in particular, and also of some bovidae.

Who knows what I expected, if in fact I expected something
concrete? From then on, the hours could have flown by, letting
us sink ever deeper into contemplation of one another, until we
fell into the numbness of mummies found years after, chame-
leonlike, between the cracked statues on the balcony and the
rotting casts of the dentist's office. But suddenly I saw that overwhelming mouth moving before me. Those beautiful curved lips

parted, hesitated, rolled back, apparently completely bewil-
dered, letting out a single word the echo of which reverberated a
long time in the emptiness of the deserted gallery: "Echidna."
That was the only time I ever heard that voice and the somewhat
singsong raucous northern accent, brought up as though with
an effort from a constricted throat.

In such a cry: "Echidna"—the *i* deep and the last syllable
suspended in the air, the *ch* guttural like a *k*—I discovered once
again the melancholy pleasure a man of the north takes in
pronouncing words ending in *o* and *a*, in Latin, Greek, or Italian
names: Sophia, Panthea, Claudio, Hermia, Honorio, Cassan-
dra, Appollonia . . . which charm him so because they seem to
contain all the poetry of white towns facing the blue sea, of
green plants entwined about gilded columns, of leafy ruins, of
cities of the dead and of the Mediterranean countryside; I discovered once again, I say, all the melancholy produced by the
south of France in the English or the Germans, the indefinable
desires born on fine summer nights under the warm winds of
the South, and the feeling of emptiness and of the vanity of
existence when they face skies cloudless at last. However, the
glance resting insistently upon mine made me understand this
was not a botanical or a zoological name, pronounced by
chance, the evocation of a climbing plant or an insect hunter, a
reminder of a recollection from literature, a mythological remin-
iscence, or simply a sigh overflowing with nostalgia, but that I
was to find in it something addressed more especially to myself.
And I was undecided whether I was meant to understand,
rather, an appeal for help, an invitation, a warning, or a threat.

The fascinating creature's eyelids fluttered as though from
an agitation held in with difficulty, and a shudder ran through
her that almost impelled me toward her; but, after gazing at me
again, she turned her back on me, then began walking with a
slight swing of the hips, for her bare feet rested on very high
thick-soled sandals. I saw her head for the big staircase where
I followed her, if not in spite of myself, then at least not altogether willingly: it seemed to me my will power had been
abolished and my faculties of observation had been increased
proportionately. I followed a few paces behind her, we went
down the steps of the staircase together, we passed by the side
opening of the Régner Gallery, we traveled along the low

gallery of the Pommeraye Arcade. Nothing escaped my attention in the fatiguing décor through which we went. I noticed and retained with a sort of frenzied greediness, as painful as the sharpened sense of sight which often accompanies facial neuralgia, all the objects, all the signs, all the inscriptions in the windows of all the shops. Bookstores forced their way into my head, with the titles of more than a score of volumes; the dance and deportment school of "Miss Robin, certificated teacher" and photos of her prettiest students. Elsewhere, "art furniture," plenty of "Grand Prize terra cotta" sadly representing nymphs in flight, loving pigeons, a poor skinny lion. Further on was a truss manufacturer's store, such as one finds in almost all arcades, which overwhelmed me with orthopedic corsets, surgical belts, paraphernalia for hernias, Galen cancers, nets to put over open wounds on the nose, supports for breasts, splints, gauntlets, wads of cotton wool, suspensory bandages, and elastic stockings. At last, just before emerging into the Rue de la Fosse, I saw the window of a gunsmith whose name I had no option but to read on the glass, above the squat automatics, the shining fat rifles. The gunsmith, the last bubble rising weakly from the Pommeraye Arcade, is called Brichet.

Turning my attention back to myself at that point, I felt frightened at the idea of the importance acquired henceforth by all the tiniest details in that sort of bizarre diorama I had just explored, details fantastically enlarged by morbid attention on my part, as if I were about to see nothing ever again, and as one would imagine a condemned man has, looking about him from the top of the scaffold to which his last movements have brought him.

Outside the arcade, the air was pleasant and warm. Little pink clouds were drifting slowly above the Place de la Bourse; two or three old women, an old man, were sleeping on the benches in a narrow public park, dirtied by the coal dust of a railroad nearby; cats were playing in the shrinking spots of sunshine left them by the increasing shadows; evening was obviously coming, a fine evening, after the fine Fourteenth of July day.

The atmosphere was so enjoyable that, for a minute, I was on the point of freeing myself from the spell cast on me by that dark-haired sorceress, like a dark silk net that, with me in it, she was drawing behind her. The moment was a brief one, during which I could no longer feel anything except an agreeable impression of warmth contrasting with the dampness of the gallery, a great tenderness for those old people as well as for those cats in the sun, an even greater weariness, and a complete absence of desire for anything. Perhaps, at that moment, I really could have saved myself, for I stopped walking and felt astonished at finding myself free and indifferent in a world as banal as usual, but the woman turned her head, and without her even having to take one step back in my direction, I was once again captive to her beseeching eyes, to her gray pupils, dotted with yellow spangles.

We set off, following the Quai de la Fosse. Unexpected, right in the center of town, a train went rumbling by on the embankment behind the railing edging it and along which we were moving, she and I. It was a slow cattle train and, very close to our heads, from all the little skylights on the trucks came the bellowing of bulls on the way to the slaughterhouse; horrible to hear in the rattle of the wheels on the rails, after the silence of the arcade and of the drowsy town.

The unknown woman crossed the embankment, took the sidewalk past the old houses, turned into an alleyway, on the right, a little further down than the Rue Neuve des Capucins. In front of me I could see her hair blown out by the sea breeze, trembling like a black bird about to take flight, like the inky jet within which the cuttlefish conceals itself. I no longer could see anything, after a moment, but the dark stain made by her hair, dancing over the wretched gray walls, opening and closing about us ceaselessly as we moved forward.

At the end of a dead-end street that turned in a semicircle, finishing up pointing toward the embankment, stands a house that seems to be tall because it is very narrow, and has only one window to each floor above a door that is narrow, in proportion to the house, and flanked by two harpies in stone. It was there that the strange creature I had been unable to resist following came to a halt: precisely between the two harpies, whose woman's breasts hung flaccid over vulture's talons.

You would have glimpsed nothing alive, in that desolate place, but that woman and me, and also a very little yellow cat, crouching on the ground near a pot of basil long since dried up. Hurriedly, I approached her while her back was turned.

"Who, then?" I heard myself pronounce these words, without really recognizing my own voice and without even knowing what I meant, as if I had been awakened with a start.

I was going to touch the woman's dress, probably, take her hand, touch her hair; I was going to take her in my arms and uncover the most beautiful secret in Nantes. But she did a sudden turnabout which brought her face for an instant against mine, and then I recoiled from the expression of torture, terror or perhaps horror now imprinted on it; at the same time, her arms pushed me far away from her. The door opened with the short click of a trapdoor and the woman was lost to sight up a narrow spiral staircase, up which I rushed as quickly as possible after her. Already unsteady at the time of our first meeting, her hairdo had come down altogether at the time she made the gesture that should have sent me away, and it filled the narrow passageway of that staircase lit from above, making it dark behind her, but her hair also spread a good odor of animal warmth and sweat which kept me on her track. My eyes still retained the extraordinarily sharp picture of the woman as I had just caught her unawares, with the shame or repulsion I thought I had read in her face, with the cruel grimace deforming her mouth like that of a nun in ecstasy.

It was on the top floor that I caught her up, apparently exhausted, for I grasped her by the wrist without her protesting or putting up any fight at all. By her side, I went into a room that would have seemed miraculously enlarged, had not the beams of the ceiling shown it simply encroached upon the neighboring houses. Three big windows were flung open over the port of Nantes, it was around eight in the evening, the sun was sinking behind the aerial ferry, the cattle train had disappeared into the suburbs and silence had returned. The black-haired woman closed the door behind me and drew the bolt, then she went cowering into a corner of the room, where she began to weep, making hardly any sound. Sobs, choked back, shook her thin shoulders, while she gazed at me with an air of remorse and pity difficult to understand. But why was she becoming so distant from me and why was she fading from my sight, why was it all at once evident to me that she had played her role where I was concerned, and that nothing else bound me to her? I was slowly regaining my senses, as if after some drunken spell or a prolonged fainting fit, and applied myself to carefully examining what surrounded me in the vast aerial place where I had been led astray by that hunt during which I no longer knew if I was the tracker or the game.

A long rectangular table filled all the space comprised between the furthermost windows. On it, I could see linen stained with brown marks, punches, needles, cutting pliers, a collection of little knives of the most unusual shapes, as well as other instruments in shining steel that were completely foreign to me. On the table there was a big red quilted cushion; on this cushion, a strange beast looking at me sadly, part pig, part cat; or, more exactly, that seemed to me to be a pig covered with the soft fur of a pink Persian cat, without a tail, equipped with a very large cat's head, fine whiskers, fine cat's ears, but the feet of a pig and little sad eyes that looked like those of both animals at once. The sadness of those little golden-yellow eyes was terrifying, making me think of that sorrow, so very strange, one sees always, in the eyes of freaks. I recall a very old six-legged sheep displayed in a booth at the Trône Fair that was the very picture of despair, contemplated down all the ages of the world.

Then, only, appeared the other creature, that had just drawn back the drapes covering an alcove where it had remained until then; hissing, haughty, gilded by the sun's last fire, it held out to me its fine arm covered with smooth scales, and the black-haired woman hid her wild-looking eyes in her hands. Outside, a pair of big albatrosses dragged their inexorable weight across the mauve sky. There was no more hope left in me, nor fear, nor even doubt, but great weakness, and a feeling of infinite peace. "My hour had come," these solemn words, that I said over to myself in a low voice, were at last taking on the true meaning they will have, one day, for each of those who will read this. Resigned to everything that had to be consummated without delay, I went submissively forward toward the creature that held me prisoner with its vermilion effulgence and that, with a nacreous fingernail, was ceremoniously pointing out the draconian table, the rending instruments prepared for me.

*

This manuscript, written by the famous human caiman and found in his baggage shortly after his death, was passed on to us by a former master mariner who used to take a menagerie of freaks around the towns of Brittany. The showman, when we met him, had got abominably intoxicated to console himself for the loss of that member of his company, the biggest attraction of all.

He had picked up the human caiman, he confided in a tale too odd for us to be able to swear to having understood it perfectly, the day following a national holiday, in the early morning, after a stormy night of pleasure, on the steps leading to the red-light district of Nantes. Rolled up in a piece of scarlet rug, thrown out in the gutter among the running garbage of brothels, the injured monstrosity was uttering wailing sounds that had made him take it, at first, for an abandoned child; with care and attention, it had soon recovered, and had been in good health for several years, although living an existence entirely deprived of speech and less human than animal.

So many people have been able to examine the human caiman that we shall not undertake to describe its deformity once again. We shall add, only, that its keeper had not read the manuscript he handed over to us—he can hardly read—and that he declared on his honor as an old sailor that he had often seen the freak, in the packing case where it lived, blackening wrapping paper, clutching in its poor little webbed hand a fountain pen given away as advertising for a funeral parlor.

GISÈLE PRASSINOS

1920–

Of Greek parentage, Gisèle Prassinos was born in Istanbul. Her family emigrated to France when she was two years old. A precocious writer, whom André Breton is credited with discovering, she was only fourteen when her first texts appeared in 1934. They were published in the French surrealist-oriented magazine *Minotaure* and in the Belgian periodical *Documents 34*. The following year, her first book came out under the title *La Sauterelle arthritique* (*The Arthritic Grasshopper*), prefaced by the surrealist poet Paul Éluard, who also wrote a postface for her subsequent collection, *Le Feu maniaque*, in 1939.

Noting that in *La Sauterelle arthritique* "enchantment beats its wings among the strange attractions of crepuscular naturalism," Éluard praised in Gisèle Prassino's work the spirit of "dissociation, suppression, negation, revolt," in which he saw "the ethics of children, of poets who refuse to improve, and who will remain freaks so long as they have not awakened in all men the wish to face squarely everything separating them from themselves." Later, *Le Feu maniaque* prompted Éluard to remark of its author, "She offers all comers a pure moment in exchange for centuries of boredom."

Breton, for his part, declared in the *Anthologie de l'Humour noir*, "Gisèle Prassinos' tone is unique: all poets are jealous of it" (p. 568). That tone marks the three earliest stories reproduced here: *Journoir* (*Blackday*) and *L'Arbre aux trois branches* (*The Three-branched Tree*), dating from 1934, and *Le Feu maniaque*, written the following year. These texts are characteristic, in that they make us witnesses to the operation of a child's imagination, as yet unrestrained by the adult's sense of the world as stable and limited by rational predictability. The narrator's attitude is consistently closer to curiosity than to horror, while no moral preoccupations color her account.

Completed more than a decade later, *Le Gros Chèque* (*The Big Bank Check* [1946]) indicates that sophistication has come with maturity. Yet sophistication in no way reduces the impact of the narrative as a confrontation with the inexplicable. Instead, the perspective of adulthood injects a note of anxiety into a tale that, we notice, still draws its substance from the child's world. We now hear communicated a sense of estrangement and displacement, giving rise to feelings that help foster a disquieting mood which the passage of time does nothing to dissipate. The long-term results may be observed in *La Robe de laine* (*The Wood Dress*), taken from the collection Gisèle Prassinos published in 1961 under the title *Le Cavalier* (*The Rider*). Time has not modified her outlook upon the world as mysterious, alien, threatening. Now, details our experience of everyday living encourages us to treat as true to life, disturbingly lend authenticity to events that overturn our comfortable idea of the normal in its reassuring permanence.

Bringing together a number of her early texts under the heading *Les Mots endormis* (*Sleeping Words*), Gisèle Prassinos spoke of them in 1967 as "the result of a certain absence": "There is a pocket of darkness in us that, with the help of a drowziness of consciousness, writing succeeds in penetrating. Once the first word has been set free, the wave breaks. Then comes the moment when the pen drops, discouraged by its own hesitation. Something has intervened; returning, consciousness reclaims its rights, wishing to put things in order. Consciousness is now surprised, sometimes filled with wonder by the word from the dark, often tempted to make a contribution of its own." Born of the *absence* brought about by the practice of automatic writing, the stories of Gisèle Prassinos lend support to Éluard's affirmation that automatism "ceaselessly opens new doors on the unconscious and, as it confronts the unconscious with the conscious, with the world, increases its treasures."

GISÈLE PRASSINOS

Blackday

One day, it was cold.

Over the river spread a white sheet, hiding the uniformly somber hues of that day.

When night fell, a man came up out of the water. He made for a hollow in the stone, where already a dog had taken refuge. In the light from a luminous corner of the sky, I could make the man out: he wore on his head an immense funnel of string, delicately worked and adorned with sharp pebbles, which he had had a tinker friend make, in exchange for a ball of red thread.

He seemed laden down with unrusted scrap iron, for which no doubt he would go searching under the water, to sell it on the bank and take in sand.

When he became aware of the dog's presence—so far as I could tell in the dark—I think his moustache, which stuck out a long way, spread even further and took on a V shape. Terrified by this change, the dog turned its eyes to the wall and felt the end of its tail stick to the stone sides of the hole. But, seeing the stranger calm the irritability of his hair with a feverish start, it was reassured and went to curl up in a corner so as not to witness its bedfellow's prayers.

The man put down his load.

He thought this was the best thing to do and, kneeling on

the wet paving stones, he invoked the solitude of the poet.

During this time, the dog, which was foraging as deep as it could in its external intestines, kept its eye half closed, the better to watch over the silence. But, seeing by its side the still, cold bulk of the crouching man, it fell asleep, not able to put up with things any longer.

. . . .

The water flowed on, its scrap iron at the bottom of its bed, awaiting only the man with his load in order to stop. There were only small waves, formed by the mechanical ebb and flow of the heavy clouds.

Day appeared with its light and its dark. The man got up, his hat on his waist and his soft moustache hardened by the night.

He went off, swept down upon the river bank and disappeared in the deep waters to look for new things.

But the dog, still young, stayed where it was.

GISÈLE PRASSINOS

The Three-branched Tree

Evening was setting in over the houses in the Rue de Tronchet. At the window of one of these buildings, two women with very long dark hair and green eyes were cutting up pieces of red material that fell in tiny scraps under the scissors. One of them had her hair in a green band that blended with her eyes. The other had whiter hands and wore no ribbon, but her eyes were covered with an opaque gray skin that extended from her eyelids. They carried on working until from inside the apartment came a desperate voice in pain, at its last gasp. They got up quietly, then, leaving material and scissors where they were. Together they disappeared, moving in unison. After a moment, the window was slammed shut and they were seen no more.

Night came and a bare arm closed the window shutters. Everything went dark. No light shone in the street.

Toward midnight, a long ominous cry rent the air, coming from the window. Immediately, loads of little red squares flew up into the air. One by one, they fell to the sidewalk below and the dirty water of the gutter carried them away. They disappeared into a black hole, at the end of the street.

. . . .

At dawn a bareheaded man, wearing only a rag around his thighs, was walking slowly along the banks of the Seine. He was pulling behind him, on a string, a large aluminum box full of some rubbish or other. Arriving under an embankment arch, he sat down on the ground, on a stone. His naked body pressed against the cold and he smiled. That smile remained on that face with soft purple cheeks. As though blind, his wild eyes rolled in their sockets, and at last came to rest on a distant object floating on the water of the river. It was something red, an accumulation of shapeless blood. A livid severed hand dug its nails into the soft substance which was changing in shape.

The thing passed by.

The water came.

Another thing passed: long black threads, hair hanging down. The strong wind, passing low over the surface of the water, touched the hair lightly and turned it over.

The man saw a white globe with two gray holes in it.

While daylight increased, the globe sank into the water, slowly, the black threads following . . .

GISÈLE PRASSINOS

The Maniac Fire

Pigée thought her son was asking her a question. And so she got up and, crawling, catching onto the corners of the furniture, she managed to grasp the foot of the armchair and leaned against it. There her child was. She took hold of his smock and held him for a time, feeling the little boy's pierced fingers scratch her lungs. He cannot have had a good memory, for, from time to time, a loud groan escaped from the full smock. Pigée would lift him up, bring her lips forward in a kiss on the soaking flesh. Then she would notice that the child had no vertebrae, that he would not last for long in the heat of the cretonne . . . Sometimes she wanted to pinch him so that he would speak, but her fingers slid over the skin and she realized he had no consistency.

She wanted to crawl some more, but as the fire reached as far as the wall, she feared the Devil who used to come sometimes and touch her blood.

She wanted to get up: the child fell back into his place under the armchair while Pigée threw her fingers into the flames, very quickly, because of her rings which gave her the shivers.

There was, behind the door, a sort of dog that wanted to get in. Since the rain had started, his precarious paws gripped the door latch that could be seen rattling from time to time.

Pigée was afraid he would upset the floorboards with his jumping. She thought the dog wanted to put out the fire and take the little boy, who belonged to him, perhaps. She crawled faster.

Going by the larder, she stretched out an arm and was able to pick up a silver spoon. She stuck it in her belt and continued dragging herself along by her fingers that ran over the floor making holes in the threads covering it. But she had not seen the fire was following her, attracted by the spoon. It held aloft the little invisible monster, whose oily skin would not burn. The fire sent out a long slender advance guard, the color of a flower. It tried to fasten onto Pigée's foot so as to catch her but she felt its breath ahead of her and tried to make holes in the threads even faster . . .

Soon she arrived at the door which she opened: the dog was no longer there, only his paws were hanging from the first plank.

Pigée could see nothing. She went down the three steps, despite the absence of thread. The fire reached out its more and more delicate tongue. It took a sudden turn, the better to bite its prey. But the latter was running, her hands torn, already almost aflame.

Soon she arrived on the unpaved earth, where she could crawl more furiously. Then the fire, which had no legs, did not manage to reach her. It withdrew its tongue and made vain efforts with the child on its rounded back . . .

Pigée took hold of the parapet. Her feet reached the top, but her diseased hands stuck to the metal. The time she lost brought the fire closer. It succeeded in fastening onto Pigée's feet. With a final effort, she managed to throw herself into the water.

The fire followed her. There was a bubbling, with a noise similar to that of a flaming match thrown into cold water. All at once, the fire was eaten up.

The child seated above it was turned into oil. He spread over the surface of the water and formed thousands of little deformed spots, in which colored houses could be seen . . .

GISÈLE PRASSINOS

The Big Bank Check

A little girl had a big bank check in her pocket. She was running in a long street lined with different kinds of vegetables that people walking gathered as they went by, after struggling a while with their neighbors.

The street was full of people right out into the middle of the roadway. There was only a narrow rocky border, slippery and winding, set with gigantic standard lamps, where the little girl, armed with her check, walked painfully. From time to time, she felt a glance rest upon her and half-opened her eyes. But most of the time it was a tomato or a fresh onion, pushed a little back of the others.

She suddenly felt a great need to wash. She went through a doorway bearing the sign "Little Fair," climbed one flight and found herself in front of a closed iron gate. A woman-spider opened up for her. It had big piercing eyes, black hair drawn up to the top of its skull in a tiny bun and held in its hands a little soft horsehair brush. It pushed the little girl inside and, without speaking, roughly pointed out an empty tub, at the far end of the silent room. To get to it, she had to go by other tubs where people were scrubbing themselves in fear, with as little noise as possible and movements of extraordinary slowness.

The little girl closed her eyes because she did not want to look, but her eyelids had become transparent and she was obliged to see that most of the clients were dead. Those who were not received blows constantly from the insect-woman.

The little girl undressed and got into the water. For a moment she lost consciousness because of the heat and, when she came to again, she saw floating in front of her an unidentified object, perhaps of rubber, that disgusted her. She caught the eye of the spider, which was coming toward her. Fortunately, an old man having spilled a little water on the floor, the animal stopped to beat him.

Without losing a second, the little girl tried to hide the object in the hole of the tub's waste pipe.

The spider was getting closer and the object was putting up a fight.

It kept coming back up.

She had to sit on it.

"What is it?" asked the menacing animal, without opening its mouth.

"Nothing . . ."

The little girl had such a tremendous voice that she took fright and fainted again.

. . . .

When she came to, everyone had gone. Only the corpses were left. The iron gate was closed. In the distance the comfortable rumble of the fair was audible, interrupted sometimes by the strident blast of a trumpet.

The child took hold of the bars of the gate and shook very hard. The house crumbled to the ground.

Once outside, starting to run again, she slipped on a rotten vegetable and tore in two, at the same time as the big bank check.

GISÈLE PRASSINOS

The Wool Dress

And there you are. Now, I don't know where to go any more, without baggage, without money, with just the dress on my back. Luckily, it's a warm one, I knitted it myself by hand, it took me, that's true, two winters of nonstop work; but I can say I'm dressed now. If that thing hadn't happened, everything would be fine, really. And I don't have an aunt in the world, not a sister, nor even a friend whose place I could go to for shelter. Nothing, I've nothing left.

This morning still, I was sitting in my room, I'd hardly finished ironing the seams of my knit dress—I'd finished the last stitch yesterday evening at eleven o'clock—when there was a ring at the door.

Opening it, I was sure, straight off, that I didn't know the three people laden with cases and the baby smiling at me with quite sincere pleasure. I couldn't lie and let them believe it was me they were looking for. Very quickly, before one of them, by mistake, jumped on me to kiss me, for I could see very well they were getting their mouths ready, I said:

"You must be mistaken, I don't know you."

However, no one listened or heard me and I had to submit to an embrace from all of them, one after the other. They even put in my arms the child the younger woman held in hers. Its face and especially its mouth was covered with scabs and patches of raw flesh. It was smiling though like the others and awkwardly laid its poor diseased cheek against mine, to the great joy of its relatives: the father, the mother, and the grandmother, no doubt.

Then they put their cases down and the two women noticed my dress on the hanger. It still gave off a light steam after the careful ironing I'd given it. The younger one looked at the other, full of mute admiration for what she could see, murmuring something in her ear. Finally, they came close to feel the wool and judge its quality, as if my dress was in a shop window and they wanted to be quite sure before buying it. I felt afraid and couldn't resist the wish to put it away safe. I summoned up my courage, I took the dress down and slipped it on in front of them, in spite of their eyes fastened to my every movement. I tell myself, now, I did the right thing.

You couldn't say they weren't friendly, on the contrary, they were even willing to help.

"Don't put yourself out for us," they said, "we'll manage, we'll even unpack our cases on our own."

And that was true. With the child wedged on the sideboard, all three of them took out their things and laid them on my bed in orderly little bundles.

"And how's your mother's cold, better?" the old woman asked me in a soft voice, as she counted the pile of baby's diapers.

She's been dead eighteen years, my mother has, but I couldn't answer, my jaws seemed stuck together forever.

And she went on:

"*He* didn't want to come, you know what he's like. Always doing the opposite of other people. I could've insisted, but because of you, because I thought he could cause trouble, I told him, 'Do as you like.' "

"He'll make up his mind to it, alright, one day," said the man in a tone of indifference and, anxiously, "Joan, it's time," he added, speaking to the young woman, after looking at his watch. "Just give it a try, all you've got to do is stretch out, I'll hand him to you."

She began to cry softly on her mother's shoulder and, with a tired air, did as she was told. Then she took out a skinny little breast and the child threw himself at it. Then the other two stood one each side of my bed to watch.

"Do you think it's going to start again?" said the old woman, while her daughter's closed eyelids trembled as if in expectation of a dreaded event.

The man remained silent and watched greedily. He looked, at that moment, like one of those fanatics photographed for movie newsreels during a boxing match or at the races.

The child was sucking and fidgeting at the end of the gray nipple it was drawing in further and further, ceaselessly letting go and taking hold again, with grunts of impatience.

"Little vampire!" said the father in a changed tone, his mouth twisted, while his eyes filled with strange pride.

"It's begun . . . ," said the old woman.

What had begun was blood. It ran around the child's mouth, soaking the breast and the sheets of my bed on which the young woman was struggling feebly.

When she seemed to have fainted away and the child quietened down, its nose in its food, its father took it in his arms and amused himself making it laugh.

"We're going to eat too?" he proposed at that point.

"Let's eat then," said the old woman, looking at me.

What could I do, but bring out the bread and the nuts for my own dinner? But as that seemed only to half satisfy them, I opened the two cans of sardines I kept in stock.

When everything had been eaten up, the father stretched and lay down by the side of his wife who still hadn't moved since suckling the baby. The old woman curled up across the bottom of the bed, after placing the baby up close to her.

They put the light out. There were a few minutes of silence during which I tried to settle on the freezing floor. Then I heard my bed squeak, once, twice, then the baby began to whimper gently, as they all do before falling asleep. In the dark the old woman had sat up, her hands crossed on her stomach.

I tried to manage to sleep on the cold floor, I couldn't do so. The moment I began to warm the wood under my body, the bed began to make a noise again, and I heard the man whisper:

"My dear, my beauty, my sweetie . . ."

"No, no!" the young woman moaned.

Récits parallèles call for no less than four players each of whom, explains Micheline Bounoure, writes down on a sheet of paper "the automatic account of one and the same event that all could have witnessed." As if the phases of this incident had been forgotten, each in turn tries to bring them to the surface of consciousness by pronouncing aloud a "reference word" that everyone now introduces into his own version. Micheline Bounoure insists that narrative automatism can be preserved, only by the rapid rhythm with which reference words (set in italic in the examples below) are voiced.

In short, the games consist in enriching automatic flow by means of stimuli that demand attention and, since they call for assimilation, serve repeatedly to reorient, for each of the participants, the narrative developing on the page in front of him.

The *récits parallèles* that follow, both previously unpublished, date from July 1973. In each case the names of the players appear parenthetically at the end.

A discussion of parallel stories, drawn from correspondence exchanged by Bounoure and Guy Cabanel, appears in the ninth issue of the *Bulletin* (December 1974, pp. 12-15), under the title "Ricochets."

The Partridge Eye: parallel story

Partridge Eye was the name of an autumn flower. It wasn't easy to find in the March bushes. But it hurt the whites of the eyes of lovers planted on the *cliff* for a few decades. Was this flower a good luck charm? *Strong Current Headland* itself, where the lovers found themselves, could not have been able to say and offered only a few *Creole* shellfish that an *outbreak* of *fire* had been unable to dissolve. You find the same kind of thing on *Gaiety* Street when the gulls come down out of the Tropics for the winter and the shops selling refreshments are short of *lemonade* because summer has been everywhere it shouldn't go, and so much the better, for where would we go if *paintbrushes* began to unveil their secrets and *go on strike*? The child painters would be reduced to painting with their fingers great dream landscapes such as one sees in pictures in still-life deception on nocturnal *glass* where desire has itself taken at its word. It would take an *Open Touring Car* to get the better of the distance and *distract in vain* a few avenues of plane trees in our usual land-scapes where we find inscribed the winding paths of customary unrealities such as one scarcely ever finds in the *Museums* of the indoctrinated mind. What a *hollow road* to get lost in with pleas-ure! The skies are *overcast* and the *mist* is barely rising. But genuine dicta do not always create a fair wind. *Calomel* scarcely has a baneful action upon the clouds ready to burst above the prehistoric *steeples* whose silhouette haunted by *eagles* is out-lined against the fronton of our extravagant thoughts.

*

The *partridge eye* is all blue this evening, it stretches toward the headland of the *cliff*. Who would have expected so much of that cloddish stupidity, of that trinket for visitors to *Strong Current Headland* or for old *Creole* women making their *début* on the occasion of the *fire* at the *Gaiety*? However, we were going to live in the middle of those baneful furrows, of those sufferings, long stirred up, in which ran *lemonade*. No it was not in the evening, at least we hoped that time had got in advance of the *pencils* of light unveiled to us by the grandiloquent storms and *strike* pickets that posted themselves on the steps of industries and of vivandière *glass*. What more would we have done that surround the *open touring cars* with hurrahs that *distracted* us, perhaps *in vain*, from the bleeding cream and the sea swell of blue tar. We would also perhaps, except for the urgency of snow *frittered away*[5] by various *hollow roads*, in the *scrambled* salad, the ears' *mist*. The flower of the pine has left for hopes of *calomel*, for *steeples* whose silhouette absents itself with what is called the *eagle*.

*

A *partridge eye* set in a platinum ring? my dear you're crazy! Mad she was and from the top of the *cliff* she threw herself into the sea, they found her at *Strong Current Headland*. She was a splen-did *Creole* whose *début* on the stage had set many *fires* in the *Gaiety* Theater and yet she never offered anything but *lemonade* to the lovers who besieged her in her dressing-room. She had never been seen naked, though, she was said to be inured to the *brush*, but since the porters *were on strike* she no longer hid her-self and it was the king of *glass* from Mexico who had carried her off the day before yesterday in his *Open Touring Car*. The men-about-town no longer being able to find *distrac*tions searched *in vain* for the beautiful Creole in all the *museums* in Brittany and it is on the *hollow road*, their eyes *blurred* by the *mist* that they had

---

5. *Musée*, "Museum," and *musé*, "frittered away," are homonyms.

to call upon *calomel* from the glove box to find once again the *steeple* lost in the underbrush but over which an *eagle* was flying.

*

Partridge Eye was not an Indian. The red ring of the eye had not been painted by the hand of the holy man. However, it could see through bushes and *cliffs*, go through the shadow of all appearances to the perception of danger and of the possible. The possible and danger. All men questioned one another. Is *Strong Current Headland* the beginning of the Land or the end of the Sea? Is *Creole* the *beginning* of the Transformation or the end of *fire*? The partridge eye unveiled nothing. Its pupil lit up with *gaiety* as its stare became more apparent. But joy remained secret. People sipped *lemonade* to put on a good front but they didn't know what to think. What *brush*, with its strokes, could unveil the *strike* of things dreamed? One must paint to discover and the partridge eye girt with its red ring was interrogation itself, a mirror, a *glass* that reflected each to himself—the noise of the *open touring cars distract*ed no one anymore. Everyone thought the external agitation was taking place *in vain* and that that wasn't the essential thing. But what could the eye see and did it belong to the partridge? You can put partridges in *museums*—you can stuff them. But their glance remains in the *hollow roads, blurred* by the *mist* of our uncertainties, hollow roads that plunge into the banks of *calomel*, that disappear in a wind contained in the ambition of the *steeples* whose silhouette tries to resemble the *eagle*, the better to fly over the dead time of definitive fixations.

(Marianne van Hirtum, Vincent Bounoure, Micheline Bounoure, Renaud)

The Dog:
parallel story

The hunter's dog was *worth*less and the worried hunter would sniff the air in place of his dog. But to *sniff* is not to hunt. And so one can inhale *camomile* or *smell* the scent of infusions but this is to *reject* forever the chance of finding the *coral* whose *gleam* shines only behind the *closing* of enchanted bushes that only greyhounds can open with the first *finger* of their forefeet. Showing the velvet finger. The hunter ran an ad in the *newspaper* and hung in the *subway* a notice that *Negresses* could *read*—but they had never *tamed* greyhounds. In spite of his *weekly* notices the hunter's requests *made off*. He decided to hunt no more and became a *head surgeon* operating on *cigarette-lighters* on the banks of the *Marne* in a *brick* hospital, of course.[6] All this scarcely roused him to enthusiasm. He had the feeling he was working on *garbage* and with the *balance* of the possible this was hardly reassuring. Singing *ritornelles*, he went into courtyards to harvest *stoppers* instead of *coal* to put in his fireplace. That didn't do either. He became a *lighthouse keeper*.

*

One *dog* doesn't make a spring, the concierge at the Orangerie

---

6. *Briquet,* "cigarette-lighter," is treated as a derivative of *brique,* "brick."

Museum used to say with *force* busy *sniff*ing that December morning air. She brewed herself *camomile* tea and began to *smell* her middle finger to know if it was time to *reject* the *coral* that was obscuring its *gleam* in an army dressing-station candle. *Closing* time having rung, she rapidly set the table before the eyes of a petrified Goya that immediately dipped its *finger* in the camomile tea and finding it too salty mopped its brow on the *subway's newspaper* just given it by the Negress playing the *tame lyre*.[7] This Negress laid a few *weeklies* on Voltaire's armchair and her evening *made off* in that way. But the *head surgeon* made his appearance and demanded the reopening of the Museum, content to use *cigarette-lighters* instead of lighting. *The Marne* had never had so many of them. A few *bricks* all but decorated the façade of the Marne opera house which was having the première of "*Garbage.*" The *balance* marked five o'clock and the *ritornelles* were becoming blurred to the sound of *stoppers* that took the place of char*coal*, for times are difficult and it isn't easy to heat a museum in the care of a *lighthouse keeper* like the one who occults the Eiffel Tower.

*

What a *dog*! what a dirty trick, what a *worth*less fellow! you've seen him, it's my grandfather stretched out in the sun on the roses to *sniff* them. He smells the *camomile* too, he goes down next toward the river bank, *smells* the feet of the willows and sometimes he drowns himself until the water *throws* him *back* on the *coral* cliff, on that gentle dying *gleam*. The dog, though, doesn't die, he gets into his *zipper*,[8] he holds himself aloof, he moves one *finger*, two fingers, he dozes, and spits into the air, he gets up and pulls a *newspaper* from his pocket, he can't find the spectacles he lost twelve years ago in the *subway*, losing track of time too with a *Negress* and plucking the strings of his *lyre*, but without going so far as to *tame* that person. But his *weekly* has not returned. He gets up with a movement that *makes off*, like the clumsy saurian and then at last he grabs his *head surgeon*'s cap which always remains for this circumstance on the beach laid on his *cigarette-lighter* but remains marked with *marl*[9] and

---

7. Said aloud, *lire*, "to read," and *lyre*, "lyre," sound the same.
8. *Fermeture*, "closing" and "closure," gives *fermeture éclair*, "zipper."
9. *Marne*, in French.

raw *bricks* where he, the dog, has fallen down during the drinking bouts. *Garbage!* he's going to get up now on his boots like great weights on the *scales* of the earth, those whose *ritornelle* makes you think of the *stopper*, of *coal*, of the burnt cork with which they make up circus funny men to give them a thrashing as the *lighthouse keepers* beat the revolving lens of our misery.

*

I bought a fine rifle at the flea market, nothing but the *dog* has colossal *value*, therefore I pulled it out to go sell it at a jeweler's on the Rue des Rosiers. Taking off his beard and his spectacles the old man *sniff*ed the dog, treated himself to a glass of *camomile* tea, *smelled*, *threw* the dog *back* behind his counter, and insulted me. The dog having broken, a great *coral* flower came out of it, as big as a palm tree I went to plant near St. Paul. There emanated from it a great *gleam* that alerted the caretakers of Viviani Square who decided its *closing*. My left middle *finger* having got caught between two *newspaper* pages I then was rushing into the *subway*, a *Negress* with large breasts put my finger between her breasts to make a *lyre* out of them. My *tamed* finger began again to live and to quiver according to its *weekly* rhythm but everything, all of a sudden, *made off*. The *head surgeon* from the Pitié Hospital, by accident in a second-class compartment, having sensed a strange tale, took out his *cigarette-lighter* and told us in a very loud voice, "I who was one of those in the taxis of the *Marne*! I'll give you a *brick*[10] if you'll kindly come home immediately with me!"—*Garbage!* we reply, my Negress and I, I don't give a rap for your brick,[11] I know the *old story*,[12] it's a bribe you want to give us, a *stopper*, and I've got enough *coal* in my pocket to end my days as a *lighthouse keeper*."

*

"*Dog*," he said and the alpha star of the Centaur dreamed. Its *value* the relationship between the lion's tooth and the thirty-two teeth that chew it in a salad, *sniff*ing the sailing-ship's saltpeter, when the sons of *camomile* awake *smell*ing the whale's

---

10. A *brique* is a million francs.
11. "Je m'en *balance* de ta brique."
12. "Je connais la *ritournelle*."

spray that *rejects* the sons and daughters of *coral*. A *gleam* to star-
board, cries the swallow. The sea is a *zipper*. Its *fingers* turn over
the pages of a *newspaper* whose columns are *subway* trains. The
Negress at gone five in the morning takes herself for a *lyre* whose
tame goat fires accents that make the rails sob. But the steel is
weekly like the catastrophes the stories of which *make off*! The *head
surgeons* are handicapped in the larynx, this is why they leave it
to their *cigarette-lighters* to call the taxis of the *Marne*, why they'll
pay three *bricks* to go get beaten up, between three ashtrays of
garbage . . .

(Renaud, Marianne van Hirtum, Vincent Bounoure, Micheline
Bounoure, Jean-Louis Bédouin)

Works Cited

(Unless otherwise indicated, the place of publication is Paris.)

1. BOOKS

(a) *Primary Sources*

Apollinaire, Guillaume. *Les Mamelles de Tirésias* [1903-1916], Éditions du Bélier, 1946.

Aragon, Louis. *Le Paysan de Paris*. Éditions de la N.R.F., 1926.

———. *Les Collages*. Hermann, 1965.

Arrabal, Fernando. *La Pierre de la folie*. René Julliard, éditeur, 1963.

Bédouin, Jean-Louis. *La Poésie surréaliste*. Seghers, 1963.

———. *Victor Segalen*. Seghers, 1963.

———. *Libre Espace*. Seghers, 1967.

Benayoun, Robert. *Anthologie du Nonsense*. Jean-Jacques Pauvert, 1959.

———. *Érotique du surréalisme*. Jean-Jacques Pauvert, 1965.

Bounoure, Vincent. *Envers l'Ombre*. Editions surréalistes, 1965.

Breton, André (in collaboration with Philippe Soupault). *Les Champs magnétiques*. Au Sans Pareil, 1920.

————. *Les Pas perdus*, Éditions de la Nouvelle Revue Française, 1924.

————. *Nadja*. Éditions de la N.R.F., 1928.

————. *Le Revolver à cheveux blancs*. Éditions des Cahiers libres, 1932.

————. *Les Vases communicants*. Éditions des Cahiers libres, 1932.

————. *L'Amour fou*. Gallimard, 1937.

————. *Arcane 17* (originally published in New York by Brentano's, 1944) *enté d'Ajours*. Jean-Jacques Pauvert, éditeur, 1947.

————. *Manifestes du surréalisme* (originally published in 1924 and 1930). Jean-Jacques Pauvert, n.d. [1962].

————. *Le Surréalisme et la peinture* [1928]. Definitive edition, Gallimard, 1965.

————. *Clair de terre* [1923]. Preface by Alain Jouffroy. Gallimard, 1966.

————. *Anthologie de l'Humour noir* [1939]. Definitive edition, Jean-Jacques Pauvert, 1966.

Bussy, Christian. *L'Accent grave*. Brussels: Les Lèvres Nues, Collection "Le Fait accompli," no. 19-20. April 1969.

Carrington, Leonora. *La Dame ovale*. GLM, 1939.

————. *En bas*. Éditions Fontaine, 1945.

Crevel, René. *Babylone*. Simon Kra, 1927.

Desnos, Robert. *La Liberté ou l'amour!* Aux Éditions du Sagittaire, chez Simon Kra, 1927.

Duchamp, Marcel. *Boîte verte*. Éditions Rrose Sélavy, 1934.

Dumont, Fernand. *A Ciel ouvert*. La Louvière: Éditions des Cahiers de Rupture, 1937.

————*La Région du cœur*. Mons: Éditions du Groupe surréaliste en Hainaut, 1939.

————. *Traité des fées*. Antwerp: Ça ira, 1942.

————. *La Liberté*. Mons: Éditions de Haute Nuit, 1948.

————. *L'Étoile du berger*. Brussels: Labor, 1955.

————. *La Dialectique du hasard au service du désir*. Unpublished.

Eluard, Paul. *Donner à voir*. Editions de la N.R.F., 1939.

Ferry, Jean. *Le Mécanicien et autres contes* [Aux dépens des Cinéastes Bibliophiles, 1950]. Gallimard, 1953.

————. *Fidélité*. Arcanes, 1953.

————. *Une Étude sur Raymond Roussel*. Arcanes, 1953.

Fourré, Maurice. *Tête-de-Nègre*. Gallimard, 1960.

Goemans, Camille. *Œuvre 1922-1957*. Brussels: André De Rache, éditeur, n.d. [1970].

Hénein, Georges. *Un Temps de petite fille*. Les Éditions de Minuit, 1947.

——. *Le Seuil interdit*. Mercure de France, 1956.

Jouffroy, Alain. *Les Quatre Saisons d'une âme*. Éditions du Dragon, n.d. [1955].

——. *Une Révolution du regard*. Gallimard, 1963.

——. *Aube à l'antipode*. Le Soleil noir, 1966.

——. *Saint-Pol-Roux: les plus belles pages*. Mercure de France, 1966.

Lacomblez, Jacques. *L'Aquamanile du vent*. [Brussels:] Éditions EDDA, n.d. [1961].

Lebel, Robert. *Premier Bilan de l'art actuel*, no. 3-4 (1953) of *Le Soleil noir. Positions*.

——. *Sur Marcel Duchamp*. Paris and London: Éditions Trianon, 1959; New York: Grove Press, 1960.

——. *La Double Vue*. Le Soleil noir, 1964.

Limbour, Georges. *Soleils bas*. Galerie Simon, 1924.

——. *L'Illustre Cheval blanc*. Éditions de la Nouvelle Revue Française, 1930.

——. (in collaboration with Michel Leiris). *André Masson et son univers*. Geneva and Paris: Éditions des Trois Collines, n.d. [1947].

——. *Masson: Dessins*. Paris: Les Éditions Braun et Cie; New York: Erich S. Herrmann, n.d. [1951].

——. *Contes et Récits*. Gallimard, 1973.

Mabille, Pierre. *Le Merveilleux*. Les Éditions des Quatre Vents, 1946.

Mansour, Joyce. *Cris*. Seghers, 1953.

——. *Déchirures*. Éditions de Minuit, 1955.

——. *Jules César*. Seghers, 1958.

——. *Les Gisants Satisfaits*. Jean-Jacques Pauvert, éditeur, 1958.

——. *Rapaces*. Seghers, 1960.

——. *Carré blanc*. Le Soleil noir, 1965.

——. *Le Bleu des fonds*. Le Soleil noir, 1968.

——. *Ça*. Le Soleil noir, 1970.

Mariën, Marcel. *Trattato della pittura ad olio e aceta*. Milan: Communicazione, 1972.

———. *Crystal Blinkers*. Harpford, Sidmouth, Devon, England: TransformaCtion, 1973.

———. *L'Ancre jeté dans le doute*. Brussels: Les Lèvres Nues, n.d. [1973].

Markale, Jean, *Les Grands Bardes gallois*. G. Fall, 1956.

———. *Épopée celtique en Bretagne*. Payot, 1971.

———. *La Femme celte*. Payot, 1972.

Nougé, Paul, *Histoire de ne pas rire*. Brussels: Editions de la revue Les Lèvres Nues, 1956.

———. *L'Expérience continue*. Brussels: Éditions de la revue Les Lèvres Nues, 1966.

———. *Journal 1941-1950*. Brussels: Les Lèvres Nues, 1968.

———. *Notes sur les échecs*. Brussels: Les Lèvres Nues, 1968.

———. *Fragments*. First Series (1923-1929). Brussels: Les Lèvres Nues, Collection "Le Fait accompli," no. 13, November 1968; Second Series (1926-1941), no. 17, February 1969.

Péret, Benjamin. *Je ne mange pas de ce pain-là*. Éditions surréaliste, 1936.

———. *La Brebis galante*. Les Éditions premières, 1949.

———. *Mort aux Vaches et au champ d'honneur*. Arcanes, 1953.

———. *Le Gigot, sa vie et son œuvre*. Le Terrain vague, 1957.

———. *Anthologie des Mythes, légendes et contes populaires d'Amérique*. Éditions Albin Michel, 1960.

———. *Le Déshonneur des poètes* [1945] précédé de *La Parole est Péret*. Jean-Jacques Pauvert, 1965.

Pierre, José. *Le Futurisme et le Dadaïsme*. Lausanne: Éditions Rencontre, 1966.

———. *Le Surréalisme*. Lausanne: Éditions Rencontre, 1966.

———. *Le Ça ira*. Éditions surréalistes, 1967.

———. *D'Autres Chats à fouetter*. Éric Losfeld, 1968.

———. *Théâtre*. Denoël, 1969.

Pieyre de Mandiargues, André. *Dans les Années sordides*. Monaco: Privately printed, 1943.

———. *Le Musée noir*. Laffont, 1946.

———. *Soleil des loups*. Laffont, 1951.

———. *Le Lis de mer*. Laffont, 1956.

———. *La Motocyclette*. Gallimard, 1963.

Prassinos, Gisèle. *La Sauterelle arthritique*. G.L.M., 1935.

———. *Le Feu manique*. aux dépens de Robert J. Godet, 1939.

———. *Le Cavalier*. Plon, 1961.

————. *Les Mots endormis.* Flammarion, 1967.

Sebbag, Georges. *Le Masochisme quotidien.* Le Point d'Etre, 1972.

(b) *Secondary Sources*

Alexandrian, Sarane. *Surrealist Art.* New York and Washington:
Praeger; London: Thames & Hudson, 1970.

Alleau, René, ed. *Dictionnaire des jeux.* Tchou, éditeur, 1964.

Duplessis, Yves. *Le Surréalisme.* Presses Universitaires de France,
1950.

Esslin, Martin. *The Theatre of the Absurd* [1961]. Revised edition.
New York: Doubleday Anchor, 1969.

Kyrou, Ado. *Le Surréalisme au cinéma* [1953]. Revised edition;
Le Terrain vague, 1963.

Matthews, J. H., ed. *An Anthology of French Surrealist Poetry.* London: University of London Press, 1966; Minneapolis: University of Minnesota Press, 1967.

————. *Surrealism and Film.* Ann Arbor: The University of
Michigan Press, 1971.

Read, Herbert. *A Coat of Many Colours.* London: Routledge,
1945.

Rubin, William S. *Dada and Surrealist Art.* New York: Abrams,
n.d.

Schwarz, Arturo. *The Complete Works of Marcel Duchamp.* New
York: Abrams, 1969.

2. MAGAZINES

A Phala (São Paulo), August 1967.

L'Archibras, no. 1 (April 1967)-no. 7 (March 1969).

Aventure, no. 1 (November 1921)-no. 3 (January 1922).

BIEF: jonction surréaliste, no. 1 (November 1958)-no. 12 (April
1960).

La Brèche: action surréaliste, no. 1 (October 1961)-no. 8 (November 1965).

Bulletin de liaison surréaliste, no. 1 (November 1970)—.

La Carte d'après nature (Brussels), no. 1 (October 1952)-no. 12
(1956).

Correspondance (Brussels), six tracts published during 1924-25.
Distances (Brussels), no. 1 (February 1928)-no. 3 (April 1928).
Edda (Brussels), no. 1 (Summer 1958)-no. 5 (October 1964).
Free UNIONS libres (London), July 1946.
Les Lèvres Nues (Brussels), First Series no. 1 (April 1954)-no. 10
   to 12 (September 1958); Second Series, no. 1 (January 1969)—.
London Bulletin (London), no. 1 (April 1938, called *London Gallery
   Bulletin*)-no. 18 to 20 (June 1940).
Mauvais Temps (La Louvière), 1935.
Minotaure, no. 1 (January 1933)-no. 13 (October 1938).
Nadrealizam danas i ovde (Belgrade), no. 1 (June 1931)-no. 3
   (June 1932).
La Part du sable (Cairo), February 1947.
Phases, First Series no. 1 (January 1954)-no. 11 (May 1967);
   Second Series no. 1 (May 1969)—.
Le Révolution surréaliste, no. 1 (December 1924)-no. 12 (December
   1929).
Le Surréalisme au service de la Révolution, no. 1 (July 1930)-
   nos. 5 and 6 (May 1933).
Le Surréalisme, même, no. 1 (September 1956)-no. 5 (Spring 1959).
VVV, no. 1 (June 1942)-nos. 3 and 4 (February 1944).

3. CATALOGS

Marcel Duchamp: Ready-Mades, etc. (1913-1964). Milan: Galleria
   Schwarz; Paris: Le Terrain vague, 1964.
Marcel Duchamp. New York: Museum of Modern Art; Phila-
   delphia: Museum of Modern Art, 1973.
L'Écart absolu. L'Œil, Galerie d'art, December 1965.
Lacomblez. Brussels: Galerie Saint Laurent, March 1962.
Marcel Mariën: Rétrospective & Nouveautés 1937-1967. Brussels:
   Galerie Defacqz, April-May 1967.
Marcel Mariën: Homogeneous Heterogeneity. New York: Landry-
   Bonino Gallery, November-December 1972.
La Peinture au défi. Preface by Louis Aragon, Galerie Goemans,
   1930.
Princip Slasti. Brno, Prague, Bratislava; n.p., January-May 1968.
Rétroviseur Phases. Nice: Galerie des Ponchettes, September-
   November 1972.